THE GLOBALISATION OF CHARISMATIC CHRISTIANITY

This book analyses the revival of charismatic Protestantism as an example of globalisation. Simon Coleman shows that, along with many social movements, these religious conservatives are negotiating their own interpretations of global and post-modern processes. They are constructing an evangelical arena of action and meaning within the liminal, chaotic space of the global. The book examines globalisation not only as a social process, but also as an embodied practice involving forms of language and ritualised movement. Charismatic Christianity is presented through its material culture – art, architecture and consumer products – as well as its rhetoric and theology. The book provides an account of the incorporation of electronic media such as television, videos and the Internet into Christian worship. Issues relating to the conduct of fieldwork in contexts of globalisation are raised in an account which is also the first major ethnography of a Faith ministry.

SIMON COLEMAN is lecturer in anthropology at the University of Durham. His books include *An Introduction to Anthropology*, co-written with H. Watson (1990), *Pilgrimage: Past and Present in the World Religions*, co-written with J. Elsner (1995), *Discovering Anthropology*, co-edited with R. Simpson (1998) and *The Anthropology of Friendship*, co-edited with S. Bell (1999). He serves on the editorial board of a number of journals.

Religion increasingly is seen as a renewed force, and is recognized as an important factor in the modern world in all aspects of life – cultural, economic, and political. It is no longer a matter of surprise to find religious factors at work in areas and situations of political tension. However, our information about these situations has tended to come from two main sources. The news-gathering agencies are well placed to convey information, but are hampered by the fact that their representatives are not equipped to provide analysis of the religious forces involved. Alternatively, the movements generate their own accounts, which understandably seem less than objective to outside observers. There is no lack of information or factual material, but a real need for sound academic analysis. Cambridge Studies in Ideology and Religion meets this need. It attempts to give an objective, balanced and programmed coverage to issues which – while of wide potential interest – have been largely neglected by analytical investigation, apart from the appearance of sporadic individual studies. Intended to enable debate to proceed at a higher level, the series should lead to a new phase in our understanding of the relationship between ideology and religion.

THE GLOBALISATION OF CHARISMATIC CHRISTIANITY

Spreading the Gospel of Prosperity

SIMON COLEMAN

University of Durham

CAMBRIDGE
UNIVERSITY PRESS

PUBLISHED BY THE PRESS SYNDICATE OF THE UNIVERSITY OF CAMBRIDGE
The Pitt Building, Trumpington Street, Cambridge, United Kingdom

CAMBRIDGE UNIVERSITY PRESS
The Edinburgh Building, Cambridge CB2 2RU, UK   www.cup.cam.ac.uk
40 West 20th Street, New York, NY 10011–4211, USA   www.cup.org
10 Stamford Road, Oakleigh, Melbourne 3166, Australia
Ruiz de Alarcón 13, 28014 Madrid, Spain

© Simon Coleman 2000

First published 2000

Printed in the United Kingdom at the University Press, Cambridge

Typeface Monotype Baskerville 11/12.5 pt.   *System* QuarkXPress™   [SE]

A catalogue record for this book is available from the British Library

ISBN 0 521 66072 6 hardback

For Leslie

Contents

Illustrations

Acknowledgements

After quite a few years of researching and talking about the globalisation of Protestant charismatics I have grown used to colleagues remarking: 'Oh yes, that lot were hanging around trying to convert everybody where *I* was working, too.' Luckily, most people seem to have an opinion on these Christians. I have benefited from many conversations with friends and fellow fieldworkers, and would particularly like to thank the following: Ray Abrahams, Eileen Barker, James Beckford, Sandra Bell, David Beriss, Barbara Bodenhorn, Fenella Cannell, James Carrier, Michael Carrithers, Peter Collins, Judith Coney, Susan Drucker-Brown, John Elsner, Paola Filippucci, Paul Gifford, Mario Guarino, Rosalind Hackett, Graham Howes, Sue Hyatt, Matthew Johnson, David Martin, Caroline and Filippo Osella, Malcolm Ruel, Nancy Schaefer, Amanda Sealy, Bob Simpson, Anthony Sinclair, Peter Stromberg, Nicole Toulis, Maya Unnithan, Harvey Whitehouse and Bryan Wilson.

Jan-Åke Alvarsson encouraged me to carry out fieldwork in Uppsala and, once I had arrived, became an essential source of good tea and even better advice. Dan Nosell and David Westerlund also imparted refreshment and knowledge in equal measure. Sigbert Axelson, Antonio Barbosa da Silva, Ove Gustafsson, Charlotte Engel, Per-Anders Forstorp, Margareta Skog and Sverre Stai shared with me their own experiences of working on Scandinavian Faith ministries. Curt Dahlgren and Göran Gustafsson answered my questions on the sociology of religion in Sweden. Tina Trenczek regularly coaxed me out of churches and into cafés. Gunhild Winqvist Hollman began by helping me with my Swedish and then became a good friend. Members of

xi

the Uppsala Department of Cultural Anthropology, the local Filadelfia Congregation and the Word of Life Foundation all tolerated a visiting English anthropologist with humour and hospitality.

The research for this book was aided by a trip to the University of California at Berkeley, and more particularly its library. I would like to thank Richie Abrams of the Berkeley History Department for lending me his office and allowing me to browse among his bookshelves, and both Richie and Marcia Abrams for providing a place to stay and a regular supply of bagels. The Special Staff Travel Fund and the Anthropology Department, Durham University, granted me the funds to visit the US. At Cambridge University Press, it has been a pleasure to work with Kevin Taylor.

My family and in particular my parents, John and Rochelle, have given me constant support since the inception of my work on evangelicals. Maury and Elizabeth Carlin have grown used to a son-in-law who switches over from the baseball to watch televangelism. Eli, my son, is a little too young to appreciate the finer points of academic debate, but has helped in his own special way. Leslie, meanwhile, has not only coped with a distracted husband, but also commented upon the whole of the manuscript in draft form. Since she is from California, she probably knows more than most people about the dynamics of mixing European and American culture. It is to her that I dedicate this book with love.

Introduction

> Hi! . . . Don't hesitate to contact me if you want to know more
> or if you want to have *intercession*. You can also find out where
> I'm preaching – just look at my *diary*. Come to our meetings,
> but I'm warning you! You might get blessed!

These words, and quite a few others, were recently addressed to me
by a Swedish preacher called Stefan Salmonsson.[1] I first encountered Stefan in the mid-1980s, when he was working as a part-time
bus driver while beginning his career as a youth evangelist. Over
the years, I have sat in the congregation and listened to many of
his sermons. This time, however, my appreciation of Stefan's
words was a little different from usual. Instead of sitting in a church
hall I was in my departmental office, in England, waiting for a
tardy student to come and see me. I had switched on my computer
and typed the name of the ministry Stefan works for into my
Internet connection. Within a couple of minutes I found Stefan
greeting me (and, of course, any number of other possible visitors)
when I located his home page. The site was new to me, but I was
impressed by what it was offering. By clicking on the highlighted
words I could gain instant access to Stefan's movements over the
next few months or ask him to pray over any personal 'need' I
might have. Another part of the site informed me that I had the

---

[1] In this book, pseudonyms will be used for charismatics unless the identity of the person is
so obvious that there would be little point in concealment. Stefan is a well-known preacher
in Sweden and his real name is given here. He works for the *Livets Ord* ('Word of Life')
foundation, the focus of much of my ethnographic analysis. The translation from the
Swedish, as elsewhere in the book, is my own.

opportunity to 'Get to know Jesus' by saying a simple prayer that was helpfully supplied. I could click on yet another button to read Stefan's favourite spiritual quotations, or even send him a favourite phrase of my own. His pages also offered the possibility of going to other, similar sites, where I could explore a seemingly boundless world of virtual evangelical information and interaction. My favourite bit of the site, however, was the graphic Stefan placed on his first page: a globe was located close to his name, spinning round and round to complement the static words of the text.

'Redneck religion', as Harvey Cox (1984) terms the new mass-mediated forms of Protestant fundamentalism and evangelicalism, has in recent decades emerged from its separatist shell in the United States and elsewhere. 'Rednecks' have increasingly been forced into white collars as believers have become more economically powerful and socially ambitious.[2] Web sites represent merely one example of the methods currently used by conservative Christians to reach potential converts as well as fellow believers around the world, and this book will examine the ways in which Christians such as Stefan are displaying a potent combination of technological mastery and self-assuredness as they spread their message to new areas of missionary opportunity.

Among many contemporary religious conservatives, faith is far removed from the privatised life-world of Thomas Luckmann's (1967) 'invisible religion'. Their religion is nothing if not visible. It is also global in its outreach. Missionary fields that experienced Christianisation along with the colonising process have provided especially fertile ground for the revised faiths of a post-colonial age, but even apparently unpromising areas in Europe have not gone untouched. Conservative Protestants from the United States have sometimes prompted but often merely witnessed the emergence of new constituencies of believers in all corners of the earth.[3] Cox argues (1995:120) that Pentecostalism is the most rapidly expanding religion of our times. His view is reinforced by Peter Berger's

---

[2] Marsden (1982); Poloma (1982:4); Ammerman (1991); Coleman (1996a); Miller (1997:5).
[3] For a recent article summarising the literature on Afro-American, Latin American and African Pentecostalism, see Corten (1997). For classic general accounts of Pentecostalism see Bloch-Hoell (1964) and Hollenweger (1972).

claim (1990) that there are today two global religions of enormous vitality – conservative Islam and conservative Protestantism.[4]

The long-term implications of such developments have yet to be established. Earlier this century, it was perhaps tempting to see conservative Protestantism as an anti-modern and anachronistic revival of tradition. At least, that is how these believers were perceived by journalists and many scholars during the 'Scopes Trial' of 1925, when a court case investigating the teaching of evolution in a Tennessee school was turned into a nation-wide debate on the intellectual and cultural standing of conservative religious beliefs (Wills 1990:106). However, one of the aims of this study of Protestant charismatics is to show that many features of their ideology and practice are well adapted to modern and even post-modern cultural conditions. These conservatives belong to the present age – and almost certainly the future, as well.

Recent developments have done more than renew flagging faiths. The re-emergence of aggressive, often doctrinally uncompromising movements raises key questions concerning the delimitation of cultural, territorial and ideological boundaries in the modern world – between the sacred and the secular, the private and the public, the religious and the political.[5] Some scholars assert that the revival of proselytising faith provides a refutation of linear models of secularisation in the West.[6] Others say we should not be fooled so easily: conservative Protestants will probably have little lasting impact on industrial, democratic societies such as that of the US (Bruce 1990a). No doubt such debates will continue to rage. In this book, I propose that the revival of conservative Protestantism in many parts of the contemporary world can be viewed in the light

[4] Brouwer et al. estimate (1996:183) that possibly over 300 million Bible-believing evangelicals exist in the world today. Miller (1997:5), meanwhile, poses the following rhetorical question: 'Who would have predicted that Pentecostalism would grow faster than, say, Islamic fundamentalism, with more than 400 million adherents world-wide, including expansion in Africa as well as South America.'

[5] To some degree, also, between electronically mediated and face-to-face perspectives on reality.

[6] Thus Peter Berger, in a rejoinder to Steve Bruce at a conference on Berger's work ('Peter Berger and the Study of Religion', held at Lancaster University, 5–7 December 1997), argued that the presence of a large body of active evangelicals and fundamentalists in the United States contradicts the notion that all Western societies are secularising.

of another body of social theory that is of vital importance but is still relatively little explored in relation to the spread of such faith: that of globalisation.

GLOBALISATION AS SOCIAL PROCESS AND EMBODIED PRACTICE

Providing an extended definition of globalisation will be a task for chapter 2. For the time being, I draw on some observations of Roland Robertson. He notes (1992:8) that 'Globalization as a concept refers both to the compression of the world and the intensification of consciousness of the world as a whole' and argues that there has also been an 'acceleration in . . . concrete global interdependence'. Implicit within Robertson's characterisations of a broad sociological process is reference to specific social activities and institutions – such as the movement of capital around the globe, the workings of world-wide media systems or the articulations of cultural identities in relation to humanity as a whole. In this book, my particular interest is in demonstrating how our understanding of the phrase 'consciousness of the world' can be extended and nuanced when analysed through the ethnographic lens of the activities, cultural assumptions and social institutions of conservative Protestants.

Of course, evangelicals and fundamentalists have a long history of travelling the world to spread the universally applicable Word. Their activities today, involving the promotion of transnational 'flows' (Appadurai 1996) of religious culture, personnel and objects across space and time, can be seen as contemporary manifestations of age-old proselytising practices.[7] Many aspects of globalisation can also be regarded as amplifications rather than fundamental transformations of previous forms of human activity. To give merely one example, pilgrimages within the world religions have long challenged the salience of national borders or ethnic boundaries as definitive markers of identity and practice (Coleman and Elsner 1995). However, to talk today of conservative Protestantism

---

[7] The word evangelical comes from the Greek 'evangelistes', meaning 'bringer of good tidings'.

as a world religion does not mean quite the same as it would have done a century, or even half a century, ago. These Christians are responding to wider social processes that are rendering former understandings of territory, society and cultural identity increasingly problematic. Rudolph (1997:1) comments that religious communities are among the oldest of the transnationals, but that, in the contemporary situation, 'religion has expanded explosively, stimulated as much by secular global processes – migration, multinational capital, the media revolution – as by proselytizing activity'. In a curious sense, then, apparently secular aspects of modernity have actually increased the scope of religion rather than rendering it irrelevant. Along with many social movements, evangelicals and fundamentalists are negotiating their own interpretations of and relationships to global and (post-)modern processes. It may be, as Rudolph argues (ibid.:1), that transnational activity creates a liminal space that cuts across conventional political and cultural divisions. Yet such a space is neither homogeneous nor neutral in its constitution. As a realm of possibilities, it juxtaposes fragmented, dynamic and often competing versions of global consciousness and practice.

I hope to show how the Christians I have studied construct a place of their own, a specific arena of action and meaning, within the shifting, liminal, chaotic space of the global. Most of these Christians do not, of course, use a social scientific vocabulary to describe what they are doing (even though sociology and anthropology are now taught in some evangelical universities). They have, however, developed ways of engaging in global activity that overlap with but are not the same as methods adopted by, say, secular businessmen or members of Greenpeace. Part of the task of the social scientist in such a context must therefore be to develop a double hermeneutic, an academic interpretation of charismatic understandings of their world that takes 'fully . . . into account the reflexivity of the other' (Csordas 1994:xi).

A further dimension of my argument is that a global, charismatic 'consciousness' should not be understood as a purely cognitive cultural system. The orientations towards the world displayed by these Christians involve not merely a set of ideas, but also engagement in certain physical and material activities, including the development of a spiritually charged aesthetic that encompasses ritual movements, media consumption, linguistic forms and aspects of the external environment.[8] The global culture of the people discussed in this book is acted out and practised as much as it is discussed or even consciously reflected upon. I attempt to show how their religious ideology is manifested in the practical constitution of everyday life as well as in worship or explicit discourse (Comaroff 1985:5). Religious activities contribute to the creation of a form of charismatic 'habitus', a form of embodied disposition (discussed in chapter 5), that is geared towards the transcendence of the local and yet can be articulated in specific contexts of belief and practice. Understanding the constitution of this habitus requires an ethnographic appreciation of charismatic constructions of the person, of sociality, even of space and time.

My proposal is therefore that the global culture of these christians does not simply involve communicating across territorial boundaries. It also involves the creation of a multi-dimensional yet culturally specific sense of reaching out into an unbounded realm of action and identity. Seen in these terms, globalisation is not merely a broad sociological process; it is also a quality of action, a means of investing an event, object or person with a certain kind of translocal value. Berger and Luckmann (1966) have famously discussed the social construction of reality in terms which present such reality as resting on collectively maintained plausibility structures. The self is regarded as always engaged in a dialectical relationship with the socio-cultural world (Wuthnow et al. 1984:38). I am arguing that processes of globalisation do not simply happen to believers; they also create them in their own image. Engagement in such processes allows one plausibly to perceive oneself as part of (and contributing to) an ultimate reality where global and spiritual transcendence of the self become mutually reinforcing, even mutually constitutive, activities.

---

[8] Some work on evangelical aesthetics does exist, even if more is needed. Stromberg (1986:33), Forrest (1988), Peacock and Tyson (1989), Richardson (1990) and Lehmann (1996) integrate some consideration of Protestant architecture into wider arguments. McDannell (1995) presents a survey of material culture amongst a variety of Christian groups in North America.

CONTEXTS: PERSONAL, INTELLECTUAL, CULTURAL

It would be tempting for the sake of narrative coherence to claim that, some fifteen years ago when I began to carry out anthropological fieldwork on conservative Protestants, I had already decided to frame my research questions in relation to theories of globalisation. The realities of ethnographic investigation rarely achieve a seamless fit between intention and achievement, however. Thus my original plans bore a rather indirect relationship to the present work. My decision to work in Europe was fuelled – so it seems to me now – by various forms of intellectual perversity. Rather than journeying to remote climes, in common with most of my postgraduate colleagues, I had decided to apply anthropological ideas closer to home. With a family background that combined Eastern European Judaism, Scottish Presbyterianism and Anglo-Saxon atheism, and an education between the ages of seven and eighteen in a school founded on Benthamite principles of secular utilitarianism, I felt that charismatics were sufficiently remote from my everyday experience to warrant ethnographic investigation.

A search through various databases for references on conservative Protestantism resulted in a daunting printout containing thousands of references, produced by numerous social scientific studies. Most of the latter, I discovered, were carried out in the United States. My response was to try to locate some as yet unresearched groups in a Western context clearly different in significant ways from North America. Salvation, or at least some clues as to where to look, came in the form of David Martin's marvellously erudite *A General Theory of Secularization* (1978). The book's schematic characterisation of Protestant, liberal democracies (now, of course, some twenty years old) places the United States and the Scandinavian countries at opposite ends of a continuum of pluralism. The US is described as federalist in politics and religion. The notion of the dissenting denomination is said to have become widespread (see also Hunter 1987:7), along with a stress on feeling and spontaneity that suits denominational ideals of voluntarism and commitment; evangelical religion therefore has the potential to function as a dominant rather than counter motif within religious circles. According to Martin's framework, Scandinavian countries contrast sharply with the pluralism and heterogeneity of the United States. In Sweden, the Lutheran Church[9] has adapted itself to changes in the character of the state, which for much of the twentieth century has constituted a Social Democratic establishment. While the State Church has served as a repository of national and historic feeling, non-socialist politicians and religious peripheries have had little success in their attempts to resist the centre, and religion has not had a cultural or ethnic base from which to resist metropolitan influence.

Sweden, a supposed heartland of secularity, homogeneity and stability, seemed a perfect fieldwork site for an anthropologist seeking to study Protestant charismatics who were trying to flourish in a context remote from the dynamic pluralism of North America. My decision was also helped by the discovery of a feature of the country that is remarkable and yet rarely mentioned in works by social scientists who do not work in Scandinavia: relative to the size of the population and the supposed secularity of the culture, Sweden maintains a large Pentecostal Movement. Currently, around 90,000 people claim membership of the Movement in a national population of a little under nine million, and many adherents are highly active in their involvement. Throughout the past century, Swedish Pentecostalists have created, among other things, a national daily newspaper, banking facilities and a television production company. Although many of these Christians retain a sense of spiritual and cultural peripherality in relation to national culture – and see such a stance as necessary to their revivalist principles – they have become an accepted part of the religious and cultural landscape of the country (Coleman 1989).

A preliminary visit to Sweden in 1985 helped me decide where I would conduct fieldwork. I had been recommended to talk to an academic based in Uppsala (a university town just north of Stockholm) who also happened to be a Pentecostalist. From him I learned not only about the local Pentecostal church that had been in the town for many decades, but also about a new charismatic group that had been set up in the early 1980s. My informant had not been to see the new group himself, but he said they were

---

[9] After many decades of debate, the Lutheran Church has, in fact, decided to become disestablished.

becoming well known – indeed, highly controversial – in local Christian circles. I soon decided that my fieldwork would involve a comparison of these two churches: one old, one new; one established and respected, the other controversial. In particular, I wanted to examine relations between the two groups alongside a study of the different ways in which they negotiated relations with wider cultural, social and political contexts in the town.

The stage seemed set for research to commence. Indeed it was, but not quite as I had expected. The newer group that I had decided to study – called the Word of Life (*Livets Ord*)[10] – turned out to be rather more than a thorn in the side of local Christians: in fact, it was fast becoming a nationally known, even notorious, cultural phenomenon. I remember, for instance, an occasion in the late 1980s when I had returned to England after my first spell of fieldwork. I tuned my radio to a broadcast from Sweden. The programme was discussing themes that had preoccupied the country's media over the previous year. The speaker claimed (admittedly with some exaggeration) that Swedish journalists had discussed little over the past twelve months other than sex or the Word of Life. Such a juxtaposition of topics might have been viewed as unfortunate by members of the charismatic group, but few would have denied that they have become something of a national obsession during their short history. The Word of Life has acted as a catalyst for the kinds of moral panics that are more usually associated with New Religious Movements (Beckford 1985; Barker 1989). It has been described in public and private realms as a brainwashing, money-grabbing, heretical, dangerously right wing, Americanised and deeply un-Swedish institution (Coleman 1989).

I decided on a strategy of working in the Pentecostal congregation and the Word of Life at the same time to gain a sense of possible interactions between the two groups, and soon discovered that relations between the two were indeed strained. Many Pentecostalists felt threatened both by the Word of Life's aggressive evangelism and by the fact that it appeared to be attracting members from more established congregations in the town, including their own. In the Pentecostal church itself, located in the centre

---

[10] The phrase appears in the New Testament. See for instance 1 John 1, where it refers to Jesus.

of town and with around a thousand members, I found people to be readily accepting of my presence. Some simply assumed that I was a Pentecostalist myself, while others, who asked me about my own beliefs, took me for what I was, a sympathetic outsider. Indeed, I soon found that I had been assigned a specific identity. I was regularly greeted with the appellation 'our English brother' by the affable head pastor who perhaps did not always remember my name but knew where I fitted into the social scheme of the church. I joined the gospel choir, helped with producing educational cassettes for children, and regularly attended services and private study groups. I became part of a relatively stable religious community that was quite impressive in the degree to which members could subject each other to a kind of benign surveillance; it was also a community that seemed relatively sure of its place not only in the Swedish Pentecostal Movement, but also in the religious, social and cultural community of Uppsala.

Fieldwork at the Word of Life proved to be a very different experience. I located the group's premises in a rather desolate industrial zone to the east of the city centre. Rumours that researchers from Uppsala University's Theology Department had been subjected to policies of non-co-operation did not encourage me, but in the event a Pentecostalist missionary who frequently attended the Word of Life offered to help me find a way in. He selected the assistant pastor of the group as the person most likely to be sympathetic to my case. After a service, the pastor listened to my explanation that I wanted to write about churches in Uppsala for my doctoral dissertation and informed me that neither he nor anybody else at the ministry would have time to help my research – they had far too much to do. On the other hand, he would not stop me from attending Word of Life events and talking informally to its members. Relieved, I started to attend twice-weekly services at the group.

Unfortunately, I could not join the Word of Life's choir, as its professional aspirations far exceeded those of the gospel choir of the Pentecostal church: my enthusiastic but entirely tuneless singing would have appeared out of place in the seamless performances put on by members of the newer organisation. I also discovered that gaining a comprehensive overview of the activities of the newer church was initially rather difficult. The Pentecostal church ran a shop, had a small radio station attached to its premises and supported various missionaries in foreign lands, but was clearly focussed to a large degree on its long-standing and locally based congregation. In contrast, the Word of Life organisation comprised far more than a congregation of approaching a thousand or so members even in 1986, when I first encountered it: an extensive media business, educational facilities for younger children and a conference centre were also in operation. Furthermore, members of the group were running what they claimed was the largest Bible School in Europe. In subsequent years, all of these operations have been expanded and augmented by a fledgling university, more extensive missionary operation, website, local radio franchise (subsequently given up) and satellite Bible Schools as well as offices in other parts of Europe. While certain personalities at the Word of Life remained constant, involving a core of people who performed pastoral, educational and business-related tasks and who were also prominent at services, I found that the group attracted many people with much more transient interests in its activities. Shorter-term visitors included: students at its schools who were expecting and often encouraged to move on after a few months or years; visiting preachers, particularly from Scandinavia and the United States at first but increasingly from other parts of the world; charismatics from various parts of Sweden or other countries who came to the group's regular workshops and conferences; members of more established churches who occasionally attended Word of Life services (and who often looked rather sheepish when spotting, and being spotted by, other members of their own church); purchasers of the many products sold at its shops; even non-Christian residents of Uppsala, curious to see a group reported so extensively in the press, or perhaps concerned to see what kind of organisation a friend or family member had joined. I remember once having to act as an interpreter at the Pentecostal church when (a rare event) some visiting North American Christians came to a couple of meetings; at the Word of Life, however, my help was certainly not required as instant translations of services into more than one language became standard practice at the group.

Gradually, over the fifteen months I spent in Sweden during my first period of fieldwork, I came to know people who attended the Word of Life as well as I knew many members of the Pentecostal church.[11] Such social contacts were achieved mostly through consciously cultivating acquaintances made at services or participating in a prayer group for Christian university students run by a group member. Yet I, in common with most other regulars at the Word of Life, could not hope to come to know more than a modest fraction of the mobile population that flowed through the group. Many of us also remained anonymous to each other. While a number of people either tried to convert me or assumed that the real reason I was there was because God had led me to the group, in practice my beliefs were rarely questioned since I became merely one more semi-familiar face at services.

Certain aspects of the relatively nameless experience of participation in the Word of Life's activities can be related to the fact that it is a fledgeling institution: a long history of mutual participation in a common spiritual project has not yet been established; the urgent sense of needing to cultivate revival rather than consolidating community is still very much present. I also want to argue, however, that the forms of sociality being cultivated at the group are partial transformations of those evident in either the institutionalised present or the revivalist past of other Christian groups in Sweden. The new ministry's adherents, led by pastors and educators, have created a religious culture constituted by modes of religious consumption and staging of social interaction that appear to be very new in the Swedish religious landscape. In fact, the group has come to embody a form of sociality that I shall be characterising as distinctly global in its orientation.[12]

My original decision to base my research in Scandinavia therefore contained a striking and significant irony. I had decided to remove myself from North American charismatics, yet regularly found myself listening to them preaching in, of all places, a

---

[11] Since then (between spring 1986 and summer 1987), I have returned to Uppsala roughly every two or three years.

[12] This is not to say that previous Christian groups have not constructed orientations to 'the global'. As we shall see, I am talking of matters of degree in relation to global 'consciousness' and 'orientation'.

medium-sized town in the southern part of Sweden. From the outside, and certainly to its critics, the Word of Life appears essentially to be a vehicle for the diffusion of unadulterated North American conservative Protestant ideas to Sweden and thence to Europe (Coleman 1989; 1993). I came to realise that an understanding of the group could not be restricted to an analysis that treated it, in classic ethnographic fashion, as a purely self-contained social and cultural unit (Lareau and Shultz 1996:3). The charismatic arena in which the group operates extends far beyond Uppsala and Sweden itself; it is part of a wider movement of broadly like-minded Christians that has been dominated in the past by North American believers but is becoming increasingly transnational with time. This book is therefore based in the fieldwork experience of a religious culture that cannot be confined to a single spatial or national context. In a way, it is concerned to understand the workings of a globally dispersed charismatic network from the viewpoint of one of its more notable points. Within the network as a whole, there exists an internal market involving the production and consumption of particular goods as well as the promotion of highly mobile preachers who circulate between numerous, widely distributed workshops and conferences. Believers create a comprehensive and comprehensible evangelistic world of mutual interaction within a broader, secular, social and cultural world that is rather more difficult to understand and control.

These remarks must not be taken to mean that I am denying the salience of local and national context to my analysis. As the Word of Life became a national talking-point before my surprised and fascinated gaze, I became interested in the ways in which its members negotiated their relationship with what they perceived as their surrounding culture. Certainly, the almost constant abuse directed at the group from a variety of bodies and individuals in Sweden has influenced the ways in which believers present themselves to people whose ideological support cannot be guaranteed. For instance, they have often attempted to 'localise' their evangelical message in order to give it particular resonance in the Swedish context. At the same time, adherents have found comfort in the fact that they belong to a movement whose scope extends beyond an immediately hostile religio-political environment. I shall be arguing towards the end of this book that one of the reasons why the group has roused such ire in Sweden is precisely because it embodies aspects of the globalisation process that appear to be deeply threatening in the specific circumstances of contemporary Sweden.

Over the years, as my interests in globalisation have developed, I have found myself writing about the Word of Life to the virtual exclusion of the Pentecostal church. This book is no exception to that tendency. Nevertheless, I regard my experience of having worked in the older church and having regularly visited other congregations in Uppsala as vital to my understanding of the newer group. In this way I have come to appreciate what is particular to the Word of Life's modes of worship and forms of sociality. Comparisons with other churches will be used at various points in the text to make my point. Furthermore, in keeping with a research strategy that assesses the significance of a given religious group in relation to multiple contexts of action and reaction, I have combined my participant-observation among churches in Uppsala with a series of other methods of gathering data. Newspaper articles and other literature produced on both the Swedish Pentecostal Movement (past and present) as well as the Word of Life have been consulted extensively. I lived in a student corridor of Uppsala University whilst carrying out my initial fieldwork, and engaged in frequent discussions concerning my work with my often incredulous neighbours. Some were Christian, some not; almost nobody had anything to say about the Pentecostal church; almost everybody had strong opinions on the Word of Life. More formally, I conducted a series of interviews with local priests and pastors in Uppsala concerning their views of the Word of Life, and carried out a small number of interviews with local residents of the town, obtained by snowball sampling, to see what they knew and thought of the local religious landscape.[13]

My somewhat schizophrenic existence – moving between churches as well as between secular student life and contexts of intense religiosity – was made even more complex by the fact that

---

[13] These interviews are discussed particularly in chapter 9, and also in Coleman (1989).

I was also discussing my work with members of Uppsala University's Anthropology and Theology departments. Such academic contexts could not be divorced from 'the field' in which I worked: local scholars (particularly theologians) helped to define the context in which the Word of Life was interpreted in Uppsala and Sweden as a whole. If, as I have argued, we need to be aware of evangelical forms of reflexivity in comprehending processes of globalisation, we must also reflect upon our own assumptions in the analysis of a religious group whose ideology appears to contradict many of the cherished principles of academic life.

THE ORDER OF CHAPTERS

The first three chapters of the book provide intellectual and historical background to subsequent ethnographic description and analysis. In chapter 1, I discuss conservative Protestantism in very broad terms, assessing its contemporary significance as a religious and cultural phenomenon. I then focus on the so-called 'Faith', or 'Health and Wealth' Movement, of which the Word of Life is a prominent member. The (largely North American) religious and intellectual roots of the Movement are outlined, along with Faith attitudes to the person, language and the material world. Chapter 2 summarises recent work on globalisation, suggesting areas where more work can be done, before reconsidering the role of Protestant charismatic religion in the light of global processes. In the next chapter I outline salient features of Sweden as a cultural and religio-political context for evangelical activity, focussing on the construction of the modern state as well as those translocal forces that are perceived to threaten national identity.

Chapter 4 provides a bridge into a more detailed study of the Word of Life, with the organisation and activities of the group presented in very broad fashion. Much of the rest of the book concentrates on the ways in which the Swedish group articulates a globalising form of charismatic ideology and practice. I examine narrative, ritualised movement, art, architecture, use of the mass media and deployment of money, showing how each reinforces a globalising, charismatic habitus. Comparisons with the ritual and more broadly aesthetic dimensions of other churches based in

Uppsala are also made. In addition to various comments on the Pentecostalists, I include in chapter 6 an analysis of a well-established free church in Uppsala, part of a denomination called the Swedish Mission Covenant, that can be shown to represent a radically different ideological position to that of Faith Christians.

Towards the end of the book, in chapter 9, I show that the group's apparent ease at playing on a global stage is highly problematic when reconsidered on a national level. Faith activity in Sweden has gained a reputation as a source of foreign-inspired spiritual and economic imperialism. It has come to represent the breaking of certain cultural taboos associated not only with conventional religion, but also with the supposed coherence of a national culture and collectivist state apparatus. The response of the Word of Life to criticism can itself be viewed as expressing a globalised orientation to its mission. In discursive terms, the group is placed within a theological and historical framework that appears both to celebrate and to transcend the immediate context of Sweden. Word of Life leaders promote a discourse of spiritualised nationalism whereby entrepreneurial, conservative Protestant values are presented as essentially Swedish. At the same time, adherents are encouraged to perceive themselves as contributors to a narrative of salvation that must be reinforced through experiences of mutual interaction between Christians from all parts of the world.

I do not propose that globalisation is the only analytic framework through which to understand contemporary conservative Protestantism. I am, however, claiming that an understanding of why these Christians are so visible in the contemporary world must take global processes into account. Indeed, the significance of the Faith Movement may go further than its contribution to religious revival. As we shall see, it has parallels with other transnational phenomena, religious and secular, that are becoming an increasingly taken-for-granted part of human organisation and self-understanding.

CHAPTER ONE

A 'weird babel of tongues': charisma in the modern world

I vividly remember my first encounter with a charismatic church. It occurred during my final year of studying for an anthropology degree. During a particularly boring undergraduate lecture, a fellow student slipped me a note enquiring if I believed in God. When I scrawled a noncommittal reply, she asked if I wanted to accompany her to a local church that Sunday. I agreed (in a spirit, I told myself, of intellectual inquiry), and a few days later found myself sitting not in the Victorian Gothic pile that I had envisioned but in a school hall on the edge of the city. The 'altar' of the church consisted of a microphone and the 'organ' was a battered and out-of-tune piano. I arrived at the hall intending to sit at the back, but was soon spotted as a newcomer by an usher and placed towards the front row of seats so that I would be directly facing the micro-phone. The sermon was preached by a visiting Welshman who had come to give a 'revival' talk, and, although I admired the force and eloquence of his oration (and was surprised by its humour), I recall being even more struck by his keen control of the choreography and tone of the service. At one point, we were singing a hymn in a lackadaisical manner, following the stumbling efforts of the con-gregation's pianist. Half-way through the hymn, the visiting preacher pushed the pianist aside from his stool, took over the playing and transformed the hymn into a boogie-woogie version of itself. The hall erupted on cue.

No doubt my student friend had intended me to convert to the faith, but something rather different happened. The day after the service, I walked past a hot-dog stall near the city market-place and glanced at the person standing behind the counter. His face looked vaguely familiar. Then I recalled that he was the young man I had been sitting (or, more often, standing) next to at the service. The previous morning, I had directed swift and surreptitious glances at him while his eyes remained closed in apparent ecstasy and his mouth uttered incomprehensible phrases that I realised were spoken in tongues. The juxtaposition in my mind of the everyday quality of the stall with the apparent 'exoticism' of the service was striking and remote from my experience. Ethnography, I decided, could be done in a school hall down the road as well as in more conventionally 'ethnographic' sites in distant parts of the world.[1] My student friend became a missionary, and emigrated to the United States in order to develop her proselytising career. I, however, became an anthropologist of religion.

This first encounter with charismatic worship took place over fifteen years ago. Although my memory of it is very clear, what strikes me now about the story as recalled is that its form, if not its end result, is remarkably similar to the narratives of personal conversion told by charismatics themselves. It may be that many years of listening to sermons have had as great an impact on my own sense of my intellectual past as they do on the spiritual self-perceptions of believers. As a final-year undergraduate, I was indeed a 'seeker' after a kind of Truth, but in my opinion I was looking for a research topic rather than a belief in God. The service made a deep impression on me, partly because it sowed the seeds for a later 'revelation' concerning my academic future which occurred as I looked at the charismatic carrying out his daily business of selling hot-dogs. These are classic conservative Protestant themes: hoping for personal guidance during a period of uncertainty; being led to an answer by seemingly coincidental and everyday but highly meaningful events; the translation of such events into a narrative that is repeated to others (Harding 1987; Stromberg 1993).

As my visit to the school hall indicated, charismatics tend to scorn the ornate buildings of conventional churches, seeing them as reminiscent of 'dead tradition' rather than living faith. The use of the hall exemplified the way any space, any context, could be

---

[1] Of course, I have reflected subsequently on the fact that I decided to work on Christians who are relatively more 'peripheral' in their society than those who belong to mainstream churches. I hope, however, that my analysis does not exoticise charismatics in an 'orientalist' sense.

converted to spiritually charged purposes. (Note that my fellow student had taken advantage of a less-than-gripping lecture as an opportunity for evangelisation.) The Welsh speaker displayed a finely tuned sense of how to gee up the service, but he benefited as well from a congregation that was rehearsed in opportunities physically and vocally to display signs of inspiration and enthusiasm. He could turn his unfamiliarity with the congregation to his advantage, imparting a feeling of novelty and freshness but also the notion that he came from a Christian community located geographically far from the local group yet clearly kindred to it in Spirit.

I soon discovered that the charismatic gathering I had encountered was a 'house church'. The latter is a term that refers to evangelising congregations, self-consciously separated from mainline Christian denominations in Britain, that Andrew Walker (1989:280) – perhaps with some hyperbole – has described as: 'The largest and most significant religious formation to emerge in Great Britain for over half a century.'[2] Theologically or politically motivated opponents of such churches, invoking themes often levelled at charismatics as a whole, have accused them of being highly authoritarian and of brainwashing their members into devotion to a rigid creed and all-powerful leader. In contrast, house church members see their role as encouraging a restoration of the New Testament pattern of the early Church, and in particular its inspiration by gifts of the Spirit as described in the Bible.[3]

Elements of belief and practice contained in the British Movement are paralleled but also transformed in contemporary charismatic and wider conservative Protestant circles throughout the world. Any attempt at a survey of the historical, theological and social connections between such Christians is a difficult task, not least because of the ambiguity of the descriptive vocabulary that must be employed. For instance, although in the United States the word 'evangelical' connotes a theological conservative, in Latin

---

[2] Assessing the exact significance of the apparent success of house churches, indeed of charismatics in general, is problematic in a number of ways. For instance, it may be that the vast majority of those actually joining house churches have already professed a Christian faith in some other context (Bruce 1998:228). According to such a view, the phenomenon still needs to explained, but should not necessarily be seen as involving mass conversion of atheist hordes.

[3] See Acts 2, Romans 12: 1 Corinthians 12 and Ephesians 4.

America the term can refer to any non-Catholic Christian (Stoll 1990:4; Spittler 1994:103). Alliances between groups themselves shift over time. However, a summary account is necessary at this stage, even if it is subsequently qualified in the light of specific cases such as the one I shall be presenting in this book.

CONSERVATIVE CHARISMATICS

So far, I have been using the term 'conservative Protestant' as a blanket term for all believers who can be characterised as 'charismatic', 'Pentecostal', 'evangelical' and 'fundamentalist'. 'Conservative' in this sense does not refer to a political orientation, even if many of the politically active Christians thus designated might nowadays be considered more rightist than socialist (most notably in the United States). It refers instead to a broad support within the Protestant rubric for 'traditional' positions on such doctrines as the Virgin Birth of Jesus, the reality of miracles as reported in Scripture and the inevitable return of Christ to rule over the earth (Ammerman 1991:2). In their rhetorical affirmation of biblical literalism and explanation of events in supernatural terms, conservatives contrast broadly with the more self-consciously symbolic, interpretative and naturalistic approaches of liberals.

Amongst conservatives, charismatic Christians occupy a particular if fluid place. Some of the roots of their present expansion can be linked to specifically Pentecostal models of worship whose Arminian, Methodist and Holiness origins were consolidated in late nineteenth- and early twentieth-century revivals in the United States and Europe. Marsden (1991:41) notes that, while liberal, modernist religion of the time emphasised the gradual cultivation of the good qualities inherent in the person, Holiness adherents argued that only the dramatic work of the Holy Spirit could cleanse the heart and overcome human nature. The perfectionism and sanctification available to the believer were wrought by supernatural means, but were always under threat if the person did not guard against future temptation.

The term Pentecostal, derived from the Greek, refers to the fiftieth day after the second day of the Jewish festival of Passover. At such a time, according to Acts 2:1–4, the representatives of the early Christian Church in the first century were filled with the Holy Spirit and spoke in other tongues. By invoking the possibility of deploying glossolalia in the present (as well as exercising other spiritual gifts such as healing), the Pentecostals of the early twentieth century saw themselves as traversing (indeed, bypassing) history in order to embody the beliefs and practices of an original, authentic Christianity. They drew a distinction between tongues as a sign of initial baptism in the Spirit and later manifestations of the gift (Williams 1984:73–4). Tongues were therefore an important indication of the reception of grace but also a form of subsequent empowerment.

According to most accounts of the origins of Pentecostalism, an outbreak of glossolalia in a Bible college in Topeka, Kansas, was followed by the 'Azusa Street' revival in Los Angeles in 1906, initiated by the black evangelist William J. Seymour. On 18 April of that year, a *Los Angeles Times* reporter described the Azusa Street Revival incredulously as a 'Weird Babel of Tongues', indicating the scepticism and hostility with which it was received in wider, polite society.[4] Much in the faith appeared to have black, slave roots, including its orality, musicality, narrativity in theology and witness, emphasis on maximum participation, inclusion of dreams and visions in worship, understanding of correspondence between body and mind and antiphonal character of worship services (Hollenweger 1997:18–19). Extensive criticism, frequently from fellow Christians, of their supposedly indecorous fanaticism encouraged some believers to form separate churches where they could worship as they wished.

In a sense, charismatics of today revive not only Acts but also the history of the early Pentecostal Church in their practices and beliefs – involving glossolalia, healing and prophesy, personal testimony and consciously cultivated liturgical spontaneity – even if they do not always call themselves Pentecostals. The connections between more 'classical' and newer styles of worship can be seen in Poloma's (1982:4–5) definition of charismatics as: 'Christians who accept the Bible as the inspired word of God, but who also emphasize the power of the Holy Spirit in the lives of those who

---

[4] Olsen (1998:10).

have accepted Jesus Christ as their Savior.' In this quotation we see the juxtaposition of two key elements – the canonical text and the possibility of personifying sacred revelation and power – that coexist in both Pentecostal and more broadly charismatic faith.

Over the past three or four decades, charismatic styles of worship have diffused throughout congregations and denominations of varied theological persuasions. An important influence in spreading the message to mainline churches and middle-class churches throughout the world was David du Plessis (1905–87), a Pentecostalist minister from South Africa and associate of Oral Roberts (Marsden 1991:78). Du Plessis had himself been touched by the spirituality of black South African Christianity with its healing, tongues, dreams and visions (Poloma 1982:11–12; Poewe 1994:3). The spread of the renewal to mainstream Christianity is also associated with the Episcopal priest Dennis Bennett, who in 1960 announced that he had received baptism in the Holy Spirit and spoke in tongues. Bennett was forced to resign from his church in California but nevertheless continued to recruit Christians for his cause. It is therefore now possible, as Spittler (1994:105) has noted, to talk of charismatic Lutherans, charismatic Presbyterians and so on, implying the ability of such a 'genre' of worship to attach itself to a multitude of theological orientations and, increasingly, to the middle classes. Particularly from the 1950s and 1960s, charismatic forms have grown and diversified, sometimes within more established denominations, sometimes in previously non-charismatic contexts, sometimes even in Catholic churches.[5]

Important as such developments are, this book focusses on the activities of more explicitly conservative, Protestant charismatics. Leading conservatives in recent years have included Pat Robertson, founder of the Christian Broadcasting Network and former presidential candidate, the televangelical healer Oral Roberts and the scandal-ridden Jim and Tammy Bakker. These charismatics – themselves embodying different styles of worship and even theologies – are merely some of the best-known participants within a huge and increasingly transnational network of Christians, comprising congregations, networks, fellowships, mega-churches and even

---

[5] On Catholic charismatics, see McGuire (1982); Neitz (1987); Roelofs (1994); Csordas (1994, 1997).

so-called para-churches.[6] Sometimes, they are termed 'neo-Pentecostals', signalling their connections with previous forms of worship but also more novel tendencies in appealing across class barriers, denominational affiliations and even towards a greater accommodation with material prosperity. Although ostensibly independent, many of the neo-Pentecostal churches have joined such associations as The International Communion of Charismatic Churches, the Charismatic Bible Ministries and the International Convention of Faith Ministries (Brouwer et al. 1996:267).

Since the 1970s, the charismatic scene in the US and elsewhere has been hit by what is sometimes called a 'third wave' of the Spirit (following first Pentecostalism and then charismatic renewal). It has often been cultivated by independent ministries, and is closely associated with such luminaries as the now deceased John Wimber (Harris 1998:80; Percy 1996, 1998). A North American, Wimber gained a following around the world that transcended denominational affiliations. In the UK, for instance, his movement and others like it have had an impact on groups ranging from house churches to Anglican congregations.[7] Since 1994, 'Airport Vineyard', a Christian fellowship based in Toronto and connected with Wimber's Ministry, has become the centre of the so-called 'Toronto Blessing' (Hunt 1995).[8] The Blessing itself is manifested in powerful physical forms, including outbursts of uncontrolled laughter, and parallel phenomena have spread to charismatic churches around the world.

Interconnections among conservatives are now highly fluid, and mutual influences between classical Pentecostals and other charismatics have become increasingly evident. Describing developments in the US, Shibley (1996:1) talks of how southern-style evangelicalism has spread throughout the country as a whole, but has itself been transformed in new, pluralist contexts. Along with

---

[6] Probably the best-known example of the latter is the Full Gospel Business Men's Fellowship, founded in the 1950s. The principle behind para-church organisations is that they can co-ordinate activities distinct from those of conventional congregations (Nilsson 1988; Hunt et al. 1997:2).

[7] Percy (1998:187) identifies John Wimber, Benny Hinn, Morris Cerullo and Reinhard Bonnke as key figures in the new revival.

[8] On the Toronto Blessing, see also Poloma (1997); Richter (1997); Percy (1998). The Canadian church's chief pastor had prepared for a renewal of his ministry by, among other things, receiving the prayers of Benny Hinn (Hunt 1995:261).

the 'southernisation' of religious activities beyond the South has come what he calls the 'Californication' of conservative Protestantism. Thus some conservatives have accommodated to the anti-institutional, therapeutic, cultural preferences of baby boomers (Hunter 1987). In Britain, meanwhile, Walker (1997:24) states: 'The sociological distinctions we might have made, even ten years ago, between classical and neo-Pentecostal are now difficult to sustain in the light of new Charismatic alignments and the syncretistic tendencies of late Pentecostalism.' Older Pentecostals may dislike the worldliness of newer charismatics, but they are increasingly likely to see such tendencies within their own congregations.

For Percy (1998:144–5), the contemporary period is one of dislocation from earlier eras. He describes early forms of Pentecostalism as expressing a relatively homogenous response to secular modernism. Contemporary revivalist forms, however, appear to compete with and borrow from a post-modern world of healing movements, the New Age, materialism and pluralism. Percy may be exaggerating the unity of classical Pentecostalism. The point remains, however, that older boundaries between charismatic life styles and those of the wider world do appear to be shifting and becoming increasingly permeable.

SACRED TEXT AND HOLY TOUCH: FUNDAMENTALISTS AND CHARISMATICS

The issue of the firmness or otherwise of religious boundaries is key to a further issue relating to charismatic identity. Charismatics are often associated by outsiders with another wing of the conservative Protestant revival – Christian fundamentalism. The drawing of such a parallel is sometimes a little misleading. Cox (1995:15) highlights the differences he perceives to exist between the two by invoking an opposition between textual and tactile orientations to faith: 'While the beliefs of the fundamentalists, and of many other religious groups, are enshrined in formal theological systems, those of pentecostalism are imbedded in testimonies, ecstatic speech, and bodily movements.'[9] Marty and Appleby (1992:43) similarly

---

[9] Hollenweger (1997:191) expresses the historical distinctions pithily: 'Fundamentalists and the neo-orthodox mounted arguments. Pentecostals gave testimony.'

see the main distinction as concerning the role of the Bible in establishing the framework of life and community. Pentecostalists are said to lay emphasis on prophecy, tongues and faith healing, with divine revelation from the Holy Spirit complementing guidance from the Bible. In contrast (ibid.): 'Fundamentalists are uncomfortable, to say the least, with the open-ended character of pentecostalism and feel that the Bible alone is perfectly sufficient in guiding Christian moral, religious, and political action.'

Fundamentalist unease at being identified with such aspects of Pentecostalism and charismatic Christianity can be explained by looking at historical factors and the (partially) separate development of these two forms of religious conservatism. Fundamentalism as a movement does not draw upon the Arminian, Wesleyan sources of Holiness and Pentecostal groups. Rather, it emerged from a coalition of diverse evangelical groups who articulated a theologically based opposition to such early twentieth-century bugbears as secular labour politics, higher biblical criticism, Darwinism and forms of modernism.[10] Arguments reflecting a Calvinist zeal to preserve doctrinal purity and stressing the inerrancy of Scripture were developed to combat historical–critical approaches to the text (Cox 1984:44; Harris 1998:4). Between 1910 and 1915, a series of pamphlets called *The Fundamentals* was produced. In the 1920s, fundamentalists rather than Pentecostalists took the lead in mounting arguments during the Scopes Trial, even though the two groups shared many of the same attitudes to the secular world (Hollenweger 1997:191).

Charismatics' supposed ignorance of Christian tradition and theology, apparent emotionalism and emphasis on the possibility of continued revelation from the Holy Spirit, remain anathema to many representatives of fundamentalism. Wesleyan-inspired concepts of the entire sanctification of the believer have also proved an obstacle to conservatives of a more Calvinist persuasion (Harris 1998:24). Unsurprisingly, therefore, charismatics and fundamentalists have often viewed each other with a certain amount of sardonic

---

[10] See Bruce (1990b:17) and Harris (1998:2). It would however be foolhardy to emphasise sociological separation too much. Marsden (1991:3) notes that the early fundamentalist coalition did include militant conservatives based in Methodist, Holiness and Pentecostalist congregations, as well as Baptist and Presbyterian ones. The lines of division gradually emerged over time as fundamentalism became more exclusively Baptist.

mistrust, and sometimes overt aggression. The fundamentalist Baptist Jerry Falwell, probably best known as the leader of a now-defunct religio-political lobby group called the Moral Majority, has referred to speaking in tongues not as a sign of the presence of the Holy Spirit but as a consequence of having eaten 'too much pizza the night before' (quoted in Bruce 1990b:201).

In practice, however, these two wings of conservative Protestantism share many convictions in their seeking for radical conversion and 'personal' relationships with God, stress on salvation through Jesus, rhetoric of biblical literalism and belief in Christ's impending return (even if the timing and nature of the return are disputed). They share a common enemy (manifestations of diabolic atheism) and a common aspiration (restoration of early, authentic Christianity). It may be that charismatics/neo-Pentecostals are generally less theologically and politically polemical than fundamentalists. None the less, in recent decades, more outwardly oriented representatives of both these groups in the United States have worked together or in parallel in order to make their feelings widely known over specific issues such as religious education in schools, abortion and family values. Differences have sometimes been suppressed in order to present an agenda that appears as united as possible. Both have defined themselves as providing guidance and leadership after the spiritual, cultural and political crises of the 1960s, including the uncertainties of the Vietnam period.[11] The lack of an established Church in the US, combined with a relatively decentralised legal and political system, has aided them in their attempts to gain power on local levels at least (Bruce 1990a). Communications technologies have been used to disseminate conservative Protestant messages to ever-broadening cultural areas. At the same time, increasing numbers of charismatics and fundamentalists have managed to reconcile the exercise of faith with the valorisation of contemporary forms of corporate capitalism (Cox 1984:60–4). Given the parallels that exist between charismatic and fundamentalist ways to be a conservative Protestant, I therefore find it most useful to describe

[11] Of course, signs of evangelical revival were evident before the 1960s. The period immediately after the Second World War witnessed the work of healing revivalists and the international work of Billy Graham. A faith founded on an apocalyptic vision of the world found resonances in the new atomic age.

charismatics, adopting Percy's term, as 'fundamentalistic'. Percy (1998:62–6) is correct to note that fundamentalism is not just a noetic phenomenon, but also a way of being in the world.

PREACHERS OF PROSPERITY

One wing of the global (neo-Pentecostal) charismatic revival has been particularly successful as well as controversial in recent years. It is known variously as the Faith, Faith Formula, Prosperity, Health and Wealth or Word Movement, and is the main focus of this book.[12] The exact place of the Movement in the broader spectrum of conservative Protestantism is disputed, since many Faith Christians maintain ambiguous and sometimes acrimonious relations with fellow charismatics. If the Movement's supporters regard it as a revival of old faiths and a reclamation of the Christian's right to have dominion over the earth, opponents see the Faith Gospel as dangerous in its irresponsible claims to solve all problems – spiritual, physical and financial.[13]

However, Faith ideas are becoming increasingly respectable and widespread in the charismatic world. Various reasons have been proposed for the apparent success of the Movement in the US. Brouwer et al. (1996:24) see it as the latest revival of an older gospel of wealth that received a fresh impetus during the later 1970s. They note that it may have benefited from widespread disenchantment with mid-twentieth-century liberalism. In addition, the Movement has spread from its bases in US ministries to become a world-wide phenomenon over the past twenty years.[14] Considerable followings are found in large urban areas with middle-class constituencies, for

---

[12] I shall normally choose the appellation 'Faith' both for the sake of convenience and because, in my experience, Swedish and American adherents are themselves happy with it as a term of self-description. Of course, a variety of terms is used in these and other countries. My choice of the word 'Movement' is perhaps more problematic. Broadly, it implies an organisation with a sense of direction, social boundaries and clear leadership. The Faith network, on the other hand, is permeable, and, although Hagin is an influential figure, it is clearly decentralised and diffuse. However, the idea of movement has the advantage of evoking a sense of charismatic fluidity combined with evangelical mission.

[13] For such critical texts, see, for instance, Farah (1978); Hunt and McMahon (1985); Barron (1987); Brandon (1987); McConnell (1988); Horton (1990).

[14] See, for instance, Poloma (1982:237–8); Gustafsson (1987); Hollinger (1991); Marshall (1991); Gifford (1993); Coleman (1991; 1993); Cox (1995:272); Hackett (1995); Coleman (1998); Gifford (1998).

instance in South Africa, South Korea, Guatemala and Brazil (ibid.:6). Faith teachings have also appealed to less-advantaged groups who have maintained aspirations for personal (and sometimes wider) forms of transformation and empowerment.

Three areas of teaching give the Movement its distinct theological profile: healing, prosperity and 'positive confession'. The first two refer the believer to a reconsideration of the Abrahamic covenant: a blessing that in the Old Testament was promised to a particular people is said to be extended to all through the atonement of Christ.[15] As a born-again Christian, the believer is a possessor of faith, and learns to draw upon new-found power not only through obedience to God, but also through specific acts that draw divine influence into the world. Thus 'positive confession' is a statement that lays claim to God's provisions and promises in the present (Hollinger 1991:57).[16] In a highly critical account, Brandon (1987:17) paraphrases such thinking as 'What you say is what you get' and sees it as deriving from the idea that humans, made in God's image, can have divine dominion over creation by deploying language.[17] A clear implication of ideas concerning positive confession is that words spoken 'in faith' are regarded as objectifications of reality, establishing palpable connections between human will and the external world. They form a kind of inductive fundamentalism (Hunt 1998:277). Believers are supposedly enabled to assert sovereignty over multiple spheres of existence, ranging from their own bodies to broad geographical regions. Emphases on both personal empowerment and the unlimited capacities of objectified language can reinforce each other when a Christian uses words to create desired effects in the self. One Faith preacher describes the principle behind this idea by using the imagery of a thermostat and timer in a central-heating system: the system (i.e. the person) inevitably reproduces whatever is programmed into it.[18] As we shall see, the association of the self and spiritual practices with mechanical processes is a common feature of believers' discourse.

---

[15] See Galatians 3:13–14.
[16] Compare Romans 10:10; Mark 11:23–4; Proverbs 18:21; Proverbs 12:13.
[17] Compare Mark 11:23–4; Matthew 9:29; Philippians 4:19. See also Hagin's *How to Turn your Faith Loose* (1985).   [18] Capps (1980) cited in Brandon (1987:25).

Faith ideas have been adopted to varying degrees by many of the most famous televangelists in the US, including Pat Robertson and Oral Roberts. The figure most closely associated with the Movement's foundation and expansion is Kenneth Hagin. The story of his life provides both a classic narrative account of evangelical salvation and a microcosm of shifts in charismatic alignments throughout the latter half of the twentieth century. Hagin was born in Texas in 1917, apparently with a serious heart defect (McConnell 1988:58). After a troubled and sickly childhood, he decided as a teenager to give his life to Jesus. In return, the young Hagin received the gift of divine revelation – Mark 11:23–4 – telling him not only that faith could move mountains but also that prayer could help him attain his desires. Hagin came to understand the divine message as indicating the importance of avoiding doubt: even while still apparently sick, he had to believe that he had already been healed for his physical condition to improve.

Having gained his health, Hagin became a preacher. Moving from Baptism to Pentecostalism, he was licensed as an Assemblies of God minister in 1937. After the Second World War he participated in healing revivalist circles and worked within the ministries of independent evangelists. According to Hollinger (1991:59), Hagin then adopted a strategy that was vitally important for his future career. In line with changing styles of charismatic worship, he shifted from older styles of Pentecostal practice (indeed, he was eventually forced out of the Assemblies of God) into less legalistic, separatistic expressions of faith. During the late 1960s and 1970s, after he transferred his ministry to Tulsa, Oklahoma, he began to develop a national profile. Alongside his Living Waters Church he initiated his 'Faith Seminar of the Air', a programme syndicated on radio stations in the US and Canada. Rhema Bible Training Center and Rhema Correspondence Bible School were founded in 1974.

Hagin claims to have had numerous personal visits from Jesus. In addition, he deploys the mass media with some skill, with his *Word of Faith* magazine and other teaching materials distributed monthly to many thousands of homes. A major part of his legitimacy and influence comes, however, from the fact that his ministry has acted as the training ground for so many preachers who have themselves become prominent within a globally ramifying movement. By the mid-1990s, almost 16,000 graduates had been produced, most of them from North America but including others from almost thirty different countries (Brouwer et al. 1996:190). Hagin may not have formal, bureaucratic control over the numerous offshoots of the Faith Movement; none the less, his influence through social, educational and mass media channels has been undeniable, even if in practice his son (Kenneth Hagin Jr) now runs much of the ministry and its associated organisations.

Other important preachers in Faith circles have developed specialised profiles through aspects of their teaching or preaching styles, but all tend to echo Hagin's entrepreneurial model of establishing an overtly independent ministry that is a vehicle for evangelistic activity far beyond the level of the local congregation. Kenneth Copeland (originally a pilot working for Oral Roberts), based in Fort Worth, Texas, is generally viewed as Hagin's successor in spearheading the Movement. He travels extensively around the world, frequently with his wife, Gloria, and has become well known for his teachings on the 'laws' of prosperity. In addition, some well-known preachers clearly echo Faith principles without necessarily being at the heart of the Movement in organisational terms. Morris Cerullo, for instance, was based in the Assemblies of God before becoming involved in post-war healing evangelism. In 1961, he started his own independent ministry, World Evangelism, in California (Schaefer 1999). Cerullo acquired the Bakkers' defunct television ministry, Global Satellite Network, in 1990, and has continued to expand his healing ministry beyond the US into Asia, Africa, Latin America and even parts of Europe. Cerullo maintains his autonomy and yet shares platforms with other preachers who disseminate their own versions of the prosperity message. The Movement on a global level does not have firm boundaries of membership or non-membership, and it is marketed via mass rallies, workshops, conferences and media products that appeal to diverse constituencies of believers.

Faith leaders tend to deny that they are part of a fixed denomination (McConnell 1988:84–5). Certain organisations that transcend the local, congregational level do however function to consolidate national and transnational networks. For instance, in the late 1970s, Hagin helped to found the International Convention of Faith Churches and Ministers. Other leading figures in the Convention have included the North Americans Lester Sumrall (now deceased), Jerry Savelle and Fred Price, the South African Ray McCauley, Reinhard Bonnke (formerly a missionary in Africa, now based in Germany), the Nigerian Benson Idahosa and Ulf Ekman from Sweden. Although the strengths of personal alliances may vary considerably, these figures share pulpits, ratify each other's prophecies and market each other's goods (Gifford 1993:179–80).

PROSPERITY GOES GLOBAL

In recent decades, Faith ideas have been transferred to, as well as transformed within, numerous contexts around the world. Certain areas such as the Muslim Middle East have proved largely resistant to the message, but generally the expansion has been impressive. Paul Gifford has traced the diffusion of Faith ideas in a number of African countries. In much of his work he argues that the effects of such teaching should be considered in political and economic as well as religious terms. He tends to emphasise the strength of North American influences on activities throughout the continent, partly through missionaries but also through economic, educational and preaching contacts. Writing of local black and West African missionaries in Doe's Liberia, Gifford concludes (1993:296): 'The message they disseminated was devised in the southern states of America and inextricably bound up with Western culture.'[19] Describing a Pan-African Crusade by Reinhard Bonnke,[20] much of which took place in a giant tent financed by Kenneth Copeland, Gifford states (1987:85): 'In this strain of religion, things like "democracy", free enterprise, individual liberty, "a strong dollar", and American military superiority acquire almost divine status.' Strong links with the United States are also said to

[19] Gifford is unlikely to be surprised by Walls's (1991) claim that, in the late 1980s, probably over 80 per cent of the world's Protestant missionaries came from North America, with the great majority of these coming from unaffiliated organisations, often Pentecostal in character.
[20] Reinhard Bonnke is the founder of Christ for All Nations. The organisation was originally based in South Africa, though in mid-1986 it was moved to West Germany.

be evident in the ministry of Ray McCauley (Gifford 1988), a preacher who trained under and was ordained by Kenneth Hagin.[21] McCauley founded the Rhema Bible Church in Randburg, Johannesburg, in 1979, and according to Gifford the Church's gospel of prosperity has helped to support state authority and therefore draw attention away from the need for social change. For prosperous white South Africans, Faith ideas are said to present comforting messages that emphasise the need for order in society and justify the possession of wealth as a sign of divine grace. For poorer blacks in Africa, on the other hand, the preachers of health and wealth do not appear to offer practical schemes for societal development but present alluring images of efficiency linked to foreign missionaries as well as forms of prosperity that do not rely on the initial possession of resources (Gifford 1993:186–9). Some Faith preachers may also present an Americanised message whilst denying its cultural origins. Thus, at Bonnke's 1986 Fire Conference in Harare (attended by 4,000 evangelists from forty-one African countries) one of the guest speakers, Kenneth Copeland, emphasised that prosperity was not inherently American. Instead, it relied on the following of universally applicable biblical principles (ibid.:152).

In a recent book, Gifford (1998) has attempted a comparative examination of Christianity, including Faith ministries, in different parts of Africa. In this work, he locates his analysis more explicitly in a consideration of indigenous factors that might influence the reception of revivalist forms. Gifford accepts that Pentecostalism has been on the continent for most of this century, but argues that a new charismatic wave has been evident since the 1970s, resulting in a situation where the Faith Gospel has become widespread (ibid.:39). While in the past missionaries have been mostly North American, there now seems to be a strategy of supporting more locally based workers, even if the influences from abroad remain

---

[21] Gustafsson (1987:46) notes that Kenneth Hagin participated in Rhema's church-consecrations in 1981 and 1985. In the *Eagle News* newsletter of 1 June 1985, McCauley wrote: 'The Lord, through prophesy, has given ample encouragement and confirmation that the impact of this ministry will be felt nationwide and internationally.' Indeed, Rhema Ministries South Africa established daughter congregations in South Africa, Zimbabwe, Swaziland, Malawi, England and Scotland (Gustafsson 1987:46) and in 1982 took part in a satellite communion, organised by Copeland, involving churches from twenty-three countries.

evident. In Ghana, one of the churches with the highest profiles is Christian Action Faith Ministries International, founded by Nicholas Duncan-Williams, son of a politician–diplomat (ibid.:77). By 1995, the congregation boasted 8,000 members and was located in a large new complex. A church of broadly similar ideology, whose name also expresses its translocal aspirations, is Mensa Otabil's International Central Gospel Church. Gifford observes that Otabil's Faith message of releasing the power of the person and Black pride, reinforced by media images of travel and communications technology, strikes a responsive chord among Accra's educated, English-speaking, upwardly mobile youth (ibid.:82). Otabil himself appears to exemplify his followers' aspirations, and he presents himself as the model of a successful entrepreneur. He has recently been developing plans for a new university.

The Faith message in Ghana emphasises the idea of power, a concept already of some significance in local discourse. Such influence, moreover, is regarded as extending beyond the transformation of the individual person. The new Faith churches subscribe to a political theology (as already seen in South Africa) by praying for a God-fearing leader who brings his people prosperity.[22] Indeed, in 1993 local charismatic churches prayed for and over Jerry Rawlings the President (Gifford 1998:86). Similar emphases are evident in Zambia through the actions of Frederick Chiluba, leader of the Movement for Multi-party Democracy and leader of the country for much of the 1990s. Chiluba is 'born-again', and received the gift of tongues from Reinhard Bonnke (ibid.:193). As the Faith paradigm became more widely accepted in Zambia, he declared the country a Christian nation on national television in 1991. During the ceremony to celebrate the fourth anniversary of declaring Zambia to be a Christian nation, he stated that because Zambia had entered into a Covenant with God the nation would be blessed to the point where it would stop borrowing from others and become a lender of resources instead. Diplomatic links were also established with Israel, and in 1994 and 1995 healing televangelist Benny Hinn visited the country and pledged to support Chiluba's re-election (ibid.:204). The preacher Nevers Mumba,

---

[22] Here we see a version of the Old Testament idea, located in the Books of Kings and Chronicles, of the connections between a godly ruler and national prosperity.

former Bible School student in Texas[23] and Zambian interpreter for Bonnke, developed Chiluba's Christian Zionism partly by emphasising the need for Christians to counter local threats from Islam and partly by creating a three-level schema for understanding the different kinds of Christian nation (ibid.:233). According to Mumba, some nations have declared themselves to be Christian (Zambia); others display a great awareness of Christ but have not actually made a declaration of identity (Ghana); in addition, a nation may actually be founded upon biblical principles, as exemplified by the United States.

An important aspect of Gifford's analysis is his pointing to differences in the way that Faith ideas are used by various preachers in Africa. For instance, he contrasts Otabil's stress on skill and training as key components of success with the approach taken by Handel Leslie, head of the Abundant Life Church in Kampala, who places more emphasis on the quasi-magical gifts possessed by the pastor and his anointing (1988:162). Healing in Leslie's church, in contrast to many other Faith congregations around the world, is a relatively peripheral concern, with business success the chief focus. Perhaps the most intriguing point made by Gifford, however, relates to his argument that, in the face of increased marginalisation in global terms, some African churches provide an important arena and vehicle for international contacts (ibid.:93). Faith churches are significant not only because they participate in translocal networks, but also because they cultivate an ideological context where the virtues and excitements of internationalism are stressed – and contrasts are often evident here with many more established independent churches, which provide fewer links with the outside world. Faith preachers are often presented as having 'just flown in today' or as leaving soon for foreign parts. Bible Schools list among their teachers anyone from overseas who has visited them, and testimonies are cultivated from people who have been abroad. A particularly important feature of Faith practice in this regard is the convention or conference phenomenon (ibid.:233). Such gatherings provide occasions for the bringing

---

[23] Bonnke arranged for Mumba to study at 'Christ for the Nations' in Dallas, Texas, between 1982 and 1984. This Bible School supported Mumba to the tune of 100 dollars a month for years after his return to Africa.

together of congregations to hear preachers from many parts of the world, as well as opportunities for international products to be marketed.

Rosalind Hackett's work on West Africa partially reinforces Gifford's emphasis on American involvement in local charismatic activity. She also reiterates his point that believers may neverthe- less present their faith as being unconfined by cultural boundaries (1995:211). She acknowledges the influence of such established North American healing revival figures as T. L. Osborn, Oral Roberts and Morris Cerullo, but also notes the activities of 'Archbishop Professor' Benson Idahosa, founder of the Church of God Mission International in Benin City (ibid.:201). Idahosa studied with Gordon Lindsay at the Church for Nations Institute in Texas in 1971 and has established a religious empire that echoes (and was partially funded by) those of his American 'Faith' counterparts. His achievements have included a Word of Faith group of schools, a Faith Medical Centre, the All Nations for Christ Bible Institute (involving students from forty nations, taught by people from the US, India, England and Nigeria) and various international crusades organised under the rubric of Idahosa World Outreach. We therefore see in Idahosa's case a common pattern in Faith ministries, and one that was evident in Gifford's observations: a 'local' organisation is set up, often aided by foreign influence or even money, and becomes a new centre of influence that defines its identity not only in terms of local outreach but also in relation to influence exercised over a transnational sphere of operations. Idahosa's reputation as 'The Apostle of Africa' is for external as well as internal consumption, providing him with a legitimacy that extends beyond the continent itself. His ministry acts not only as a new centre, but also as a point of mediation between Africa and the external world, whilst bringing together and training Christians from different countries in the continent itself. Nicholas Duncan-Williams, for instance, was a student at Idahosa's Bible College in the late 1970s before he set up his own 'international' church in Ghana.

In explaining the emergence and apparent success of Faith styles of preaching and worship in African contexts, Hackett pro- poses a number of interlinked factors. Clearly the missionising actions of American evangelists are important, as is the role of the mass media in disseminating the message. It may be that economic recession combined with political disillusionment encourages people to seek alternative source of power and life-style transformation (1995:205), while she notes that the strong Muslim presence in, for instance, Nigeria, has encouraged some Christians to renounce their apolitical stance in order to bring their own agenda to the fore through lobbying candidates in elections. At the same time, Hackett places more stress than Gifford does (at least in his earlier work) on the role of indigenous styles of relating to and appropriating Faith Christianity. She notes (ibid.:211):

We [should not] forget the predominantly American origins of the pentecostal and charismatic revival in Africa. Yet in its present phase, the forces of appropriation and negotiation seem to be more active, with more evidence of agency by African evangelists. It is hard to resist gospel ships and their cargo, but indigenous inspirational literature is now beginning to proliferate and some African evangelists are becoming well known on the global circuit. At one level they appear to be content to reproduce the theological tenets of the movement (a skill much admired in certain cultural contexts), but it is in the process of selection that we find an African emphasis and creativity – in the importance attributed to deliverance, healing and experience, for example.

Here, we see the ambiguities associated with the cultural status of transnational religious revivals such as that promulgated by the Faith preachers. A theology whose origins lie predominantly in the United States is sometimes 'reproduced', sometimes selectively appropriated, in a new context. The development of the revival into a world-wide movement provides a set of numerous recursive channels through which Faith ideas, interpreted through (in this case) an 'African' lens, are then disseminated beyond that continent into the global networks of preachers, conferences, media products, and so on. In this sense Faith ideas may have clear North American origins and be associated with highly powerful ministries in the US, yet they are subject to constant forms of cultural appropriation, repackaging, and redissemination into the transnational realm.

Work carried out on Faith churches in Latin America expresses similar concerns in relation to issues of personal and political effects, as well as ambiguities of cultural location.[24] Chesnut (1997) perceives one of the attractions of Pentecostalism in Brazil to be its apparent ability to provide spiritual power that will provide healing as well as freedom from material deprivation:[25] 'In the context of declining real wages and high levels of underemployment and unemployment, the health and wealth gospel of postmodern Pentecostal churches . . . reverberates through the slums of Brazil' (ibid.:65). Members of the Universal Church of the Kingdom of God and the Four-Square Gospel Church, both of which preach forms of prosperity theology, have been attracted by the idea of running their own businesses (ibid.:21). In fact, the Universal Church (founded in 1977, boasting over a million members by the early 1990s) devotes two days of its weekly schedule of services to preaching the virtues of entrepreneurship. 'Prosperity campaigns' are run where preachers lead worshippers in prayers for those who desire to be self-employed (ibid.:112) and the approach here seems to be more dynamic and direct in seeking work than that of the much older, Pentecostal group, the Assemblies of God. The Universal Church also owns one of the largest television networks in Brazil and has shown signs of (anti-left-wing) political engagement through block voting and seeking allies in government (Freston 1994:544 and 1996:148; Brouwer et al. 1996:205). In these senses the Universal Church looks like Faith ministries in the US, and yet again it cannot be interpreted as a simple vehicle for an unadulterated message of North American evangelical ideology. Chesnut notes, for instance, that the Universal Church syncretises practices of classic and modern Pentecostalism with elements of the more 'indigenous' healing cult of Umbanda, even if it is more dynamic than Umbanda in seeking

---

[24] Even while he discusses how Pentecostalism takes on local colour as it interacts with indigenous religious and social systems, David Martin (1990:53, 76) notes how modern means of communication and forms of competitive religiosity derived from the US have been deployed by Latin American believers. Note also that Lionel Caplan (1995), reflecting on the fact that Pentecostalism exhibits the fastest growth of any Christian group in South India, sees developments there as partially reflecting the commodification and expansion of North American religion to a new market, and is struck by the ways in which Tamil translators duplicate every gesture of their Western exemplars.

[25] Commenting on the current religious market-place in Brazil, Chesnut (1997:3) notes that 'such is the ascendancy of this charismatic branch of Protestantism that other Christian churches have had to "Pentecostalize" to survive the fierce competition'.

contexts into which to spread its message. Its engagement in politics occurs in a country where the Church–State separation of the US is not present and thus engagement in public life takes on rather different implications (Freston 1996:166). In addition: 'Reversing the traditional direction of missionary work, the [Universal Church] has established eleven temples in the United States, one of which occupies the old Million Dollar Theater in downtown Los Angeles, the birthplace of Pentecostalism' (Chesnut 1997:47–8). As in the African case, the ramifying and ultimately uncontrollable networks of Faith activity reach into areas conventionally seen as net exporters of the message, such as the US. In fact, the Universal Church has established itself in some forty countries (Freston 1996:154).

Lehmann (1996:129) identifies the strategy of the Universal Church as concentrating on large congregations in urban contexts (see also Freston 1994:539), producing standardised forms of religious discourse and demarcating between the organisational core and the mass of followers who maintain only a loose, non-institutionalised identification with the organisation. We see here the adaptation of worship to new forms of religious consumption that are paralleled, albeit with different emphases, in churches around the world. Thus Faith ideas have also taken root in many areas of the Pacific Rim, such as the ministry established by the Korean Paul Yonggi Cho (originally an Assemblies of God minister). Cho's Yoido Full Gospel Church, with its membership of somewhere between half and one million people, operates a Bible Institute, video and closed-circuit television links between worshippers and language translation services for foreign visitors. Yet, again, the resonances of such teachings cannot be considered as mere replications of American models, but are understood as emerging from understandings of consumption, demonology and shamanism that can be traced to more obviously local Korean cultural categories (Mullins 1994:92).

The influence of the Faith Movement can even be felt in supposedly secular Europe. Missions from the United States and elsewhere have been active in Eastern Europe over the past few years (Hunt 1995) and in the UK many of the more established Pentecostal and charismatic churches have been influenced by

Faith ideas. Morris Cerullo World Evangelism has alienated many middle-class evangelicals as a result of its extravagant claims to healing and apparently brash Americanism, and yet it has received sponsorship from Kensington Temple, a member of the Elim Pentecostal denomination and purportedly the largest church in Britain[26] (Schaefer 1999). As we shall see in much of the rest of this book, Sweden has also provided an important if surprising context for the dissemination of Faith ideas in Europe.

This brief survey of Faith activities world-wide indicates that broadly similar ideological themes and practices are carried along by the loosely organised Faith network. Adherents can choose from a package containing the following: entrepreneurship, education, organisation of conferences, deployment of the mass media, material consumption and desires for personal empowerment that may shade into reflections on national and international arenas of actions and identity. The United States acts as a key point in the network of activity, not least through its training programmes for budding preachers from around the world, and it may also evoke spiritual imagery, such as Mumba's depiction of the US as founded on biblical principles. However, the global hierarchy of nations is fluid, and other nations (or at least their representatives) are perceived as possessing important spiritual callings, even involving missionary activity within North America itself.

The Faith Movement is sustained not only by the actions of local congregations but also through activities that set up the possibility for exchange and communication on transnational levels, such as conferences and the marketing of spiritually edifying products. The global reach of the Movement means, however, that Faith messages are constantly being re-located in contexts of reception and interpretation that are divorced from the control of distant preachers. For instance, Gifford (1988) notes that African expectations concerning the relationship between public and private life are rather different from those prevalent in many Western countries, and a similar point is made by Freston for Brazil (1996); Latin American conflicts between Catholic hierarchy and Protestant activism have a flavour that is not replicated elsewhere; according

---

[26] With 10,000 members and 100 satellite congregations.

to many Faith adherents in Africa, a major ideological enemy is Islam, whereas in Europe the main perceived threats have been communism and atheism. The Faith Movement provides multiple arenas and frames of action for its adherents, and the contexts of impact and reception for any one preacher or even message can be multiple: a service located in a conference hall in Harare may introduce an American preacher to a Zimbabwean audience; the same service may be shown on video to the preacher's congregation in Texas a month later, or broadcast on a satellite television channel to other countries in Africa, and so on.

Although literature on Faith churches often contains reference to the ways in which adherents are encouraged to support current regimes as well as cultivating pride in the nation-state, we should not underestimate the capacity of Faith and related ideologies to be transformed into symbolic resources of resistance. Some churches in Brazil have expressed a form of popular liberation from old Catholic hierarchies (Freston 1994:538). Van Dijk (1999:181), meanwhile, argues that charismatic religion in Malawi has helped to create autonomous fields of organisation through which young people have instituted non-gerontocratic forms of authority. As we shall see, in Sweden Faith Christians appear to articulate a message that combines conservative support for the nation-state even as it presents a radical reinterpretation of the meanings of governance and territorial belonging.

THE ORIGINS OF FAITH TEACHING

It seems likely that most Faith adherents around the world, whatever their concealed theological and cultural differences, would argue that the Movement's message transcends history in its expression of spiritual truths and immutable laws. Contemporary believers often express the conviction that they are returning to the Early Church in their search for an authentic faith. However, the controversial status of the Faith Movement has prompted some rather more sceptical analysts to reassess its specific historical roots (McConnell 1988). The fact that the Movement has emerged from the United States seems generally to be agreed. At issue is whether it can be seen as truly Pentecostalist or even genuinely Christian in its origins.

The Movement's emphasis on prosperity is hardly novel within Christianity. Images of material success have a long history in North American evangelical circles and beyond.[27] In the US of the nineteenth century, economic success, Divine Providence and millennial hopes for the coming of the Kingdom of God were frequently conflated (Wauzzinski 1993), and the connections between living a correct life and gaining bountiful wealth and prosperity were pointed out by clergy as well as lay people. Famous preachers such as Dwight Moody assumed that diligent Christians would reach their individual goals, including material success, and his Arminian gospel of wealth appealed to middle-class congregations who sought spiritual justifications of entrepreneurial attitudes (Brouwer et al. 1996:9, 26).

Early Pentecostalists did not emphasise the material aspects of prosperity, although miraculous cures as a sign of God's grace were always assumed to be possible. After the Second World War, adherents of the North American healing revival movement, led by such figures as William Branham, Oral Roberts, Jack Coe, A. A. Allen, Gordon Lindsay and T. L. Osborn, proclaimed the notion that God always wished to heal the faithful (Hollinger 1991:58). More general themes of prosperity also began to emerge in the revival, including the idea that financial blessings could be provided for the believer. A key figure here was Oral Roberts, who claimed that in 1947 he had 'discovered' 3 John 2 with its message that 'thou mayest prosper and be in health, even as thy soul prospereth'.[28] In the mid-1950s, at a time when he needed financial resources to fund his television ministry, Roberts created the 'Blessing-Pact' (Barron 1987:62-3). Subscribers who contributed $100 to his work were promised a refund if they did not receive the gift back from a totally unexpected source within one year. Roberts also published a book

---

[27] Brouwer et al. (1996:22) argue that reverence for riches has been legitimated by both secular and religious beliefs in the US. The industrialist Andrew Carnegie, an atheist, wrote *The Gospel of Wealth* in the late nineteenth century and convinced many well-placed Protestants of the merits of the philosophy of Social Darwinism. The main Protestant denominations and industrialists co-operated in incorporating this gospel of wealth into American civil religion.   [28] King James Version; as recounted in Barron (1987:62).

called *God's Formula for Success and Prosperity* (1955), and similar messages of material welfare were proposed by, for instance, A. A. Allen and Gordon Lindsay.

Some twenty years later Roberts developed the 'seed–faith' concept. He claimed that Old Testament tithing to God out of obligation was replaced by a New Testament version – giving in order to expect a blessing. Thus the television viewer could plant a 'seed' (i.e. a donation to him) and would later be rewarded by a large financial return. As Roberts put it: 'You Sow It, Then God Will Grow It' (Brouwer et al. 1996:24), and similar imagery has been deployed by Hagin, Copeland and others. Roberts has also maintained social and preaching contacts with many of the main Faith teachers[29] and invited them to preach at his university in Tulsa, although he has also been careful to maintain his independence from the Movement.[30]

The Pentecostalist or at least evangelical roots of prosperity teachings are evident, at least in broad outline. They are also claimed by members of the Faith Movement. Hollinger (1991:54) quotes Kenneth Hagin Jr as stating the following in a personal letter: 'Our major tenets of faith are held in common by those in the evangelical world – beliefs such as the virgin birth and deity of our Lord Jesus Christ, the absolute necessity of the new birth through faith in the atoning work of Jesus on the cross, and other fundamental doctrines of the church.' However, another set of influences appears to have given the Movement something of its particular character. We need to return to the nineteenth century at this point, not to evangelical Protestantism but to a clock-repairer from Maine, called Phineas Parkhurst Quimby (1802–66). Quimby suffered from bouts of neurasthenia, and from the 1830s he worked on methods to cure himself, with apparent success. By the 1860s he had become well known in local circles as a healer,

---

[29] According to Brouwer et al. (1996:24–5) in 1979 a dispirited Oral Roberts, in the midst of financial problems, attended Hagin's Tulsa Camp Meeting at the Rhema Bible Training Center. Hagin dedicated that night's collection to him.

[30] Some members of Oral Roberts University, indeed, seem actively hostile to or sceptical of the claims made by adherents to Faith ideas. Apart from McConnell's book, in 1979 ORU professor Charles Farah wrote *From the Pinnacle of the Temple*, criticising the 'faith-formula' of the Movement. This book was characterised as a 'negative confession' by the Faith teachers.

'Dr Quimby', even though he lacked a formal education (Meyer 1966:15–16; McConnell 1988:39).

Quimby's 'mind-cure' psychology involved the assumption that mind affected body. Spiritual matter contained within the person acted as a storehouse of past experiences. However: 'Exposed to Truth, the erroneous, faulty, disease-producing, worry-inducing items were eliminated. Thereafter, by the use of conscious, deep and correct thinking, and the exercise of mental suggestion, future experiences could be screened before being allowed to become spiritual matter' (Meyer 1966:70–1). In Quimby's view, human divinity was located in the 'soul', and soul ranked above mind. The conscious mind of common sense, rational inquiry and sense experience was not equipped for the comprehension of divine Truth; its role was to surrender so that the soul could rule. Thus mind-cure or 'New Thought Metaphysics' taught the importance of dominion over consciousness and individual personality. On the one hand, true reality was seen as being created on a spiritual level prior to its manifestation in physical realms; on the other, the potential immanence of the divine was stressed and freedom from disease and poverty was regarded as possible through developing the spiritual nature of humans (McGuire and Kantor 1988; Hollinger 1991:61). Jesus's kingdom could truly be located within the person (McConnell 1988:40).

Quimby was more of a practitioner than a writer, but his ideas were disseminated eloquently by some of his patients. One such was the Reverend Warren Evans of Boston, an ex-Methodist (also influenced by Swedenborg), who in 1869 published a book called *The Mental Cure*. Evans argued in this and subsequent works that healing was not the fruit of finite human thoughts but was spiritual, and according to Meyer (1966:16–17) such reasoning encouraged followers to make 'the leap of faith in the new religion, from therapy to theology'. Around the turn of the century, a number of national associations were formed to promote New Thought ideas, and these helped attract followers who often retained their old Protestant or even Catholic and Jewish affiliations (ibid.:19).

One figure who proved at least partially susceptible to the new 'divine' science was E. W. Kenyon (1867–1948), a New England preacher–educator. Kenyon was to form a vital ideological link in the chain linking New Thought Metaphysics to Faith teachings, and yet his exact connections with either Quimby's ideas or Pentecostalism are far from clear. Kenyon's denominational loyalties moved from an upbringing in Methodism to an adult life promoting forms of Baptism. In the 1890s, he attended Emerson College of Oratory, an educational establishment located in Boston that was closely connected with New Thought Metaphysics.[31] McConnell (1988:34) notes that one of Kenyon's classmates in Boston was Ralph Waldo Trine, subsequently author of the best-selling New Thought text, *In Tune with the Infinite* (1970). After leaving the College, Kenyon worked as an evangelist in New England and Canada. He founded the Bethel Bible Institute in Massachusetts and gradually became a nationally known preacher and author. In 1923, he moved to California, starting a church in Los Angeles, before founding the New Covenant Baptist Church in Seattle in 1931. A radio programme, 'Kenyon's Church of the Air', was also started in the early 1930s (McConnell 1988:33).

Kenyon's career contains many of the elements that would become significant in the ministries of Faith preachers and, indeed, other evangelists of the latter half of the twentieth century: teaching combined with preaching; movement from rural to urban-based evangelism; cultivation of the mass media (both electronic and printed) as well as local congregations; willingness to shift denominational affiliations; and indeed an attempt to build up a constituency of followers that transcended conventional forms of religious membership. In common with Faith preachers of today, he appears to have denied the existence of connections between his ideas and those of New Thought, despite the obvious parallels between the two (McConnell 1988:44). Kenyon stressed the notion that God's nature and the human spirit could be conjoined, so that the divine could become part of the believer's consciousness. Kenyon's book *The Two Kinds of Knowledge* (1942) argues that Revelation Knowledge enables humans to transcend the limitations of the senses or intellect, and to act in faith. The expression

---

[31] McConnell (1988:36) states that the leader of the school, Charles Wesley Emerson, held to the basic tenets of Spencer's Social Darwinism and was an admirer of the Transcendentalism of Ralph Waldo Emerson. Ralph Waldo Emerson emphasised the divinity of the person (Hambre et al. 1983:30).

of the inner person through words appears to mediate between physical and spiritual realms, and indeed Kenyon is the source of a phrase popular in the Faith Movement itself: 'What I confess, I possess' (Hollinger 1991:61).[32]

McConnell (1988:105) concludes that a dualistic epistemology (derived from New Thought) is constructed in Kenyon's teachings, with the Spirit constituting the essential, ideally all-powerful, divine identity of the person. Certainly, the notion that healing occurs in faith before it manifests itself on the material level, a point emphasised by both Kenyon and subsequent Faith preachers (and already seen in the revelation granted to Hagin on the occasion of his original cure), presents a hierarchical construction of reality according to which the spiritual realm is both blueprint for and anticipation of events in the physical world. The individual person becomes a site for contending forces of limitation (physicality, human error) and transcendence (the boundless identity of the divine). A point of some ambiguity in such teachings is the relationship between the conscious mind and the inner Spirit of the person: in one sense, the mind is activated through its deployment of sanctified language and articulation of evangelical desire; in another, it is not to be trusted as a vehicle for ratiocination, and must give way to the guiding power of a Spirit that is the locus of contact with divine force.

Just as Kenyon cannot be regarded as a spokesman for New Thought ideas even if his teachings promoted many of their essential tenets, so his relationship to Pentecostalism was complex and ambivalent. He was critical, for instance, of the idea that glossolalia could be seen as the exclusive initial evidence of Spirit baptism, and he apparently did not encourage the exercise of the charismatic gifts at his meetings (McConnell 1988:22–3). None the less, in his later years he visited Pentecostal meetings and was invited to speak at Aimee Semple McPherson's famous Angelus Temple in Los Angeles. Although he died just after the end of the Second World War, many of the prominent healing revivalists of the postwar years were clearly influenced by him and quoted his work.

An important figure to consider in assessing Kenyon's role as a

---

[32] See also Kenyon's *The Hidden Man: An Unveiling of the Subconscious Mind* (1970).

forerunner of the Faith preachers is, unsurprisingly, Kenneth Hagin. Hagin acknowledges some impact of Kenyon's ideas in his own teachings, but the exact relationship between the works of the two men has become a point of heated debate. A major aspect of McConnell's (1988) thesis is that Hagin's claims to be the founder of the Faith Movement obscure the extent to which the main Faith doctrines were posited by Kenyon long before Hagin's supposed reception of them through divine revelation. Hagin states that he first encountered Kenyon's books in 1950, some seventeen years after he had received the revelation that launched his ministry, and that both he and Kenyon are simply expressing a common truth that is derived from a single source: God. McConnell argues, however, that numerous examples of plagiarism from Kenyon can be discerned in Hagin's work.

The politics of these claims and counter-claims must be considered. As McConnell points out (1988:13), in conceding that he took his theology from Kenyon, Hagin would have to admit that his teaching was of human origin rather than a result of personal revelation. McConnell's claims are themselves associated with a recognisable theological agenda, however. He writes as a committed charismatic (though not a Pentecostal as such) who is highly critical of aspects of Faith theology. By linking Hagin's work so closely to that of Kenyon, he establishes a further intimate connection to New Thought Metaphysics. McConnell can then attempt to argue that the (from his perspective) heretical aspects of Faith teaching – its crude emphasis on prosperity, its conferral of complete power on the believer – have primarily 'cultic' rather than Pentecostal or charismatic origins (ibid.:xviii).

McConnell's work does demonstrate Hagin's debt to Kenyon beyond any reasonable doubt.[33] Less convincing is McConnell's downplaying of the influence of Pentecostal revivalism on the Faith Movement (Hollinger 1991). Many Faith preachers clearly have roots in some version of Pentecostalism and consequently can hardly be said to derive their emphases on miracles, the believer as

---

[33] However we choose to assess its veracity, Hagin's defence that he is drawing only from the same ultimate, divine source as Kenyon is significant in the sense that Faith adherents often depict themselves as able to embody and express precisely the same spiritual power and understandings as fellow believers.

vehicle for divine power, the performative power of language or the body as site of both wholeness and holiness purely from Quimby or his followers. In addition, themes of material prosperity are evident not only in New Thought Metaphysics, but also in elements of nineteenth-century evangelical Protestantism (although not early Pentecostalism). Evangelical and New Thought sets of ideas concerning the divinity of the person and the human right to prosperity have certain mutual affinities and, to some extent, common origins in the ideological streams of late nineteenth- and early twentieth-century North America.

Significantly, Quimby's ideas (and their offshoots) proved resonant for other significant figures in the history of religious and therapeutic cultures in the US. In 1862, the founder of Christian Science, Mary Baker Eddy, was apparently cured by Quimby and subsequently undertook to become his disciple (Meyer 1966:20). Although she was to claim that her book *Science and Health with Key to the Scriptures* (1875) was written through inspiration, it seems clear that she drew heavily on Quimby's notes, New England spiritualism and her knowledge of the Bible (Meyer ibid.:55).[34] Norman Vincent Peale (a Methodist-ordained minister and Christian Reformed pastor) achieved great success after the Second World War with *The Power of Positive Thinking* (1952), an adaptation of some mind cure ideas, psychiatry and Christianity. Peale presented the divine as an unlimited, inner spiritual resource to be tapped through correct techniques, for instance the releasing of power through words. Thus Peale and Eddy, like Kenyon, certainly drew on ideas contained within New Thought Metaphysics, but combined such ideas with other influences to produce distinctive forms of self-help and (spiritualised) therapy.

CONCLUDING REMARKS

In this chapter, I have provided a sketch of charismatic Christianity in general and the Faith Movement in particular. The bare bones of theology and history have been provided since they provide

---

[34] McConnell (1988:15) quotes Hagin: 'When I preach on the mind, it frightens some congregations. They immediately think of Christian Science' (in *Right and Wrong Thinking* (1966)).

necessary background for subsequent, more multi-dimensional analysis – for instance an approach that takes into account the relationship between normative description and specific practice. Most importantly, I hope to have raised some questions that will be addressed more fully in subsequent chapters. I am concerned to inquire, for instance, how it is possible to study a movement that is clearly so fluid and transnational in its scope. I examine the significance of the US in the Faith network, and ask to what extent missionisation (particularly within one context in Sweden) can be seen as pure Americanisation. I hope also to have raised issues relating to matters that transcend religion, concerning the consumption of culture, the nature of transnational movements and the meaning of the international and the global. In the next chapter, I focus more fully on globalisation and suggest how we can begin to understand the Faith Movement in terms of this theoretical paradigm.

CHAPTER TWO

'Faith which conquers the world': globalisation and charisma

Charismatic Christianity is flourishing in the contemporary world. It is a fluid culture that is seeping into numerous social contexts and even permeating supposedly secular practices such as economic consumption and the deployment of technology. Charismatics often view such developments in both defensive and triumphalist terms: they regard themselves as reclaiming territory lost to the devil at the same time as they are spreading the Good News of the Gospels to all nations. The phrase 'Faith which conquers the world' is a quotation from the Bible (1 John 5:4–5); it is also the title of a book by Ulf Ekman, founder and head pastor of the group we shall be focussing on in later chapters, the Swedish 'Word of Life' Ministry.[1] Ekman is referring here to 'the world' as constituting not only the fallen domain of secular humanity, but also the collection of all societies and cultures – including many believers who are already 'born-again' – towards which charismatics should direct their enthusiastic gaze. My aim in this chapter is to juxtapose charismatic understandings of their calling with social scientific analyses of broader developments that are also occurring on a world-wide scale. In other words, I shall begin the task of exploring some of the affinities and connections between charismatic culture and globalisation.

Globalisation became a highly fashionable concept during the 1990s. If the buzzword of the previous decade – post-modernity – highlighted the fragmentation of cultures, a superficial consideration of globalisation would seem to indicate that it redresses the balance by moving towards cultural, political and economic

---

[1] See also Coleman (1991) for a use of this phrase.

integration at a greater level than ever before: that of 'world society'. However, no matter that particular movements might develop their own utopian views of world domination, globalisation taken as a whole need have no inherent direction since it is neither a consciously orchestrated project nor a single, lawlike process (Albrow 1996:95). It can initially be seen as composed of a set of sociological processes and technological developments which aid communication and contact across social and territorial boundaries. Key components include the growth in power and effectiveness of the mass media, increased levels of physical and economic mobility and the burgeoning development of transnational social, political and cultural alliances (Lash and Urry 1987, 1994).[2]

Roland Robertson's famous definition (1992:8) – 'Globalization as a concept refers both to the compression of the world and the intensification of consciousness of the world as a whole' – takes us a vital stage further because it refers not only to the idea of increasing economic, social and communicative interconnections, but also to changing forms of reflexivity and perception. Processes of globalisation are as much about personal and cultural identity as they are about physical mobility, and current developments are particularly notable for their production of new forms of self-awareness in relation to the world. Robertson (ibid.:104) also makes the important point that many discussions of the world-system have ignored the contemporary construction of individualism for the apparent reason that globalisation refers most obviously to very large-scale matters. He rightly disagrees with such a separation of micro- from macro-sociological approaches and insists that 'individuals' are as much a part of the globalisation process as any other basic category of social–theoretical discourse. Overall, the 'global field' is regarded (ibid.:27) as constituted by four, mutually interacting, reference points: selves, national societies, the world-system of societies and humankind.[3] Particularist and universalist tendencies

---

[2] In an influential formulation, Appadurai (1996:33) describes globalisation as being made up of a series of 'perspectival constructs': ethno-, media-, techno-, finance- and ideo-scapes.

[3] Robertson notes (1992:270): 'In an increasingly globalized world there is a heightening of civilizational, societal, ethnic, regional and, indeed individual, self-consciousness.'

thus coexist, often uneasily. The individual self is defined as a citizen of national society and also as a member of humanity as a whole, while people 'can and do increasingly form their identities trans-societally through . . . non-government organizations and social movements, tourism, migration, foreign work, and indeed inter-ethnic and inter-cultural contact within societies' (summarised in Beyer 1994:28).

Despite the richness of Robertson's analysis, his use of the term global 'consciousness' is unduly limiting to the degree that it encourages us to view personal and group identity in purely cognitive terms. He refers (1992:8) to consciousness as involving receptiveness to and understanding of cultures other than one's own, and stresses (ibid.:183) its reflexive character. Intellectual, discursive and semantic factors are emphasised to the exclusion of other perspectives (Friedman 1994:196, 198). The treatment of consciousness as a largely mentalistic state is common in Western scholarship and is presumably bound up with historical distinctions between mind and body.[4] However, an alternative social scientific perspective (influenced by phenomenology and anthropology) is to explore its connections with processes of embodiment. Thus Kapferer (1995:134), drawing on Husserl, argues that consciousness is 'always embodied and constituted and expressed through the action of the body' just as it is formed 'through its engagement with other human beings in the world'. Consciousness is not restricted, therefore, to reflective thought as such, although it does involve (ibid.:135) 'a body directed and oriented towards the horizons of its life-world' (see also Berger and Luckmann 1966:34).

Although I do not intend this book to be an extended exercise in phenomenology, I shall be arguing that charismatics construct an attitude towards the global circumstance that is composed of specific aesthetic and embodied elements as well as conscious thought. Much of this attitude is deliberately orchestrated, especially by leading preachers, but much of it emerges more implicitly out of forms of worship and evangelisation. Charismatics therefore construct *a* world within *the* world, setting up arenas for action, agency and imagination that invoke the global circumstance in a

---

[4] On this theme, see Strathern (1995:117) and Parkin (1995:199).

way that is distinct, even 'sub-cultural',[5] in its combination of noetic, material and physical elements. In doing so, they compete with other, equally 'universalising' and yet distinct ideologies, each containing a different version of what it means to be global.

TRANSFORMATION OR INTENSIFICATION?

Does globalisation really represent an important shift in human activity, or is it merely a novel way to describe old and familiar social processes? Social scientists and historians certainly acknowledge that significant interactions between cultures and nations have occurred throughout many centuries of human history. Eric Wolf (1982) adopts a Marxist perspective in arguing against the 'myth' (propagated not least by anthropology) of the isolated tribe or region, in favour of a perspective that acknowledges the importance of long-established processes of cultural contact, commercial transaction and colonisation in relations between European and other societies. Similarly, Hannerz (1996:18) points out that the image of a world-wide mosaic, where each culture is a territorial entity with sharp, enduring edges, has never really corresponded with ethnographic realities. It can even be argued that the so-called 'world religions' have encouraged people to cultivate non-parochial forms of identity for thousands of years.

World-wide interconnectedness, then, is not new in itself. However, the pace has been hotting up in recent centuries. Haynes (1999:15) identifies three main historical roots for current developments: (1) the emergence of the international states system, stimulated by the geographical spread of European influence and colonisation to the Americas, Asia and Africa from the sixteenth century; (2) the effects of technological and industrial revolutions in the eighteenth, nineteenth and twentieth centuries; (3) the gradual growth of a world capitalist economy. Waters (1995:4) would probably agree with such observations but notes that, if we are to assume that globalisation is at least partly a reflexive process,

---

[5] By using the term 'sub-cultural' I mean to imply that charismatic culture can be shown to have a degree of internal consistency. Adherents clearly vary in the degree to which their lives are enveloped within this culture/sub-culture, and most encounter alternative modes of existence on a daily basis.

the Copernican revolution is likely to have played an important role in convincing large parts of humanity that it inhabited a globe. Here, Waters is invoking a version of globalisation that has some parallels with Robertson's notion of global 'consciousness'. Robertson himself (1992:6), while emphasising that globalising processes have been occurring for centuries and even millennia, feels that the world has moved very rapidly towards 'wholeness' since about 1870. While globalisation should not be confused with modernisation *per se*, it is clearly given extra impetus by the latter's promotion of concepts of new technologies, internationalism, cosmopolitanism, the abstract citizen and contractually based social relations as opposed to status hierarchy (Turner 1994:136).

If processes relating to global interconnectedness have been evident for many centuries of human history, it is also the case that classical social theorists developed concepts of the development of society that parallel those often invoked by scholars of globalisation. Some of these theorists, such as Georg Simmel and Walter Benjamin, will be discussed in later chapters.[6] For the time being, I note that Marx's characterisation of capitalism presented it as providing the grounds for stages of universalism:[7] world-wide class exploitation would lead to revolution and genuinely enlightened world order based on the unity of the human species. Durkheim claimed that, as individuals, we would soon have little in common but our humanity, and speculated that modern societies would have to discover a new set of universally significant moral bonds. Weber, meanwhile, viewed Western rationalism as the basis for an all-encompassing form of modernity.[8]

Admittedly, there are clear limits to the extent to which early theorists can be seen as anticipating current theories of globalisation. For instance, Turner (1994:140) notes that Marx had no appreciation of the universalism of Islam. Marxist analysis was therefore tempered by a somewhat orientalist, Western-centred perspective. Durkheim, meanwhile, came to the conclusion in *The*

---

[6] See, for instance, the references to Benjamin in chapter 7 and Simmel in chapter 8.

[7] See, for instance, his *German Ideology* (1964), written with Engels.

[8] On Marx, see Albrow (1990:9); Robertson (1992:17); Kilminster (1997:265). On Durkheim, see Lukes (1973:338ff.); Featherstone (1990:4); Robertson (1992:22). On Weber, see Turner (1994:141).

Elementary Forms that Christianity could actually be replaced by *nationalist* symbols and rituals. More explicit attempts to understand global order (and disorder) did not emerge until a period much closer to the present day. In the 1960s, McLuhan introduced the highly resonant concept of the 'global village' (1964). His position was that culture was heavily determined by its medium of transmission (Waters 1995:34) and that technologies of transportation and communication extended the human senses. Thus, the new electronic media could create a shared simultaneity of experience, with rapid communications systems allowing instantaneous and domestically appropriated awareness of events occurring in all parts of the globe.[9] McLuhan's views, combining utopian and apocalyptic perspectives, clearly overstressed the extent to which message was determined by medium, and did not take into account the forms of resistance and contested interpretations possible within and between social groupings. The global village can more accurately be described as a predominantly urban social landscape, formed and re-formed by restless, sometimes cosmopolitan, sometimes inward-looking populations which compete for space and political representation. However, the sense of instantaneous communication and mutual awareness highlighted by McLuhan remain useful perspectives.

Another precursor to current theories of globalisation also places considerable emphasis on a single, determining factor; not communications technology, as in McLuhan's work, but rather the economy. World systems theory, associated with the work of Wallerstein (1974; 1979) adapts Marx's analysis of global exploitation by postulating that the earth's nations and societies are being consolidated into an evolving, unequal system of economic–political relations (Shupe and Hadden 1989:115). The driving force for world-wide integration is capitalist expansionism as new forms of polarisation come to transcend national boundaries, creating an increasingly internationalised bourgeoisie versus an impoverished, marginalised and fragmented periphery (Randall 1999:50). Parts of Wallerstein's work (1974) maintain Marx's utopianism by suggesting that, under world socialism, both the

---

[9] See Shupe and Hadden (1989:116–17); Robertson (1992:8).

nation-state and capitalism would disappear, while permitting a multiplicity of cultures to exist (Waters 1995:23). Quite apart from the teleological aspects of systems theory, Wallerstein's perspective has been criticised by commentators such as Robertson (1992) for its inability to take non-economic factors into account. Its analysis of the power-relations involved in a globalising world is valuable and yet too one-dimensional.

DIMENSIONS OF GLOBALISATION

I clearly do not regard globalisation as representing a sudden paradigm shift or transformation in human relations. However, I think it is evident that certain developments involving contacts between individuals, cultures and societies in the modern world are exceptional in their current force and ramifications. New boundaries of belonging are being constructed to an extent never seen before. Connections between people, aided by physical or virtual vehicles of mobility, are becoming more intense and more widespread, and are having an impact on forms of identity and mutual awareness. I suggest that it is useful to think of globalisation as having three interrelated dimensions. These refer to the technological *media* through which cultural flows occur; the forms of *organisation* that have emerged to direct such media as well as other kinds of mobility; and the impact on consciousness, identity and experience – the combination of which I shall call *orientation* – that global processes have the potential to produce. In other words, processes of globalisation can be seen as emerging, with many different and unpredictable outcomes, out of a combination of technological, social and subjective elements.

Media

The past century in particular has seen a huge increase in the number, effectiveness and widespread availability of vehicles for communication and physical movement, ranging from the telegraph to the train, car, plane, telephone, television, fax, e-mail, website and so on. For Giddens (1990, 1991), both 'symbolic media' and 'expert systems' are key factors in the restructuring of social relations across time and space. The former are universal media of exchange such as money, which can under current conditions transfer value from context to distanced context within an instant. Expert systems, meanwhile, consist of repositories of technical knowledge that can be deployed across a wide range of actual situations.

Forms of organisation

Media distanciate human relations across time and space, so that many 'local' events can be regarded as shaped by developments occurring hundreds or thousands of miles away. The social matrix of the transmission of knowledge is transformed as sender and receiver of any given message are physically separated (James 1995:9). In such a world, the freedom to move people or objects and symbols in controlled ways becomes a vital but unequally distributed commodity. Indeed, distance itself can be seen as a socially constructed product rather than an objective, physical given, with its length varying according to the speed with which it may be overcome (Bauman 1998:2, 12). Hannerz (1996:84) draws on Robert Reich's book *The Work of Nations* (1991) to argue that members of certain professions become leaders within particularly mobile webs of enterprise. Those engaged in symbolic–analytic services, including scientists, engineers and journalists, construct centres for global exchange such as convention centres, research parks and international airports.

Certain regions possess the material, social and cultural resources to become favoured venues for the production and distribution of objects and ideologies. 'World cities' develop – concentrations of global financial and culture industries – although one cannot assume that cultural centres will always correspond to social, economic and/or political ones. In fact, a frequent consequence of global flows is a divorce or at least loosening of relationships between social organisation and territoriality (Ahmed and Donnan 1994:7; Scott 1997). It has become increasingly difficult for the state to create a unified culture within its physical boundaries, while nation-states may express different levels of openness to processes of 'de-territorialisation'.

In addition, various forms of organisation are emerging that reflect and take advantage of increases in cultural and social flows associated with the detachment of production, consumption, communities and even identities from local places. Touraine (1981) speculated two decades ago that the social movement rather than the nation-state might become the basic category for social scientific analysis, while other authors have emphasised the emergence of the transnational corporation as a new source of solidarity and collective identity as it develops markets and sites of production across national boundaries.[10] Many movements or organisations – ranging from Greenpeace to the Disney Corporation to the Moonies – can be seen as directing and acting as conduits for 'diverse cultural flows which cannot be merely understood as the product of bilateral exchange between nation-states' (Featherstone 1990:1). They are often assisted by the way certain media and means of forming relationships, such as money, financial markets, contractualised labour, the law and scientific discourse take on transnational reality and scope.

The result of such organisational developments is well summarised by Hannerz (1996:102): 'There is now a world culture, but we had better make sure we understand what this means: not a replication of uniformity but an organization of diversity, an increasing interconnectedness of varied local cultures, as well as a development of cultures without a clear anchorage in any one territory.' Nor should we make the mistake of assuming that globalisation spells the end of the nation-state. Robertson (1992) argues that national societies will continue to be prime, but no longer hegemonic, determinants of identity in the global system. He also points out that the emergence of the nation-state was itself the product of the world-wide diffusion of a particular way of organising social, political and economic relations.[11] Bergesen (1990; see Featherstone 1990:5) agrees on this point, and criticises Wallerstein for assuming that individual states acquired their properties prior to participation in the world-system. In fact, for most of the world's states, the international system necessarily *preceded* their existence.

[10] See Sklair (1991); Hannerz (1996:86).
[11] Regarding these characterisations of Robertson's views, see Beyer (1994:27) and Friedman (1994:196).

Orientation

'Orientation' is an inelegant word.[12] I use it because it can imply both explicit awareness (of one's connections with others as well as of the material environment) and a physical attitude. The term points, perhaps more obviously than 'consciousness', not only to cognition, but also to an embodied stance within a cultural, social and physical context. It also allows for the possibilities of change and mobility: a person or group can shift their orientation towards a given set of ideas, physical environment or group of people according to circumstances. In the following, I shall spend some time exploring the connections between elements that might make up an orientation towards the globe, concentrating on notions of awareness, subjectivity and embodiment.

Transformations in self-awareness can be prompted by transnational and/or transcultural encounters. Albrow (1996:4) refers to 'the reflexivity of globalism, where people and groups of all kinds refer to the globe as the frame for their beliefs'. Similarly, Roland Robertson and Frank Lechner (1985) allude to the 'thematisation of globality' in people's lives. Undoubtedly, the mass media and other global processes have helped create and disseminate images of the world against which increasing numbers of people define themselves and their communities. Transnational contacts encourage 'relativisation' whereby members of any given culture are prompted to consider their own identity in relation to alternatives.[13] Hannerz (1996:48) describes what he calls the 'global ecumene' as an open landscape, so that 'the habitat of an agent could be said to consist of a network of direct and indirect relationships, stretching out wherever they may, within or across national boundaries'.

Perhaps the most comprehensive depiction of subjectivity and identity under conditions of globalisation is provided by Appadurai (1996).[14] He regards electronic media as offering new

---

[12] It is often deployed within Weberian or Weberian-influenced sociology to indicate a sense of motivation and directedness (for instance in relation to aims that are ultimately 'worldly' or 'other-worldly' (Freund 1969:176, 212ff.)). Compare also Csordas's (1997:64) phenomenological analysis of 'orientational processes'.

[13] On relativisation, see Robertson and Chirico (1985:234); Robertson (1992:27); Turner (1994:111).   [14] Though see also Giddens (1990).

resources as well as new disciplines for the construction of imagined selves and worlds. As with electronic media, so with physical migration (ibid.:4): 'When it is juxtaposed with the rapid flow of mass-mediated images, scripts, and sensations, we have a new order of instability in the production of modern subjectivities.' If Anderson's (1983) highly influential work indicated the ways in which nations could be imagined, Appadurai is extending the analysis to the construction of a post-national political world (1996:22). On an individual level, 'More persons in more parts of the world consider a wider set of possible lives than they ever did before' (ibid.:53); and, on a higher level of social organisation, there are also a growing number of 'diasporic' public spheres being imagined and virtually created by people who are separated from their homeland or ethnic group by geographical distance but who often retain contact (and even maintain nationalist ideologies) via electronic means.

We have to remember, however, that for many people the social landscape (to invoke Hannerz's image) remains an enclosed, even claustrophobic environment. It may be the case that in a world of constant change we are on the move even as we stay still in physical terms, but there are still massive differences in the degree to which people feel that they can direct such change or indeed their own forms of mobility. It is notable, for instance, that those who are in the vanguard of creating Appadurai's diasporic public spheres are frequently university students, who have the cultural resources as well as the motivation to carve a cultural space for themselves through advanced technological means. Reactions to defining identity in relation to global processes can range from a cosmopolitan[15] acceptance of pluralism and 'creolisation' (Hannerz 1996:66) to an assertion of the validity of a single view of the world. Indeed, contained within or prompted by processes of globalisation, apparently anti-globalist impulses can develop.[16] The 'Rushdie affair' can be interpreted, for instance, as an attempt

[15] Hannerz (1996:103) characterises genuine cosmopolitanism as an orientation, a willingness to engage with the Other that involves an aesthetic openness towards divergent cultural experiences.

[16] Beyer (1994:3) notes that the global system corrodes identities in one sense but also encourages the creation and revitalisation of particularistic senses of self (see also Robertson 1992:97ff.).

by Khomeini and other Muslims to counter perceived inequalities within the global system through the reclamation and revitalisation of Islamic particularity. Similarly, Bauman argues (1998:3) that neo-tribal and fundamentalist tendencies reflect and articulate the experience of people on the receiving end of globalisation. He is correct to see the reassertion of neo-tribalism as inherent within the global circumstance, and it is true that such a reaction may come from people who feel left out of the cosmopolitan ecumene (or who object to its existence in the first place). As we shall see in the case of charismatic Christianity, however, it is possible to regard a rhetoric of 'tribalism' as positively and actively seeking to redefine the global condition, and not simply as a defensive reaction in relation to it.

Given that some parts of a community or society are likely to be more explicitly open to global cosmopolitanism than others, a possible effect of globalisation might be to create connections across territorial divides but simultaneously to increase fragmentation at the local level. One inhabitant of a croft on a geographically remote Scottish island might earn a living by dealing in stocks and shares, using computer technology to link up with markets in London, New York and Tokyo. In contrast, the cultural and social horizons of the person next door could well, even today, extend little further than the village down the road. This example of neighbours who are 'worlds apart' in orientation also raises the question of whether 'virtual' relations conducted at a distance need by definition be regarded as less meaningful than those based on co-presence (Albrow 1996:138; Hannerz 1996:95; Shields 1996:5). If communications technology (such as that favoured by many charismatics) can make the distant and foreign seem present and tangible, we have to ask whether new social formations and orientations are being constructed that no longer rely on spatial proximity for their power. 'Imagined' communities can be made to appear much more closely knit and concrete now that they can be represented by the moving, speaking image of the video or satellite link-up.[17]

---

[17] Hannerz (1996:96) even refers to the creation of so-called 'tertiary relations' between people – those mediated entirely by technology.

Vehicles of communication that cross cultural boundaries frequently promote relatively abstract and generic ways of producing meaning. The 'symbolic media' and 'expert systems' described by Giddens fall under this category, while Waters states (1995:63–4): 'Under globalization individuals extend trust to unknown persons, to impersonal forces and norms (the "market", or "human rights") and to patterns of symbolic exchange that appear to be beyond the control of any concrete individual or group of individuals.' We do not need to subscribe to McLuhan's technological determinism to accept that the mass media often encourages certain generic ways of classifying and framing events. Such media are likely to involve, among other things, forms of miniaturisation, integration (of text, sound, visuals and sometimes response) and diffusion (Waters 1995:147). It can even be argued that the media have reconfigured many peoples' senses of space and place, as spatial barriers to simultaneous or virtually simultaneous interactions have been reduced (Harvey 1989:293–5). Referring to forms of television, Morley and Robins (1995:11) claim that: 'Audiovisual geographies are thus becoming detached from the symbolic spaces of national culture, and realigned on the basis of the more "universal" principles of international consumer culture.' Visual media can prompt the staging of spectacles such as 'Live Aid' that appeal to a world audience, potentially providing a technical transformation of experience that is as important as the overt articulation of specific values in conveying the impact of globality. Certainly, the experience can have a greater immediate impact than printed forms in the contemporary age.

Appadurai notes (1996:52) that the task of ethnography is to question the nature of locality as a lived experience in a globalised, deterritorialised world. In my opinion, part of the answer to such questioning must be that the subjective appropriation of locality remains on an embodied level. Globalisation can offer not only expanded ways to develop the imagination, but also potentially new ways to experience and orientate the self towards the world in physical as well as aesthetic and broadly material terms. Coney's (1995) analysis of belonging to the 'global religion' of Sahaja Yoga is notable in this regard, as she talks of how (ibid.:111) 'the somatic experiences induced in ritual provide members with an intimate feeling of belonging to an international "collective"'. Sahaja Yogis claim that their development of what is called 'vibratory awareness' unites them to the 'collective consciousness' of the group. The somatic response to global influences can include but also go beyond ritual forms, of course. Appadurai (1996:31) suggests as much in his account of the imagination as an organised field of social practices as well as a form of negotiation between sites of agency (individuals) and globally defined fields of possibility. He invokes a modified version of Bourdieu's (1977) influential concept of habitus, with the latter seen as a tacit (and embodied) realm of reproducible practices and dispositions that is culturally specific in its manifestation.[18]

In completing my depiction of the notion of global 'orientation' I also draw on elements of Bourdieu's work, not least his concern through the idea of habitus to trace the connections between culturally derived classifications, embodiment and material practices. Actors are regarded by Bourdieu as learning a set of practical cultural competences and tastes, expressed in assumptions concerning the social world, bodily movements and language, that are appropriate to and derived from a given social field. The body is therefore seen as the vehicle for 'practical taxonomies' concerning basic social divisions (e.g. male versus female) and sensory experience (e.g. up versus down). Through deportment, stance, gesture, etc., people express a culturally specific habitus, thus expressing the links between the subjective world of the individual and the group and/or class into which they are born or have been inserted. Even something as personal as a gesture takes on a publicly derived dimension (cf. also Mauss 1979). Social life becomes mutually intelligible and collectively orchestrated since individuals' systems of dispositions develop as structural variants of the group habitus (Bourdieu 1977:86; Csordas 1994:12). Such competencies are learned as much by experience as by explicit teaching, and, indeed, social performances are produced as a matter of routine, without explicit reference to codified knowledge. Part of the power of the habitus, then, is that it involves the reproduction of cultural

---

[18] Jenkins (1992) informs some of my depiction of Bourdieu's work in the following paragraphs.

schemes whilst providing a basis for the generation of apparently spontaneous, even improvised, practices by individuals. People react in culturally predisposed ways even to novel situations (Shilling 1993:129).

Many questions are left unanswered by the idea of habitus. Bourdieu does not provide a satisfactory account of the structures that mediate between practising individuals and the broad, ambiguous level of the 'social field' (Jenkins 1992:90).[19] The exact mechanisms of 'socialisation' or training remain unexplored. The degree of the actor's self-consciousness towards the elements of habitus is not fully discussed (although it might be argued that a virtue of Bourdieu's concept is that it challenges dualities between the conscious and the unconscious). Nor does he indicate the possible interrelations or conflicts between the different habituses that an individual may encounter through membership of different social groupings. Furthermore, global processes may be rendering anachronistic the potentially static nature of habitus. Appadurai states (1996:55–6):

> Some of the force of Bourdieu's idea of the habitus can be retained (1977), but the stress must be put on his idea of improvisation, for improvisation no longer occurs within a relatively bounded set of thinkable postures but is always skidding and taking off, powered by the imagined vistas of mass-mediated master narratives. There has been a general change in the global conditions of life-worlds: put simply, where once improvisation was snatched out of the glacial undertow of habitus, habitus now has to be painstakingly reinforced in the face of life-worlds that are frequently in flux.

Appadurai's argument about improvisation is likely to be more or less salient according to the specific circumstances of the individual. The important point is that we can see involvement in cultures and sub-cultures – such as charismatic Christianity – as socialising members into adopting certain physical orientations towards and material practices in relation to the global realm. Even communication in virtual space is, after all, initiated and then interpreted in

---

[19] Shilling (1993:138–9) sees Bourdieu's concept of the social field as a set of dynamic organising principles, maintained by social groups, which identify and structure particular categories of social practices concerned with art, fashion, sport, etc.

'real' space. Cultural models become reinforced by social inter-action in which such models become resonant with subjective experience (Friedman 1994:76). On a similar theme, Hannerz states (1996:27): 'If there is now a growing celebration in social and cultural theory of the body as a symbolic site of self and continu-ity, and of the senses, a greater concern with the body and the senses in their contexts might help us understand some of what "place" is about.' Perceptions of self and local context are nego-tiated under globalising conditions. Any given locality, as experi-enced by the individual actor, will be 'constituted by a series of links between the sense of social immediacy, the technologies of interactivity, and the relativity of contexts' (Appadurai 1996:178). Engagement in globalising forces may involve interactions between the embodied self and mobile, abstract symbolic tokens; between physical and mediated experience.

Thus the spatial metaphor implicit in the notion of orientation is meant to encompass various interrelated elements of human life. Orientation is directed *towards* some other point or points in a social or physical environment, so that any given position is always understood in relation to others; such relationships are constructed in the context of particular forms of social organisation and are often mediated by technologies of communication; they also combine cognitive and embodied elements. Of course, considera-tion of physical engagement raises issues concerning the body as site of social regulation. Appadurai (1996:14) refers to the way in which certain large-scale cultural forms (in the case he describes, the global and colonially diffused game of cricket) come to be inscribed on the body through a variety of practices of increasingly smaller scale. He draws on the work of Foucault, Asad (1983) and van der Veer (1989) to argue that sensory experience and bodily technique – indeed, habitus – emerge as parts of historically con-stituted regimes of knowledge and power. Thus (Appadurai 1996:148): 'This body of work works from the top down, or from the macro to the micro, suggesting that power is largely a matter of the imprinting of large-scale disciplines of civility, dignity, and bodily control onto the intimate level of embodied agents.' Such a view of culture as imprint is criticised by, among others, Friedman (1994:77), who attributes it to a modernist tendency to assume that cultural schemata have an independent existence beyond human experience.[20] While we must accept Friedman's warning that schemata are always our own abstractions from experience (see also Stromberg 1986), we should be alert to the ways in which global processes become implicated in regimes of power and discipline. Charismatic Christians are particularly interesting in this regard because they maintain an emic model of impressing sacred language (the Bible, tongues) upon the self, so that physical person and verbal inscription are regarded as becoming merged. More broadly, charismatic engagement in globalisation involves a politically charged negotiation between physical, material and symbolic elements. Believers subscribe to a democratised notion of the Spirit but also regard some preachers as 'great men' or 'great women' of God; they deal with relativisation of identity and yet seek confirmation of a universalising system of truth; they construct global frames of reference and action while celebrating the sacredness of locality; they appropriate abstract symbolic tokens as well as language not merely on the level of cognition, but also on the level of tangible, embodied experience.

THE CHARISMATIC MOVEMENT

The social and technological processes I have described provide fertile ground for religious and political movements to produce their own definitions of the global circumstance. While accepting the likelihood of the emergence of such movements, Robertson (1992:69–70) notes that few social scientific attempts have been made to understand them. Beyer (1994) does provide an overview of a number of relevant groups, including the New Christian Right in the US, the Liberation Theological Movement in Latin America, the Islamic Revolution in Iran, New Religious Zionism in Israel and Religious Environmentalism. He indicates the power of new or revived religiosities in a world whose mobile and interconnected nature provides many arenas for religious action, but he

---

[20] Csordas (1994:239) argues that 'to say that divine power is embodied does not mean it is "inserted" into or "imposed" upon the body, which is merely a more subtle form of the representational argument, but that it partakes of the bodying forth that defines the body as the orientational locus of self'.

can only provide brief sketches of complex social phenomena. My contention is that the re-emergence of the charismatic movement can be analysed and partially understood in relation to the dimensions of globalisation that I have highlighted, and that in-depth ethnographic analysis is an invaluable means of understanding the sub-culturally specific resonances between certain religious practices and global processes. In the remaining part of this chapter, I shall briefly re-present charismatics in terms of my three dimensions – media, organisation and orientation. Throughout the rest of the book the interactions and interconnections between these dimensions will be illustrated.

Charismatics and other conservative Protestants have clearly adapted their faith to the deployment of mass communications technology. Hunter (1987:6–7) notes that such Christians dominate religious broadcasting in the US, and speculates that their success or otherwise in North America is likely to have an important impact on the diffusion of conservative Protestantism on a global level. Cotton (1995:2) describes charismatics as a 'prototype of the global culture envisaged for the twenty-first century, a network linked by computer, jet and fax'. Faith Christians – who really constitute a sub-movement within the global charismatic movement – are particularly striking even among fellow conservatives in their use of new forms of communications technology in information processing and dissemination (Lindermeyer 1995:28).

The relationship between the use of communications media and certain forms of social organisation can obviously be a close one. According to Poewe (1994:xi): 'The term *global* refers to the unbounded spatial, temporal, institutional, and linguistic reach of charismatic Christianity. The latter has become a global culture or way of life based on perceptions and identities that are transmitted world-wide through high-tech media; international conferences, fellowships, and prayer links; and megachurches.' Some mega-churches function like international corporations, serving as the advocates for smaller, affiliated churches as well as exporting literature, tapes and videos to external markets (Hexham and Poewe 1997:45). Global contacts across networks of evangelicals, meanwhile, can disseminate 'current' ideas or practices in an instant. Thus the Toronto Blessing can be interpreted as involving the globalisation of religious ecstasy along these lines. Outbreaks of uncontrollable laughter amongst Pentecostalist Christians are in themselves nothing new. When they occurred in Airport Vineyard Church, Toronto, however, within a few months it was possible for thousands to share the experience and take it back with them to countries across the globe.

More broadly, styles of worship among charismatic Christians display striking parallels.[21] Of course, one could argue that such similarities are due to the same Spirit infusing different populations around the globe; or one might wish to claim that common psychological phenomena are being manifested, even though the cultural meanings of such phenomena vary considerably. It is at least as plausible an approach, however, to examine the social and communicational links between complex and shifting networks of individuals and groups.

What kind of 'global orientation' might therefore be cultivated by charismatics? Beyer (1990; see also Waters 1995:129) argues that Protestantism carries with it a positive contribution to globalisation on a very basic level. To the extent that belief is a matter of individual conscience, the community of the faithful is dotted across the world and is not confined to a locality or subjected to spatial constraints. Such a view has particular salience amongst charismatics whose ideology usually abjures overarching, centralising structures of governance.[22] These Christians are concerned to prompt the 'flow' of people, ideas and material objects across the globe, and the idea of cementing interconnections between believers united in 'Spirit' is powerfully articulated by them in sermons, oral testimonies and literature. Conferences, prayer networks and media are valued partly because they sustain a sense of participation in impermanent, free-flowing structures. For Poewe (1994:xii): 'Charismatic Christianity is a *global* culture because it is experiential, idealistic, biblical, and oppositional. Being experiential, it is

---

[21] Lehmann notes (1996:8): 'Pentecostal churches all over the world, in the most diverse cultures and societies, exhibit astonishingly similar patterns of growth, use similar techniques of oratory and proselytization, and similar forms of organization and leadership, and also resemble each other strongly in their ritual practices.'

[22] Which is not to say that centripetal expressions of authority are absent – see, for instance, my discussion of Hagin in the previous chapter.

not tied to any specific doctrine nor denomination. Being idealistic, it embraces the whole person and the whole world.' Where church structures and theologies are mistrusted as opponents of spiritual spontaneity, it should become easier to reject specific organisations in favour of an apparently unconfined, all-embracing and endlessly mobile force for personal empowerment. Biblical truth can also be viewed as offering a transcendent model of opposition to confining cultural mores.

If a global, charismatic 'meta-culture' is thus in existence, certain features of believers' ideology and practice might encourage widespread diffusion and openness to local appropriation – for instance, notions of the generic 'seeker' and the emphasis on (often commodified) experience. Cox (1995:147), indeed, marvels at: 'Pentecostalism's phenomenal power to embrace and transform almost anything it meets in the cultures to which it travels.' Roelofs (1994:230) adds that selected examples of exemplary religious talk and ways of behaviour are broadcast via the media to an international public, and such strategies 'may encourage world-wide imitation of religious praxis at the cost of individual and culture-specific expressions.' The necessity for the ability to invoke images and ideas that can appear to be shared across many groups of people is clearly evident, while at the same time (ibid.:231) strong experiences can be taken to refer metonymically to God in ways that go beyond specific expressions of language.

We come back to the idea of charismatic culture articulating an orientation to the global that includes but is not confined to explicit declarations of identity or theology. Poewe (1994:249) emphasises that the charismatic Church is global partly because it is iconic, and in this context she means that it encourages believers to find their way to God through all five senses. Such comments are very suggestive, and they raise as many questions as they answer. How, we must ask, is the mobilisation of the senses related to specific charismatic understandings and experiences of the body as vehicle for Spirit and soul? How does embodied charismatic experience connect with wider aspects of the (globalising) environment, involving for instance the appropriation of geographical or architectural space, or the incorporation of media images into worship? And is it possible to view such processes as 'prompting' certain interpretations of power and knowledge within the physical person? In other words, if globalisation is in part an embodied aspect of charismatic action, is it as much a technique of disciplining the self as it is a means of personal empowerment?

One reason to pose questions concerning the mobilisation of power in relation to the body and concepts of the self is to point out that the idea of charismatic culture somehow transcending locality and denominational constraints is also an ideologically charged claim. Conservative christians generally react to the global circumstance not by accepting pluralism but by emphasising the need for their faith to spread to all corners of the earth as well as to all aspects of the individual psyche. Their efforts in this direction are at first sight, as Lehmann (1996:8) argues, more 'global' than 'cosmopolitan' in the sense that they are aiming to broadcast a universally applicable message rather than seeking accommodations with alternative customs or points of view. In most cases, the message must be protected from dissonance or definitive contradiction for it to sustain plausibility, at the same time as accommodating inevitable variations in local interpretations and practices. The job of the researcher must be to understand the theological underpinnings and media representations of (globalising) charismatic culture alongside the micro-sociological processes whereby such representations achieve authority and resonance in particular people's lives. Systems of spiritual legitimacy are inevitably constructed, through which believers are not only encouraged by others but also voluntarily and sometimes unconsciously submit themselves to reinforcing certain cognitive and physical orientations.

We must remember that 'flesh' is highlighted in charismatic culture itself as a key site of action and surveillance. Wilson and Clow (1981) present the body as the locus of themes of spontaneity and control within Pentecostalism, and the rational ordering of the physical self in Protestantism has been identified by various authors as having affinities with the disciplines of factory production (Shilling 1993:90; Turner 1984:100). Csordas's work (1994, 1997) on charismatic Catholics provides an insightful and sophisticated approach that is heavily informed by phenomenology. He explores the creation of the sacred self through the integration of language and body, representation and being-in-the-world (1997:191). Most importantly, he argues that ritual acts and the practices of everyday life should not be separated too sharply in any consideration of the construction and transformation of the charismatic habitus (ibid.:198–9).[23] Indeed, one of the advantages of habitus as a concept is that it encourages us to consider the ways in which cultural dispositions can extend across fields of activity (a fact that might aid the 'disciplinary' process, of course).

My strategy will therefore be to examine a globalising ideology from the grassroots level of everyday practice as well as from higher levels of social and cultural articulation. We should not assume that global discourse can only be understood from a lofty analytical perspective: mass consumerism, media technologies and notions of the transnational are given particular forms and meanings in accordance with charismatic understandings and assumptions, but also within specific social contexts of human interaction, such as congregations, Bible Schools or domestic spaces, as well as specific acts such as prayer, bodily movement or evangelisation. My approach cannot simply be described as understanding how 'the global' is appropriated by 'the local' because an implication of globalisation, as I understand it, is that crude divisions between these two realms are unsustainable. A given charismatic organisation such as the one I shall describe can, however, constitute a powerful reference point for and locus of socialisation into a particular global orientation. It can act as an arena for the construction and dissemination of ideologies that derive resonance and salience from regional as well as national and global frameworks of spiritualised belonging and identity.

My training as an anthropologist leads me, of course, to read the general out of the particular. I accept that my discipline, through its advocacy of small-scale, ethnographic fieldwork, has tended to associate essentialised cultures and ethnic groups with fixed places (Appadurai 1996:37–9). Such rooting of persons in places has, as I have explained in this chapter, been challenged by processes of cultural flows and virtual co-presence, with the role of place as a

---

[23] I am also more explicitly concerned than Csordas with global processes, although see his consideration of such issues in Csordas (1997).

metaphor for culture becoming weakened or at least transformed (Olwig and Hastrup 1997:7). One way of dealing with such a situation in relation to a study of charismatics would be the development of techniques for multi-locale fieldwork in order to follow the various paths of cultural flow (Marcus and Fischer 1986:91). This is not the approach I adopt here. However, whatever method of research is adopted, some way of acknowledging the significance of the geographically distant for everyday life must be developed. The members of the charismatic 'culture' represented by the Word of Life Ministry in Sweden combine a keen sense of the importance of national context with the desire simultaneously to transcend such a context in many of their practices and much of their rhetoric. These Christians will be shown to construct a specific cultural space that is also oriented to 'the world'; they create contexts of practice which both extend the self out from 'parochial' space and time and make the distant and remote seem understandable – even controllable – from their own perspective. Gradually, then, believers learn to adopt modes of behaviour that provide their lives with a personally meaningful framework that is also global and transcendent in orientation.

CHAPTER THREE

Sweden: national 'state' and global 'site'

I now wish to discuss Sweden as a cultural, social and political context for globalising, charismatic Protestantism. In doing so, I attempt to convey a sense of the broad institutional and ideological background that has played a considerable part in influencing not only Word of Life members' understandings of their mission, but also the opinions of those who oppose the group with such force. More generally, I provide a perspective on a tension that runs throughout the book as a whole, concerning the extent to which understandings of national identity – cultivated by religious or other interest groups – mesh with or contradict more universalising orientations towards the idea of 'humanity' as a whole.

Let me begin by presenting two images of Sweden, separated widely in time and context of production. The first is provided by an ambitious Swedish scholar of the seventeenth century, Olof Rudbeck (1630–1702). Attempting to curry favour in the present by depicting a convenient vision of the past, he published a book in 1672 that purported to demonstrate that Sweden was the cradle of world civilisation (Gaunt and Löfgren 1984:221). Sweden, according to Rudbeck's scholarly ruminations, was actually the real Atlantis. The country had apparently been founded soon after the biblical flood, and could therefore be considered the world's oldest kingdom. Rudbeck's text included an engraving with a globe – and of course the author – in the centre of the picture. The Swedish scholar is shown staring confidently at the reader and pointing out the centrality of his country to a group of admiring sages, including Aristotle and Plato. Two angels look down approvingly whilst helpfully adjusting some curtains at the back of the room.

The second image comes from a much more recent period of

Swedish history. It is a photograph I took in the winter of 1986 and depicts a mass of flowers piled on to the otherwise pristine pavement of a street in central Stockholm. The flowers marked the spot where the Prime Minister of Sweden, Olof Palme, had been assassinated one evening in late February. Palme, in the company of his wife but without a bodyguard, had been shot when returning home from an evening at the cinema. The identity of the attacker remains a mystery, almost fifteen years later.

My point in juxtaposing these two images is to say something about representations of Sweden within a global, or at least international, framework. Rudbeck's book was produced at a time in Swedish history when the country could be regarded as a relatively important military power in Europe. This period of influence was to prove short-lived, however, and by the beginning of the nineteenth century Sweden had lost its Finnish provinces to Russia. Since that time, the country has not been directly involved in sustained military conflict. The notion of Sweden as a great centre of civilisation and empire has not become part of civil religious mythology. Rudbeck's triumphalist work, to the extent that it is noticed at all in contemporary Sweden, is most likely to be viewed with bemused irony.

In contrast, the abrupt and tragic manner of Palme's death, symbolised by flowers that interrupt the flow of pedestrians as they hurry along a busy street, has provoked a series of troubling questions in public and private discourse.[1] At issue has been the question of whether undesirable developments evident elsewhere in the world were finally afflicting a country renowned for its freedom from violence and disorder. As Kälstad (1986:2) puts it, the shock over Palme's death has led to discussions concerning the sustainability of a 'national axiom' – that of an 'open society' where political leaders can be treated as normal citizens, accessible to and trusting of the general public. For many, Palme's bloody fate implied that global chaos could no longer be kept at bay. During his life, he had been a controversial figure in Swedish society. His aggressive personal style seemed out of place in a political culture dominated by ideals of compromise and consensus. Yet he had also

---

[1] See discussions in Ejerfeldt (1986); Haste (1986); Kälstad (1986).

come to represent an important and familiar face of Sweden to outsiders – one not of conquest and empire but of mediating between positions, promoting peace and attempting to eliminate economic inequality within and between nations.

In Palme's life and death we see reflected some of the contradictions evident in contemporary Swedish society. The common idea – expressed within Sweden and elsewhere – of the country as a relatively isolated, northern nation coexists with a widely acknowledged (and to some extent consciously cultivated) image of it as a global exemplar of peace and order.[2] At the same time, the possibility is increasingly mooted in political, academic and media circles that Sweden's existence as a supposedly autonomous, neutral entity is unsustainable in a world where global influences – ranging from Hollywood films to patterns of violent behaviour – are liable to penetrate the borders of any society. The assassination served to crystallise a series of concerns and forms of self-reflexivity concerning nationhood and the articulation of culture that have been of particular concern in Sweden over the last two to three decades (Coleman 1991). It was notable that, during the widely reported police investigation of the murder, a number of 'foreign' suspects emerged, only to be discounted for lack of evidence: these ranged from Kurdish immigrants to a lone man, said in some newspaper reports to have been connected with American-inspired ecstatic religion – that of the Faith Movement.[3]

The link briefly suggested in the press between Faith Christians and Palme's murder inquiry provides one, admittedly outlandish, illustration of an obvious point: the Word of Life and fellow charismatics do not exist in a social and cultural vacuum, isolated in global splendour from national or local interests and constraints. Of course, in discussing the significance of Sweden for such Christians, I am aware of the potential irony of having a nation-state be an 'anchoring referent' of a book dealing with globalisation (Appadurai 1996:18). I do not, however, assume that a single, static, Swedish culture can somehow be mapped on to the

---

[2] Perhaps the most notable figure in the post-war period was Dag Hammarskjöld, Secretary General of the United Nations. Sweden is also, of course, the home of the Nobel Peace prize.

[3] For a discussion of these press reactions see also Coleman 1989:193.

geographical and political outlines of the nation-state; nor do I assume that the Word of Life can be seen as an essentially Swedish (or, for that matter, American) phenomenon. Rather, Sweden can be seen as a significant structural context for the case I am studying because its laws and institutions have constituted a juridical, economic and politico-religious framework that has undoubtedly had an effect on the activities of the Word of Life. In addition, most of the active members of the group are Swedish citizens, and have tended to assume that public presentation of their beliefs is part of a national 'calling' to convert their own people as well as those of other nations. The result has been a series of negotiations and often heated debates as to the 'Swedishness' or otherwise of such charismatic practices.[4] Faith actions have been variously interpreted by adherents and external observers as taking on significant meanings in relation to the activities of other, more established churches in Sweden as well as 'mainstream' life styles, attitudes and behaviours.

Below, I provide a picture of some of the elements of the Swedish state that are most salient in a consideration of influences on the Word of Life. I also point to some of the ways in which events and institutions in the country appear increasingly to be influenced by developments beyond its borders.[5] Sweden can therefore be analysed as both a 'nation-state' (in political, cultural and legal terms) and a 'site' for transnational processes.

BUILDING THE MIDDLE WAY

Rudbeck's mythical vision of global influence has little in common with the Sweden of the early nineteenth century. By northern European standards, economic development was at a low level. The predominantly agrarian population was at the mercy of a number of crop failures and these, combined with a soaring birth rate, contributed to the creation of what Connery (1966:352) calls a 'Nordic Ireland': around one and a quarter million Swedes, a

---

[4] See chapter 9.
[5] I am not, of course, claiming that a golden age of national autonomy has ever existed. For instance, the Hanseatic League which linked North German trading cities was a major influence on Sweden in the late Middle Ages.

fifth of the population, emigrated to America between 1860 and
1930. Although Sweden had supplied metals and timber to other
European countries from the Middle Ages, the first major waves of
industrialisation occurred in the 1870s, involving railways, hydro-
electric power and mechanised mills. This early period of industrial development was also characterised by the emergence of a
series of mostly working-class movements, whose members sought
a voice independent of established political, ecclesiastical or aris-
tocratic hierarchies.[6] The so-called *folkrörelser*, or 'popular movements', eventually came to consist of temperance groups, trade
unions, consumer co-operatives, tenants' associations, grassroots
educational organisations and various 'free' churches.[7] Generally,
the expression of particular forms of religious and/or political
individualism was combined in these groups with a concern
for social reform and participatory democracy. Reflecting on
the lasting significance of the popular movements, Stromberg
(1986:99) remarks: 'Although founded on the *form* of a radical and
deeply entrenched individualism, [modern Sweden] has preserved
strong communal values.'

During the early part of the twentieth century, great tensions
between popular movements and state or employers' organisations
were evident. However, by the 1920s and 1930s political and economic power-holders began to be more conscious of social duties.
In 1938, representatives of the Swedish Trade Unions and of the
Employers' Confederation created a ground-breaking agreement
in which members of labour and employer organisations laid
down the rules through which collective bargaining would take
place (Hadenius and Lindgren 1990:51).[8] In effect, the *negotiation* of
disputes became obligatory. Per Albin Hansson, the Social
Democratic prime minister in the pre-war years, also won broad
political support for the creation of an extensive welfare state,
which he called the *folkhem*, or 'people's home' (Himmelstrand
1988:19). The foundations of the so-called 'Swedish Model' of

---

[6] Deviations from Lutheran orthodoxy were strictly monitored and conversion to another
doctrine could be punished by deportation up until 1860. Opposition to the State Church
was tantamount to political protest, at least in the eighteenth and nineteenth centuries
(Stromberg 1986).

[7] See discussions in Rydén (1985:11) as well as Hadenius and Lindgren (1990:29).

[8] Known as the Saltsjöbaden Agreement. The Agreement came at a time when some economic stability had been achieved after a period of economic depression.

identifying pragmatic, collective solutions to problems were being laid, and were famously described by an American journalist of the time, Marquis Childs (1936), as constituting a 'middle way' between capitalism and communism.[9] The new welfare state would ideally allow individual citizens to break out of old dependencies and yet retain their commitment to social responsibility.

As a neutral country, Sweden emerged relatively economically and politically unscathed from the period of the Second World War. Tage Erlander, who became Social Democratic Prime Minister in 1946, advocated the notion of the 'strong society', in other words the idea of central and local governments commanding extensive economic resources for social programmes. Hadenius and Lindgren (1990:6) identify egalitarianism as one of the dominant social themes in Sweden in the post-war years, and it was an objective supported not only by an extensive welfare system, but also by high marginal taxes and relatively small income differentials. Other aspects of governance practised over the past half century have also reinforced ideals of equality and mass participation in national projects. Trade unions, farmers' organisations, consumer associations and at times even churches have been able to contribute to the formation of social policy as a result of the procedure of sending out proposals in advance to relevant organisations (Coleman 1989:315). Education has been characterised by the almost total absence of private schools and a high degree of uniformity in the curriculum (Hadenius and Lindgren 1990:82). For many years, media output in Sweden was dominated by a public-service ethic, modelled on the British Broadcasting Corporation.[10]

At the same time, the expansion of privately owned businesses has been encouraged. Wilson (1979:17) writes that politicians have aimed for 'socialization of incomes rather than rationalization of the means of production in the belief that private enterprise would produce more efficiently the economic growth on which its welfare policies depended'.[11] The adoption of capitalist policies may also

---

[9] See the discussion of Childs in Svensson (1988) as well as Childs' second work (1980).

[10] The independent but government-controlled Swedish Broadcasting Corporation was formed in 1925. The Corporation has provided air-time and technology for churches (Linderman 1996:100–2).

[11] See also Scase (1977). In fact, nearly 90 per cent of industrial output comes from private firms, even if Sweden has also developed the largest public sector in the Western world (Hadenius and Lindgren 1990:40–1).

have been influenced by the need to co-operate with opposition parties. Social Democrats, the political heirs to the Labour Movement, have held power for remarkably long periods of modern Swedish history since the early 1930s – for a total of around sixty years – but have often had to rule without an overall parliamentary majority.

The role of religion in the development of contemporary Sweden is more complex than the frequently invoked picture of the country as a haven for secularised modernity might imply. None the less, levels of practice are low by international standards.[12] The Swedish Church of the nineteenth century was seen by many people who were located outside its hierarchies as dogmatic and opposed to innovation (Scobbie 1972:89). Tolerance of even slightly deviant religions does not have a long history in the country and Sweden appeared to be a religiously monocultural country up until recent times (Gustafsson 1988:467).[13] Only in 1951 was a law created that facilitated voluntary exit from the State Church without requiring the citizen to join a Christian denomination. The (admittedly increasingly diluted) union between the Lutheran Church and the state is obviously not comparable with the much more decentralised conditions that have spawned North American religious activism.

Gustafsson concludes of Swedish religious practice (1988:462): 'Despite the high percentage of the population who are members of the churches and denominations, organised religion, for instance with regard to frequency of attendance at services, does not have any great significance in daily life.' Of course, such a description does not take into account the non-institutional articulation of religious beliefs or practices. Data from the mid-1980s indicate that over 40 per cent of the population believe in 'a God, a divine force or power', although around 20 per cent profess no

---

[12] Thus Hadenius and Lindgren (1990:101) state that 'only five percent of the overall population attend church each week . . . Few countries have such low percentages of regular worship. The Church of Sweden is not a major factor in public discourse or politics.'

[13] New Religious Movements, which emerged in Sweden in the 1960s and 1970s, have only attracted a few hundred members each (Gustafsson 1991:100). In 1990, the Mormons had some 7,500 members and the Jehovah's Witnesses just under 22,000 (ibid.:93): such numbers should be interpreted in the context of ageing memberships and missionary efforts that have lasted for over a century.

belief at all (Gustafsson 1991:25). Furthermore, the Swedish Church has managed to retain the vast majority of the population within its ranks up to the present day, even including many Christians who are active members of the free churches.[14] It has proved a sufficiently uncontroversial – and, one might say, powerless – symbol of national belonging, provoking attitudes of benign apathy rather than militant opposition.[15]

Higher levels of active participation in congregational life have been evident in the free churches, whose membership comprises just above 3 per cent of the population (Skog 1994:57; Linderman 1996). However, all of the established free churches have ageing populations. In general, people have been born into membership, though some movement between denominations has been evident. The Pentecostal Movement is younger[16] and more conservative than most other nonconformist organisations, and has also tended to be the most successful at retaining members over recent decades (Gustafsson 1991:62). Women tend to make up the majority of members of free churches, but less so within Pentecostal congregations. Data that compare the social make-up of free church members from the 1930s and 1970s imply that working-class participation has become relatively less evident in all churches except among the Pentecostalists, where levels have remained about the same and therefore become more marked in relation to a total population that is moving towards middle-class, professional status.[17]

Overall, post-war Swedish society has come to express a certain vision of efficient modernity. High levels of literacy, take-up of higher education, technological capability, newspaper readership and good health have combined with considerable participation in

[14] Until 1996, a child automatically became a member of the Church if one of the parents was a member.

[15] Around 7,500,000 belong to the Church out of a total population of a little under 9,000,000; over 75 per cent of infants are baptised and 90 per cent of funerals conducted under the auspices of the Lutheran Church (see the Report published by the Swedish Institute, May 1999: 'The Swedish Population').

[16] Both in terms of its arrival in Sweden, in the early years of this century, and in terms of its membership profiles.

[17] In 1930, 55 per cent of Pentecostalists were 'working class' (roughly in line with the general population). By 1978, 53 per cent of Pentecostals were working class (total in population 38 per cent). For figures on class membership of all the free churches see Gustafsson (1991:71).

voluntary organisations. The vision, however, has been interpreted in different ways. Huntford, in his book *The New Totalitarians* (1971), accuses Swedes of accepting an all-embracing bureaucracy and a consensual culture which have suppressed individualism and freedom. He traces such self-subordination all the way back to the emergence of a powerful, well-organised polity in the sixteenth century.[18] Despite his politically motivated hyperbole, Huntford does point to a feature of Sweden that has been rather different to more obviously fluid and pluralist Western democracies. As Ulf Hannerz (1996:158) points out, for many years in Sweden the slowly expanding state cultural apparatus – Church, schools, media – has mostly worked on the assumption that Sweden is monocultural. The Social Democratic concept of *folkhemmet*, 'the home of the people', combines the ideas of a unified nation and collective welfare state in a way that can be represented as stifling – a 'computerised prison' as opposed to a 'secure paradise' (Gaunt and Löfgren 1984:7). On the other hand, the Canadian political scientist Donald Milner (1990:4) characterises Social Democracy as a desirable cultural and social practice that transcends party politics in its achievement of a 'fit' between values and institutions. In a country of small size and, according to Milner's view, relative homogeneity (ibid.:19), it has seemingly been possible to cultivate solidaristic values that are reinforced by ubiquitous voluntary organisations.

AN IDEOLOGY OF MODERNITY

Thus far, I have combined an account of the development of the modern Swedish state with a description of some of the more significant voluntary organisations in the country. In fact, I could retell the story from a rather different perspective, in which everyday processes of cultural debate, construction and reproduction are taken more fully into account. Such an approach is adopted by the ethnologist Orvar Löfgren (1987:77), who begins his attempt to

---

[18] Writing in the same decade. Dorothy Wilson (1979:20) attempts to describe Swedish attitudes in more moderate tones than Huntford: 'Perhaps some of the disenchantment with the welfare state in the seventies has come from a feeling that . . . self-reliance has been sacrificed to the all-embracing welfare-state.'

'deconstruct Swedishness' by noting that many observers of the country – including Swedes themselves – have stressed its cultural homogeneity. Certainly, economic differences have in recent decades been less marked than in other European countries and the language of class has seemed rather muted. A consistent set of labels has been applied to and often reproduced by Swedish people (ibid.:78): they are nature-loving, conflict-avoiding, obsessed with self-discipline, orderliness, punctuality and rationality. For Löfgren, these characteristics are significant partly because they represent the dissemination of middle-class values into broad sections of society. As part of the diffusion process, such values have been expressed not only in explicit discourse, but also in the embodied routines of daily life.[19] Admittedly, during the inter-war years, the political initiative in Sweden was taken over by the working-class Labour Movement through the newly emergent Social Democratic Party. However (ibid.:85–6):

The individual was integrated into a wider, national community through new forms of interaction with the state and its many institutions. New forms of mass media invaded the home at the same time. Much of this communication came to be dominated by middle-class definitions of normality . . . The Social Democrats, who came to power in 1932, were so busy building a new, modern society, that they rarely had time to think about where the cultural definitions of this modern living were taken from.

Löfgren's depiction of Sweden should not be taken to imply that Swedes were brainwashed into mass conformity. Rather, he is pointing to the creation of a multi-faceted apparatus for constructing ideal citizens in which the authority of the state combined with other, class-related means of influencing society. Intellectuals and the state co-operated in a way that contrasts with the more open, commercially driven regimes of the USA. During the inter-war years, for instance, the idea of mental and physical 'hygiene' provided an often-invoked, medically defined vocabulary of describing recommended behaviour (even a 'habitus') in Sweden. Moral

---

[19] The years of early Swedish industrialisation can therefore be seen as involving the movement of bourgeois sub-culture into a dominant position, in contrast to the less powerful efforts of the crumbling aristocracy, disintegrating peasantry and emergent working class.

and scientific arguments combined in a powerful way, reinforcing the legitimacy of new professional classes of 'experts'. Frykman (1993:167ff.) also notes that, from the 1930s, the role of the body in the new society was further explored through mass sporting movements. Morning exercises became available on the radio, and even today around two million Swedes belong to Sports Clubs.

Löfgren (1993:53ff.) refers to the self-produced image of Social Democrats as internationalists who wished to remove a cultural inheritance that was seen as corrupt, inegalitarian and stultifyingly traditional. He notes that they introduced new means of 'becoming' Swedish through weaving together ideas and practices relating to democracy, citizenship and modernity. The idea of the modern involved learning to be rational, classless consumers – an important issue considering that the average person's buying power doubled between 1950 and 1975. After the Second World War in particular, the interplay between welfare nationalism and consumption practices grew stronger. The state became involved not only in planning the market, but also in helping to structure the aesthetics and routines of modern life (Löfgren 1997).[20] Similarly, for Daun (1988:323), the powerful equation of modernity with democracy, equality and rationality has itself been a product of particular cultural and structural forces evident in the country. Representations of pragmatism, objectivity and planning not only involve appeals to supposedly universal principles and practices, they have also taken particular shape and resonance within the institutional frameworks of Swedish society. According to this perspective, even the stereotype of the 'neutral' Swede who suppresses cultural idiosyncrasies and mediates successfully in international affairs has traceable ideological roots within the development of the Social Democratic state.

FROM THE MIDDLE WAY TO A PLURALITY OF PATHS?

An important aspect of the approach represented by ethnologists such as Löfgren, Frykman and Daun is that they present a picture of culture and society in constant process. The 'middle way' and

---

[20] A globally renowned example of a Swedish aesthetic associated with consumption is IKEA, the furniture store.

'Swedish Model' of political discourse are shown to be translated into everyday praxis and therefore located in embodied orientations to the world, and yet they are always seen as open to renegotiation and contestation through the emergence of alternative cultural, political and economic influences. In recent years, various representations and structural foundations of the *folkhem* have certainly received increasing challenges on a number of levels. Loyalty to political parties has become less evident[21] and the early 1990s saw the emergence of a new party called New Democracy, which attracted attention through its emphasis on economic *laissez-faire*, reduction of centralised government and opposition to immigration. New political outlets outside the party system have also gained higher profiles, involving for instance participation in global environmental movements and the peace movement as well as support for local action groups (Hadenius and Lindgren 1990:25–6). Membership of the European Union was established, after considerable debate, in 1995. During the 1980s a greater consensus among parties became evident concerning the financial unsustainability of large-scale government social welfare programmes (ibid.:66), particularly during a period of oil crisis, labour-cost explosion and decline in industrial production. In 1991, one of the foundations of such welfare, the high level of income tax, was considerably lowered. In the same year, the deregulation of higher education was initiated, allowing greater autonomy for pedagogical institutions.

Cultural pluralism has also become more evident in Sweden (Ehn et al. 1993:9).[22] Today about 10 per cent of the population are classified as immigrants in the sense that they were born abroad or have at least one foreign-born parent. Many such people are from the other Nordic countries, but the flux of incomers was dominated in the first post-war generation by people from Yugoslavia, Italy, Greece and Turkey who moved to Sweden looking for work. More recently, after the government started to place greater restrictions on job seekers from abroad, newcomers have often been political refugees from Latin America, Africa and Asia. Hannerz (1983:122) concludes that Swedish society has changed

---

[21] Non-socialist cabinets were in power from 1976 to 1982 and 1991 to 1994.
[22] Of course, the Saami have long been present in the north of the country.

considerably since the second half of the 1960s and has become much more influenced by ideas and life styles from around the globe. Older notions of state-supported cultural management have been questioned. During the 1970s, official attitudes to resident immigrants also seemed to change, from encouraging assimilation into a monolithic model of Swedish culture towards promoting a greater degree of multi-culturalism (Ehn 1993:242–3).

These developments have set their stamp on religious culture, particularly in larger urban areas (Straarup 1994:6). Roman Catholic and Orthodox Churches have grown in numbers, as have the numbers of Muslims in the country.[23] In such a context, the recent decision that the Swedish Church should become disestablished can be interpreted as partly symptomatic of a shifting, increasingly heterogeneous religious landscape. The mass media, too, have undergone profound changes in response to such factors as internationalisation and technological innovation (Hultén 1984:58). Linderman (1996:79) argues that Sweden is moving towards a more pluralistic institutional media environment in television, in other words to a situation more similar to the American media environment. Local radio was introduced in the 1970s and immediately became an important resource for free churches, particularly Pentecostalists. By the end of the 1980s, a fifth of the population could watch foreign television programmes via satellite and cable, and such developments also introduced commercial types of broadcasting to the Swedish audience along with some of the top-rated American electronic church programmes, including those of Schuller and Copeland. The Pentecostal television corporation, TV-Inter, has become highly involved in the introduction of American media ministries to the Swedish audience (ibid.:108). Even the Church of Sweden introduced a help-line programme on a cable channel in 1992 (ibid.:109). Nowadays, the amount of com-

---

[23] Skog (1994) compares national memberships of non-established Churches. While the Pentecostals have over 90,000 members and are the largest 'free church', 'immigrant' Churches such as the Roman Catholics have some 150,000 members, and Orthodox and Eastern Churches have a combined total of nearly 100,000. She (ibid.:57) has also examined attendances at services in Greater Stockholm and finds that, while the Swedish Church still dominates (despite rapidly falling attendances) with some 31.5 per cent of the total, Roman Catholics have 9.8 per cent, with Muslims coming fourth with 7.8%. (The Pentecostals come second with 11.9 per cent.) These figures are based on a survey conducted on 13 and 14 November 1993.

mercial religious television available is much larger than that of non-commercial output.

Many of the changes I have outlined are expressions of globalising forces: they involve movements of populations, the pluralisation of the media and new linkages to cultural, political and economic processes beyond Sweden. One effect of such developments has been the emergence, in certain sections of society, of a new sense of self consciousness in relation to 'national culture'. Daun and Ehn (1988:11–13) note that cultural and bureaucratic encounters with the immigrant 'other' have posed newly urgent questions concerning boundaries between public and private life, contexts for the expression of emotions and the cultural foundations for ideas of objectivity, common sense and planning. Concern over an intensified Americanisation of culture has also grown, although such a debate has been present in Sweden for many decades. The name of a recent book by Ehn, Frykman and Löfgren (1993), *The Swedification of Sweden*,[24] refers to a process of cultural construction, dramatisation and invention that has become particularly salient. They note (ibid.:8–9):

> The . . . interest in reflecting upon national identity has grown as Sweden has become a land of immigration. In a number of contexts, Europe and the world have come close to our lives. During the last decade alone more books and articles have been published that variously take up the theme of 'Swedish culture' than in the whole of the rest of the century.

Of course, international contacts and processes of globalisation can be manifested and perceived in many different ways. They can be seen as an enrichment of culture, a means of adding to forms of local experience and awareness. Frequently, they can be appropriated by sub-cultures and given very particular meanings. O'Dell (1993), for instance, notes how American cars have long been used by Swedish youth to signify working-class rebellion. My own experience of enduring country-and-western music sung in a southern Swedish dialect at a midsummer party convinced me that I was observing a cultural event that could hardly have been described as 'American', despite the genre of singing. Externally derived influences can also be seen as a threat, and here we return briefly

---

[24] My translation of *Försvenskningen av Sverige*.

to a reconsideration of the fate of Prime Minister Palme. In his life, Palme could be seen as an actor on a global stage, a major political figure who had been educated in both Sweden and America, who forcefully and eloquently expressed a Swedish openness to the needs of people from other cultures. In his death, however, he might have fallen victim to forces – embodied in foreign extremists – that threaten national security and coherence. Indeed, we now turn to examine a cultural phenomenon that has been interpreted by many in the country as embodying dangerous influence from abroad: the charismatic Protestants who, even as they provoked controversy and opposition, also found Sweden a fertile site for expanding their version of a globalising faith.

CHAPTER FOUR

The Word of Life: organising global culture

The flat landscape around Uppsala is dominated by the profiles of two ancient buildings, which lie close to each other in the centre of the city.[1] One is the medieval cathedral, housing the tombs of a number of famous scholars and kings. The other is a castle, originally designed as a stronghold in the 1540s by Gustav Vasa, the king renowned for having brought the Protestant Reformation to Sweden. Located alongside these buildings are departments of Uppsala's venerable university and a number of museums, forming a heritage complex on the city's only hill. Across the river in the commercial district are most of the free churches, many of them founded in the late nineteenth and early twentieth centuries at a time of increasing industrialisation and democratisation.

The casual visitor is not likely to be encouraged to visit an area on the eastern border of town, away from the historic landmarks, shops and fashionable suburbs. Here is situated a large industrial estate, whose high-rise offices and warehouses are beginning to clutter up some of the skyline previously monopolised by the castle and cathedral. Most of these newer buildings have sacrificed architectural beauty for the sake of cost-effectiveness. One structure does stand out from the rest, however. It is composed of concrete, metal and glass, and its walls are a gleaming white colour (Figure 1). Outside, a large sign proclaims the corporate identity of the occupants: the Word of Life (*Livets Ord*). The group's distinctive

---

[1] Uppsala was once the capital of the country. The urban area, located 70 km north of Stockholm, now has about 185,000 inhabitants.

Figure 1 The new Word of Life building, just before its completion in 1987.
The logo and name of the group are prominently displayed.

logo, consisting of an open Bible, a sword and a rainbow, is also on display.[2]

The Word of Life occupies a geographically peripheral location in Uppsala. However, it is at the centre of a charismatic revival in Sweden that has caught the attention of mainstream political, academic and ecclesiastical representatives. It has also acted as a conspicuously successful and influential part of the world-wide Faith Movement over the last two decades. This chapter provides a sense of how the group emerged in Sweden and how it compares with apparently similar organisations in Scandinavia and elsewhere. We begin to see how the structure of the group relates, in a distinctly charismatic way, to one of the dimensions of globalisation I highlighted in chapter 2: the creation of an organisational form that can control, and even construct, global flows of culture.

---

[2] The Word of Life's logo appears on most of the group's products. The rainbow can be taken to represent the notion of covenant, as revealed in Genesis, as well as salvation after the Flood; the open Bible represents the central text of the group being put to use; the sword recalls Paul's letter to the Ephesians (6:11), encouraging them to 'Put on the whole armour of God' and take up (6:17) 'the sword of the spirit, which is the word of God'.

ORIGINS

Charismatic preachers from abroad, and in particular the United States, have often visited Sweden. Since the Second World War, free churches (predominantly but not exclusively Pentecostal) have hosted such well-known personalities as David du Plessis, Billy Graham, Dennis Bennet, Derek Prince, Yonggi Cho and Kathryn Kuhlman. The post-war years have also seen the establishment of a series of sometimes home-grown, sometimes internationally derived, 'para-church' movements in the country.[3] Among the best-known of such groups is the Full Gospel Business Men's Fellowship International, which came to Sweden in 1965.

As elsewhere in the West, the 1960s and 1970s were times of widespread charismatic renewal in Sweden. The Jesus Movement proved especially popular among younger people, and was viewed as a largely positive and ecumenical phenomenon by more established Christian organisations (Gustafsson 1991:111–12). More controversial was the Maranata Movement, which emerged in Sweden in the late 1950s and early 1960s. Its leaders were influenced by a minor revival among Swedish Pentecostalists as well as by conservative Protestant preachers in Norway and the United States. Stress was laid on the extensive use of tongues, revivalist songs and prayers for the sick. The importance of local congregational independence – free from denominational or state hierarchy – was perceived as paramount. More traditional Swedish Pentecostalists were said by Maranata supporters to have been compromised by bureaucratic centralisation and ecumenical relations with other religious and secular organisations. As Dahlgren (1982:99) comments: 'Maranata did not claim to present any new doctrine, on the contrary it regarded itself as the true Pentecostal Movement.' None the less, by far the majority of Pentecostalists stayed with the main body of the Movement.[4]

These historical developments have played a role in the emergence of the Swedish Faith Movement. One way to contextualise the new wave of charismatic activity is to see it as part of

[3] 'Para-church' means here an organisation that is not based in a local congregation.
[4] Pentecostalists still do not officially regard themselves as belonging to a denomination. They stress – at least rhetorically – the paramountcy of the local congregation.

Pentecostalism, incorporating clear impulses from the US but also building on previous Swedish revivals (Skog 1993:94). Certainly, some of those who were active in the earlier movements have taken important positions within local Faith organisations.[5] 'Prosperity' ideology itself was most obviously introduced into Swedish religious circles in 1956, when Norman Vincent Peale's *The Power of Positive Thinking* was published in translation (Hambre et al. 1983:39). By the end of the 1970s or so Yonggi Cho's and Robert Schuller's preaching was beginning to make an impact, partly as a result of their personal visits to the country.[6] The person who is sometimes named as the first Faith preacher in Sweden is the English pastor Harry Greenwood (Bjuvsjö et al. 1985:20).[7] Greenwood claims to have received a calling from God to preach in Sweden. He made his first visit to the country in 1967 and came back frequently over the next few years, though some free church congregations refused to give him a platform. He and Ulf Ekman both preached at a 'Family' conference in 1983, and it was at this point that Greenwood announced that he felt God had told him that his mission in Sweden was at an end – there were others who could preach in the same spirit.

Ekman's personal career path into effective leadership of the Faith Movement in Sweden – and indeed Scandinavia – did not have pious beginnings, even if it soon took on classic charismatic form. He was born in Gothenburg, Sweden's second largest city, in 1950. His self-reportedly happy childhood in a respectable but not particularly religious home included a year in the US as an exchange student. On 28 May 1970, Ekman was converted by a friend and, soon afterwards, miraculously cured of a kidney com-

---

[5] Although other, closely related charismatic impulses are evident in Sweden, such as that of the Vineyard Movement, these have not constructed the extensive organisational forms evident in Faith Christianity (Skog 1993:125–6).

[6] Indeed, group journeys were organised from Sweden to South Korea. The main local representative for this kind of preaching was a maverick, but generally respected, Pentecostalist pastor called Stanley Sjöberg. In practice, however, the recent expansion of specifically Faith beliefs, practices and organisations has taken a rather different line to that represented by Sjöberg.

[7] Another early Faith preacher in Sweden was the Swedish–American Bill Löfbom, who was influenced by Hagin's teachings and was based in California. He made his first preaching tour in 1980 and initiated a prayer day in front of the Swedish Parliament on 1 May 1981 (Bjuvsjö et al. 1985:21).

plaint at a meeting led by a Pentecostal evangelist (Bjuvsjö et al. 1985:19–20). In the same year he moved to Uppsala University to study theology, and came in contact with the Swedish branch of The Navigators, a para-church organisation founded in the US that encourages both student-evangelisation and biblical erudition. Ekman estimates that between 1970 and 1975 he committed between 400 and 600 Bible verses to memory (ibid.:26). As an undergraduate, he went to different churches and contributed to a research report, entitled 'Jesus the Healer', which included reference to such charismatic preachers as Cho, Kenyon and Hagin. After graduation he was ordained in the Swedish Church and worked with success – although not without controversy – as a student-priest in Uppsala between 1979 and 1981.[8]

In 1978, Ekman had been given some American Faith material by his father-in-law, the well-known Methodist pastor and missionary, Sten Nilsson. The two also journeyed to the US together in order to observe developments there. Ekman decided to enrol in a course at Kenneth Hagin's Rhema Bible Training Center. He was one of four Swedes who studied in Tulsa during 1981–2, and all were to have an involvement in the building up of the Swedish Faith Movement. Ekman, however, became the dominant figure. After his return from Tulsa he preached in various places, most notably at *Södermalms Fria Församling*,[9] a Pentecostal church in Stockholm whose pastor had reportedly felt a calling from God to ask Ekman to preach (Bjuvsjö et al. 1985:24). According to his own account, Ekman soon felt that his own divine mission was to create an organisational base for God's Word in Sweden. As he recalls the origins of the Word of Life (1992),[10] Ekman states:

The Lord spoke to me about starting a Bible School where the basic subjects would be faith, healing and the believer's authority, together with a strong emphasis on mission. God's specific address to us was: 'Equip my people with my Words of Faith, show them what weapons they have, teach them to use these weapons and send them out into victorious battle for me.'

---

[8] Ekman worked for *Sveriges Evangeliska Student- och Gymnasiströrelse* (SESG), an organisation founded in 1925 to evangelise among students. His preaching did lead to some conflicts over theology and SESG refused to sell works by Hagin and Nilsson.
[9] Literally, 'Södermalm Free Congregation'.   [10] See Skog (1993:106).

STRUCTURES

The Word of Life was founded in Uppsala by Ulf Ekman and his wife, Birgitta, in March 1983 (he resigned from his position as priest in the Swedish Church in December of that year). In legal terms, the ministry was classified as a non-profit-making foundation (Brandell et al. 1986:31).[11] Other members of the foundation's board were Sten Nilsson (Ulf Ekman's father-in-law), Maj-Kristen Nilsson (his sister-in-law) and Robert and Åsa Ekh. Robert Ekh, originally an ordained priest in the Swedish Church, was himself a student at Hagin's Training Center in 1982–3. The congregation was formed in May 1983, with Ulf Ekman as chief pastor and Robert Ekh as assistant pastor, and a few months later the Bible School opened its doors to 190 students. With two exceptions all of the teachers at the School had studied at Hagin's Center.

Over the past fifteen years, the Word of Life's activities, contacts and, to some extent, membership, have grown steadily.[12] Well over 100 people work in various administrative positions. The group's main hall is probably the largest charismatic church in Europe, with seats for more than 4,000 people. The congregation now has around 2,000 members, but Sunday-morning meetings also attract hundreds of non-members and are translated into foreign languages on request. Other activities available to members include working with children and youth, evangelisation through knocking on doors or preaching in town squares, sports, summer camps and the production of music. The congregation is also divided into around 100 groups whose members meet on a weekly basis to pray, hold Bible-study sessions and evangelise.

The Bible School, which claims to be the largest in Europe, has had over 6,000 graduates since 1983. Apart from first-year and optional second-year courses, it has an English-speaking, international programme and has attracted students from around forty countries to Uppsala. Students are also eligible, after a year's study, to take a summer course in missionary studies, followed by a period

---

[11] On the unusual nature of the 'foundation' form in Swedish congregations see Skog (1993:92).

[12] Some of the following figures are taken from the Word of Life web pages of July 1999. The site is maintained by Jonathan Ekman, one of Ulf's sons.

assisting Word of Life operations in the field. Various other educational facilities are provided by the group, ranging from a Christian nursery to a university. Secondary and High schools cater for Swedish pupils as well as for those from abroad, and include teaching in English and German.[13] The university offers undergraduate and Masters degrees, and since 1996 has been able to offer internationally recognised qualifications as a result of a partnership with Oral Roberts University in Tulsa. The university's four faculties specialise in humanities and social sciences, media, biblical studies and education. Courses such as 'American Foreign Policy' and 'Cultural Anthropology' are taught alongside 'The Life and Teachings of Paul' and 'Bible Principles for Abundant Living Through Faith'.

Entry to all of these institutions implies acceptance of Faith principles and active participation in a Christian life style. For instance, school children are expected to engage in up to half an hour of prayer in class on most days, and Christian topics such as the history of revival movements in Sweden or creationist accounts of the origins of humankind are taken up along with more conventional subjects and approaches. All are private educational institutions, a phenomenon still relatively rare in Sweden.[14] In fact, the university was formed only after a recent change in Swedish law which relaxed central control over tertiary-level curricula and organisation.

The group's business activities include the printing of books and course literature as well as the production of audio-cassettes, videos and television programmes. 'TV Word of Life' produces video and television programmes which are broadcast on satellite, cable and local stations throughout Europe. Most services and conferences are recorded in various media and made available for subsequent purchase, and subscribers can join monthly audio- or video-cassette clubs (for adults as well as children). Texts by Swedish and foreign, most often American, preachers are available in various languages, and a shop has been opened in the centre of

---

[13] The High school estimates (1999) that 15 per cent of its pupils come from outside Sweden. The Secondary school has around 500 pupils, and the High school around 100.

[14] Although after a long struggle to gain national recognition, the Secondary school has earned the right to receive county and state support (Skog 1993:107).

Uppsala to sell these and other 'brand' products. Besides newsletters sent out to congregation members and other subscribers, the group also produces a monthly magazine aimed at reaching a broad evangelical public.[15] Editorials are written by Ekman, and the publication provides a morally conservative view on various social and religious issues.

As well as two regular services and a youth meeting during the week, the Word of Life organises various seminars and workshops throughout the year. Its leaders take part in an annual anti-abortion march through the streets of Stockholm together with pastors from older free churches and some politicians. A 'Jesus-festival' is held in the spring, in order to reach out to inhabitants of Uppsala, and involves preaching in the street, concerts, drive-in-cinema and parades. A summer 'Europe Conference' attracts over 10,000 people, while a New Year conference is aimed specifically at a younger constituency and also attracts many thousands of delegates. The highlight of the winter conference is a prophecy for the coming year, delivered by (or perhaps one might say *through*) Ekman on New Year's Eve. The ministry claims that representatives of over fifty countries participate in these meetings, and invites numerous speakers from the Faith network around the world. Satellite link-ups are sometimes used on such occasions to connect congregations dispersed around Europe.

Specific projects are also set up. 'Operation Jabotinsky'[16] helps Jews from the former Soviet Union to emigrate to Israel. The ministry even bought its own ship, the *Restoration*, in order to facilitate the process. Similarly, the project 'Prayer 2000' was set up by Swedish Faith groups, including the Word of Life, to produce a chain of continuous prayer up to the start of the new millennium. The project was envisioned when Ulf Ekman received a prophetic message, during the 1997 Europe conference, that unity in prayer was important for Sweden. It was also boosted by a prophecy

---

[15] The newsletter usually has multiple editions a year and is published in Swedish (40,000 copies) and English (20,000 copies). 'The Magazine for a Victorious Life' (*Magazinet för ett segerrikt liv*) is a monthly, published in Swedish and Norwegian, with a total print run of over 10,000.

[16] Named after a Russian Jew who in the 1920s and 1930s attempted to warn of the coming Holocaust.

apparently pronounced in Swedish by two unrelated people, based in Zaïre and Jordan respectively. Their message was that God was about to start an important revival in Sweden.

Although the Word of Life is headquartered in Uppsala, its growth has involved the co-ordination of a considerable number of activities beyond Sweden itself. Around seventy full-time missionaries are sponsored, primarily for work in Eastern Europe, and Word of Life preachers take part in revival campaigns around the world. Three subsidiary Word of Life Bible Schools are run in Moscow, Tirana (Albania) and Brno (the Czech Republic) respectively, and the Word of Life also co-operates with hundreds of congregations around the world. Posters put up in hallways in the Uppsala offices frequently include maps, representing foreign countries as undifferentiated spaces to be touched with the Word.

Besides activities that take place under official Word of Life control, numerous other projects and organisations have been started over the years by members who perceive that they have a special calling to work in a particular direction. These include particular missions to certain sections of the population, such as Muslims or students. The newspaper *Trons Värld* ('World of Faith') provides news of Faith congregations around the country and beyond. There is now even a travel agency that, among other things, offers group journeys to places such as Israel and the USA.

Ulf Ekman is perceived by group members as being an inspiration for most of the activities I have described. This perception is reinforced by the structure of authority incorporated into organisational structures. As Skog (1993:113) puts it, describing the pattern in Faith congregations as a whole: 'The congregation "is" its pastor and the pastor's preaching, in a different way than is the case with a free church or a congregation within the Swedish Church.' Ekman subscribes to the so-called 'One Shepherd' principle commonly expressed in Faith churches. He does not have to answer to higher ecclesiastical structures or a body of elders. He does not claim particular technical expertise in relation to the Word of Life's many activities – indeed, the group has often relied on specialists (preferably Bible-believing Christians) in developing its business strategies, technological communication and

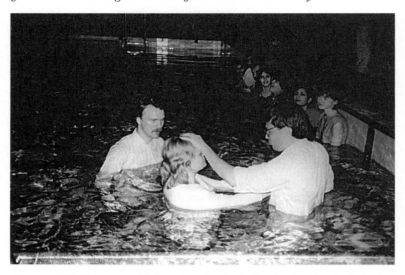

Figure 2 Ulf Ekman conducting a baptism in the local swimming baths in the centre of Uppsala. The picture was taken before the new building was put up, complete with facilities to carry out baptisms on Word of Life premises. Ekman is shown praying, one hand on the forehead of a female convert; behind her stands the Ministry's youth pastor.

bureaucratic organisation (see also Gustafsson 1991:117). Nor, in contrast to some North American figures, does he display great trappings of wealth, but lives in a comfortable suburb – with many other leading figures in the Word of Life as his close neighbours – a little way outside Uppsala. Ekman's authority relies fundamentally on the basis that he was given the original 'vision' for the group. In addition, his training in Tulsa has clearly provided a vital link – socially and symbolically – to Faith contacts abroad.[17]

Certain personal qualities of Ekman also contribute to his success (Figure 2). His preaching style is lively: he does not hector his audience, but speaks at a fast pace and frequently includes elements of humour, even of a self-deprecating sort, in his sermons.

---

[17] Although, in common with Hagin and many other charismatic leaders, Ekman's conversion experience was accompanied by miraculous healing, he tends not to stress this episode in his life.

At a face-to-face level, he is able to convey charm, authority and enthusiasm. I remember standing next to him at an evangelical student meeting held in a university hall, early in my fieldwork. I inadvertently dropped some books at his feet and within the space of perhaps a minute he had managed to help me pick up my possessions, ascertain that I had come to Uppsala from England and suggest that I should enrol in his new international Bible School for the next study year. Congregation members and Bible School students sometimes refer to him as 'Ulf', although many will not have had the opportunity to get to know him personally, and clearly regard meetings with him as having special significance. Even disillusioned adherents have described in interviews the sense of dread they have felt in leaving the group: the fact that they were required to have a personal meeting with Ekman in order to withdraw membership was often perceived as a major hurdle in the final decision to leave.

CONNECTIONS

Formally, the Word of Life is an independent ministry with no ties to any overarching organisation. In practice, it is at the centre of a network of similar but smaller groups in (mostly urban areas of) Sweden and Scandinavia as a whole. By cross-tabulating different sources of information produced by Faith sympathisers, Skog (1993:104–5) estimated some six years ago that around 90 congregations existed in Sweden, involving perhaps 8,000 members. The figures may well have grown since – for instance the Word of Life congregation has increased in size by perhaps 10–20 per cent since then. Nor do Skog's figures take into account the large numbers of Christians who have participated in Faith activities without joining one of the new congregations. Stai (1993:7) notes the possibility that by 1990 between 20,000 and 30,000 people had participated in Swedish Faith services or similar activities.

The vast majority of Faith-oriented congregations in Sweden, although not all, have close ties to the Word of Life. Faith pastors and preachers are generally very mobile, travelling the country to speak at each other's conferences, and Ekman has an especially busy programme involving preaching engagements, teaching at Bible Schools around the country and frequently acting as guest of honour at the consecration of new Faith locales. In general, Bible School students are encouraged to leave Uppsala after their studies have been completed, and some decide that they have their own calling to start up a ministry of some sort. For instance, I remember meeting Lena in a medium-sized town to the north-east of Uppsala. She was a woman in her early twenties who had graduated from the Bible School the year before (1985), and kept in touch with the Word of Life through its literature and videos. Over tea in her modest kitchen she told me that she had decided to start a congregation with a friend who had also studied at the Word of Life. This step, she felt, was entirely 'natural' and 'biblical'. The congregation would be independent of any denomination, since all mass-movements were the work of people opposed to God, and therefore threatened 'individual spiritual initiatives'. Although there were just five people involved in her plans at the moment, she was convinced that the numbers of supporters would grow. New groups like her own were necessary in Sweden at the moment, she said, because other Christians did not preach 'the full gospel'. Sixty years ago, the Pentecostalists had done exactly the same, but now they had become too much like other, established denominations.

In Lena's story, we see many of the elements I was to hear from other Bible School students. The work of revival is seen as an act of restoration, providing the 'full' Gospel and in the process replacing now quiescent and compromised congregations such as those of the Pentecostalists. In addition, it is a form of spiritual entrepreneurship, carried out by spiritually empowered people who are not controlled by overbearing and overly centralised administrative structures. To the outsider, the echoes of Ekman's career are evidence that such initiative is not quite as autonomous as it seems; to the believer, however, it primarily demonstrates that the Spirit moves in similar ways in different contexts.

Many congregations or Bible Schools in the country not only have theologies that are very similar to those of the Word of Life, they also sell material acquired from the Uppsala ministry as well as from foreign Faith organisations. Nilsson (1988:211–12) attributes the relative confessional and constitutional conformity of Swedish Faith congregations to the ability of the Word of Life to act as a distribution centre; certainly, the Word of Life has benefited from collections around the country and the broadcasting of Ekman's sermons over local radio and cable (ibid.:213). Although leaders of local congregations tend to deny official attachment to the Word of Life, the naming of such groups is often significant and a tell-tale sign of theological affiliation – including for instance 'Bread of Life', 'Way of Life' and 'Water of Life'.[18] In 1991, around 100 pastors organised themselves into a Nordic-wide 'Faith Movement's Preachers' Organisation'.[19] The expressed aim of the group was not to form a denomination but rather to provide a forum for common pronouncements in relation to the state and authorities (Gustafsson 1991:120). Unsurprisingly, Ekman was chosen to be the organisation's first convenor, and indeed he was referred to as an 'apostle' by a fellow Faith pastor (Skog 1993:95).

Thus, we see how a new religious landscape is being formed out of Faith groups in Sweden and Scandinavia as a whole. Elements of the all-encompassing Word of Life model (congregation, Bible School, media business, etc.) are selected and mirrored, at a smaller scale, in other parts of the region. Any given group, for-mally independent and the product of the particular 'vision' of its founder, is ideologically and socially oriented not only towards similar organisations in Scandinavia, but also towards the Faith Movement at a world-wide level. Describing Trondheim Christian Centre (TKS),[20] a Norwegian congregation of nearly 300 people, Stai (1993) notes how some members receive the Word of Life's publication *Magazinet*, go to conferences in Uppsala, perhaps train at the Swedish Bible School and purchase Ekman's books. They may also subscribe to *Word of Faith* magazine (produced by Rhema in Tulsa) and purchase American Faith products in their local media centre. The Trondheim group has received visits not only from Swedish pastors, but also from leading figures from

---

[18] *Livets Bröd, Livets Väg* and *Livets Vatten* respectively.
[19] *Trosrörelsens Predikantorganisation i Norden.*   [20] *Trondheim Kristne Senter.*

Germany, the USA, Armenia, Brazil and Kenya; the chief pastor
of TKS himself trained at Rhema Bible Training Center, and in
1981 visited Yonggi Cho's congregation in South Korea. To some
degree, then, the Word of Life acts as an important mediator
between Scandinavian Faith groups and others in the global
network. However, it can only ever be regarded as the first among
spiritual equals, given that charismatic ideals tend to eschew
explicit recognition of permanent, centralised structures of organisation. In addition, other Scandinavian groups may themselves
develop into important points in the network. Oslo Christian
Centre, for instance, has become a national focus for Norwegian
Faith groups.[21] *Södermalms Fria Församling* in Stockholm, the Pentecostal church that played an important part in developing Ekman's
profile in the early 1980s, is presented in its own newspaper as 'a
local congregation which is part of the Body of Christ, the world-
wide congregation'.[22] The church claims to have members from 5
continents and 34 different nations, holds large conferences, has its
own company for producing books, cassettes and music, and translates meetings into Spanish, English and French (Skog 1993:109).
The Stockholm church's profile may not be as high as that of the
Word of Life; clearly, however, the trappings of global, and not
merely Stockholm-wide, significance are evident for all its
members to see. An awareness that apparently 'local' events can
have widely ramifying consequences is a unifying ideological
orientation among all Faith groups, large or small.

The Word of Life is itself a partial mirror of Faith groups elsewhere in the world, and particularly those in the United States (see
chapter 1). Its name is the same as that used by some North
American (and British) Faith ministries. Ekman resembles many
other charismatic leaders (Hagin, Roberts and so on) in the way he
has surrounded himself with family and close friends in the formation of his ministry. The very model of the mega-ministry, encom-
passing many functions, is taken from US examples, and Word of
Life retail outlets act as important vehicles through which Faith

---

[21] Stai (1993:7–8) notes that by 1991 there were around 45 Faith groups in Norway, involving perhaps 7,000 people. Oslo Christian Centre, a leading group, had its own Bible
School and almost 2,000 members.   [22] *Genombrott*, or 'Breakthrough'.

literature from around the world reaches Scandinavian homes. If Ekman and other Word of Life leaders are frequently drawn upon in national circles in order to lend spiritual authority to particular events or activities, they themselves introduce foreign pastors into events in Uppsala. The group's new building was itself consecrated in 1987 by Lester Sumrall, then a major figure in the Faith Movement with a large ministry in South Bend, Indiana.[23]

An awareness of other groups and their place within a largely implicit Faith hierarchy is evident among many adherents. Fred Nilsson, a pastor within an older free church, the Swedish Mission Covenant, describes (1990:45) a journey he made with Faith adherents to Hagin's Bible Center (and a week-long meeting series there): 'When we got out of the terminal in Tulsa the Swedish journey leader, the Pentecostal Pastor Bertil Svärd, said "Now we are here! Heaven's forecourt!"' Nilsson found that students whom he met at Hagin's school – as with Faith Christians elsewhere – tended to develop a sense of a global religio-political framework into which they could insert themselves and their actions. His party bumped into Carola Häggkvist, a famous Swedish singer and convert to the Movement, and together they felt impelled to pray 'for Sweden' whilst on American soil (ibid.:52). Nilsson also met one young man from the US who said that he and his fellow students in Tulsa all wanted to 'go out' in to the world, and that he had a particular calling, or 'burden', for missionary work in the Philippines and Peru. Or again an American woman, who was interested in Faith efforts to help Russian Jews return to Israel, heard that some of Nilsson's party came from Finland. She noted that her new Finnish friends lived 'near the border' and asked if they had read Exodus (ibid.:46).

Thus social contacts between members of the Movement are often expressed in a language and ritual etiquette that involves a mutual acknowledgement of, and prayerful attitude towards, the

---

[23] The latest (1999) Europe Conference claims Yonggi Cho from South Korea as its main speaker. As far as I am aware, Hagin himself has not been a visitor to Sweden. According at least to adherents, Ekman and Hagin have had some differences over certain doctrines, including Hagin's claim that Jesus died spiritually before being restored to God with the Resurrection.

spiritual and strategic significance of different parts of the globe. I found that, when believers learned I was from England, many asked if I had heard of particular congregations that were seen as 'significant'[24] contributors to revival in my country. In practice, such congregations tended to be those that had hosted missionary groups of Word of Life Bible students. More broadly, visits from important foreign preachers can be seen as catalysing revival. The following extract from a Bible School student's notes (made in preparation for a newspaper article) describes the impact of Reinhard Bonnke on a visit made to Sweden in the late 1980s:

> Stockholm exploded at Bonnke's first visit to Sweden . . . 'It felt like one was in Europe' said a delighted Birgitta Edström after the meeting . . . Bonnke's message to Sweden was JUST BELIEVE . . . The revival in Sweden and Stockholm has definitely started after this meeting. Bonnke, who has moved his activities to Frankfurt, was in Sweden to link together Sweden with his world-wide evangelisation work.

Note how this passage links events in Sweden to a wider sense of revival gathering around Bonnke: the event is depicted as making one participant feel that she was connected to Christians beyond Sweden – 'It felt like one was in Europe' – just as Bonnke is himself seen as linking the country to a world-wide frame of action.

Of course, other free churches in Scandinavia have long been involved in consolidating movements constructed from national and international networks of congregations, educational establishments, media communications and conferences. As in so many other respects, the Pentecostalists show the most striking similarities to Faith activities. Conservative in life style and charismatic in theological orientation, they have promoted active evangelisation within and beyond Sweden, and throughout their history have been heavily involved in using electronic media as a tool of missionisation (Andström 1966:86; Sahlberg 1985). As long ago as 1939, the massive Filadelfia Church in Stockholm, effective headquarters of the Movement under the leadership of its powerful chief pastor, Lewi Pethrus, played host to a European Conference of Pentecostalists that at one point was planned as a gathering of

----

[24] *Betydelsefull* – a favourite word of Ekman.

representatives from around the world. (A possible reason for the scaling down of the conference was, ironically enough, fear that it would be dominated by North Americans (Lindberg 1985:217).) More recently, a report in one of the Movement's yearbooks (Asp 1986), describing the fourteenth World Pentecostal Conference, notes that a gift of a mobile satellite television station has been given to European Christians. Traditional Pentecostalists are clearly not fleeing the missionary field, leaving it open to their Faith counterparts. One of the things that is so distinctive about the organisation of the Faith Movement in the Scandinavian context, however, is its development of the model of the multi-purpose organisation in which congregation, Bible School and media business combine to form what, in the Word of Life case, is a mega-ministry. Ekman's group is clearly not a simple, free church congregation of the type commonly recognised in Sweden, and is a prime exemplar of mixing congregational and para-church activities under one roof. Such activities are reinforced by the constant emphasis on establishing links with congregations or preachers from abroad. Numerous Word of Life publications emphasise the importance of being based in a strategic location in order to gain maximum evangelical influence and often note that the group is situated next to a motorway, close to an international airport, near to a renowned university, just an hour's train ride from the capital city, Stockholm.

ADHERENTS

The act of joining the Word of Life can easily be seen as an act of bravery as well as protest in a country where conservative Protestant beliefs are hardly mainstream: Uppsala is not exactly the US Bible Belt. I want here to give an initial overview of the kind of people who are attracted to Scandinavian Faith activities. Perhaps the most striking aspect of Word of Life adherents has been their relative youth – on average around thirty during the early years of the group, though with some younger and indeed much older people also becoming involved. The ministry and many of its allies in Scandinavia are therefore differentiated from more established free churches not only because they have been expanding, but also on the grounds of generational appeal.[25] Word of Life and other Faith rhetoric is highly conversionist in orientation. The role of the Christian is to a large extent defined by its evangelical, missionary aspects. However, what evidence is available suggests that a significant proportion of active participants already have a committed Christian background, with Pentecostalist churches providing the highest numbers of 'crossovers'.[26] Many Bible School students and regular visitors to the Word of Life are actually members of older, more established congregations. Remarkably, at no point during an ordinary service (as opposed to a conference) have I ever observed anybody

[25] According to Skog (1993:128), Ekman himself estimated in 1990 that the average age of adherents was around 30. My own examination of Bible School yearbooks from the mid-1980s revealed that most students appeared at least to be younger than middle-aged (Coleman 1989:31), while Bjuvsjö et al. (1985:104) found that the average age of the Bible School's intake in 1983–4 was just under 30. All of these figures and estimates correspond quite closely with Stai's (1993:16) observations on Trondheim Christian Centre in Norway, in 1991, where the average age of members was 27. That of Oslo Christian Centre was 34 (ibid.:16). These figures can be contrasted to those available for the 'most youthful' of free churches, the Pentecostalists. In 1930, just 25 per cent of all Pentecostalists were over 50 (thus probably closer to the current Word of Life model); by 1978 that figure had reached as high as 53 per cent. Fred Nilsson's (1990:51) admittedly anecdotal observation from his visit to Tulsa in 1988 was that fewer younger people were evident in Hagin's congregation than at Ekman's. One can assume that Faith congregations in Sweden will age as the Movement itself grows older.

[26] Bjuvsjö et al. (1985:27) record an estimate from Ekman himself, made in the early 1980s, of the origins of members of his congregation. At the time, the Word of Life could claim 110–120 members and Ekman reckoned that 10–15 came from established churches. According to Bjuvsjö et al., however, the figure must have been much greater: close to half at the very least. In Uppsala alone they found 20 had come from free churches, including 15 from the local Pentecostal church. Around 10 were previously active in the Swedish Church and perhaps 20 had previously lived elsewhere or were also active in another congregation. The authors (ibid.:105–6) also investigated the backgrounds of the 190 Bible School students of 1983/4, and found that most had free church affiliations, including 49 from the Pentecostals, 26 from the Swedish Mission Covenant and 18 from the Swedish Church. (In 1987, the pastor of the Pentecostal church in Uppsala told me that he thought perhaps 40 of his own congregation had gone over to the Word of Life since the latter's foundation.)

    Such figures, taken from the early days of the Word of Life, broadly correspond with the implications to be drawn from more recent data on Scandinavia. Skog (1993:129) mentions a report carried out by a Faith congregation in Uddevalla (western Sweden). Of 316 members, a third came from other congregations, a third were already Christian even if they lacked a specific fellowship, and a third were converted by the group itself. Stai (1993:48) notes that most members of Trondheim Christian Centre had belonged to one or more Christian groups before, mostly Pentecostal in affiliation.

responding to the 'altar-call' to give their lives to Jesus; in contrast, calls for people to come forward to be healed are usually met with widespread enthusiasm.

Unfortunately, no firm data are available on class membership of Faith congregations in Sweden, although clear trends away from national averages are not immediately apparent.[27] A similar position is evident in relation to gender divisions.[28] Skog (1993:129) remarks that the numbers of foreigners at Faith occasions is striking, although of course it is difficult to differentiate between visitors, international students and immigrants without the possibility of questionnaire surveys.

Various authors have speculated as to the motivations for involvement in Faith Christianity, particularly in the light of its controversial reputation in Scandinavia. From the viewpoint of the psychology of religion, Sjöberg (1988:5) notes that many people see involvement in the Word of Life as the 'kick' they needed in their spiritual life. Certainly, that is one of the characteristic ways in which adherents come to describe the effects of participation.[29] Gustafsson (1991:122) implies that enrolment in the Bible School can be fitted into more conventional patterns of youthful rites of passage: 'The economic surplus that other youth invest in journeys to distant countries can be deployed by those engaged in Christianity in a year at the Word of Life's Bible School.' Engel (1989), in a report based on twelve interviews, distinguishes between those who see the Word of Life as the 'ultimate objective' (*slutmål*) in their spiritual lives and those who see it as 'a step on the way'. Stai (1993:48), meanwhile, differentiates between those who

---

[27] Nilsson (1990:51) does remark with surprise upon the relatively few people in Hagin's congregation who appeared to be middle class, implying perhaps that he perceives a contrast to equivalent congregations in Sweden.

[28] Skog (1993:128–9) remarks that, compared to the Swedish Church, the number of men is striking – they are possibly sometimes in a slight majority in Faith congregations. Her observations contrast with those of Bjuvsjö et al. (1985) who note that slightly over half of Word of Life Bible School students were female in 1983–4, and my own examination of Bible School yearbooks that implies an intake of women slightly greater than that of men. Overall, these proportions indicate, albeit very crudely, that neither gender greatly predominates, at least in terms of numbers of people present. On the other hand, Faith principles tend to emphasise that men have authority in most contexts, although several women have achieved prominent positions as preachers and administrators.

[29] Of course, the reasons adherents give on a *post hoc* basis for engagement may be rather different to factors originally predisposing them to join a Faith group.

come over to the Movement from another Christian group and new converts who are frequently also conquering alcohol or drug addiction (ibid.: 86). The former, unlike the latter, tend to view participation in terms of a perceived *lack* in their previous fellowship.

If there is a common feature to the observations of these authors it is that involvement can variously, but not exclusively, be linked to forms of personal development.[30] Certainly, once involved, believers often use powerful metaphors of growth and mobility to describe the changes they perceive in themselves. We shall encounter various examples of such transformation in later chapters, but for the time being let me provide just one. I first met Peter, a neatly dressed man in his early twenties, in the bookshop of the Pentecostal church in Uppsala. I asked him what he was doing in Uppsala. He explained that his sister had originally studied at the Word of Life Bible School, and had 'prospered'. When after a year she had gone back to their home town in the west of Sweden, she had become involved in a new congregation which was sympathetic to Faith ideas rather than the Pentecostal congregation their parents had favoured. When he saw the new level of enthusiasm in his sister, Peter suspended his engineering studies and came to study at the Bible School. His misgivings over the bad press the ministry was receiving soon disappeared once he had arrived. Moreover, he was convinced that God meant him to be in Uppsala just then, since a job and accommodation had proved so easy to arrange. My first encounter with Peter occurred just a month after he had begun his course, and over the next few months I often saw him at services, acting as an usher. One evening, I sat next to him in the café of the Pentecostal church. He had spent the whole of the day evangelising on the streets of Uppsala, and explained that although it was difficult to start talking to people on the streets, the Holy Spirit always helped him to approach the kind of people who were prepared to listen. In the café, he soon became involved in a heated discussion with a young Pentecostalist man regarding the

---

[30] In describing how they came to hear of Faith activities in the first place, adherents of the Word of Life have mentioned a variety of methods: they might have been given a book or a video by a friend, seen Ekman speak, been introduced to a congregation by a member of the family, etc. Stai (1993:47–8) notes that its members often got to know of TKS through Pentecostal contacts, or had friends and family in Trondheim Christian Centre or other Faith groups.

relative merits of various Bible Schools in Sweden. Peter's conclusions were that Pentecostalist schools were deficient because they had ceased to preach from *all* of the Bible. At the Word of Life, in contrast, he had learned to rely on the Bible; to 'grow' in Faith; to become aware of his legal right to salvation from God. He had, of course, much still to learn, and he was forced to work hard to combine his studies, a part-time job and the need to evangelise as much as possible. However, he regarded the Word of Life as more 'fun' for young people than Pentecostal churches, and he was convinced that the Bible School itself would 'grow and grow'. Peter certainly won the argument if judged in terms of fluency and forcefulness of delivery. The last time I saw him, in the summer of 1987, I asked him when he intended to return to his engineering studies in Gothenburg. He replied that he had decided to stay for the second-year course at the Bible School. He felt he simply could not miss the opportunity: students on the course had told him how 'exciting' it was.

Peter echoes many fellow adherents in describing his initial attraction to the group in personalised terms: often, of course, it is the charismatic figure of Ekman, perhaps encountered preaching at a conference or on video, who provides the 'hook'; Peter, however, talks of the obvious transformation in his sister as helping him decide to change the immediate course of his studies. His story, in common with that of Lena described above, then characterises Faith adherence in terms of an image of completeness: the 'full' Bible is preached. At the same time, the believer must continue to develop in order to approach the perfection of holy writ. Peter experiences a sense of growth within himself, just as he is convinced that the ministry itself will expand – and just as Lena was sure that her congregation would grow from the five people it currently attracted.

Both Lena and Peter define their attraction to Faith ideas partly in terms of their disillusionment with Pentecostalism – or at least the institutionalised elements of the Swedish Movement. The new revival has more life, more 'fun', more of the Bible within it. Pentecostalists themselves whom I interviewed[31] often perceived

---

[31] See more discussion of these interviews in chapter 9.

links between their own spirituality and that of Faith Christians, even if they were usually critical of or at least cautious about aspects of its theology and ritual practices. Some also attempted partially to explain the motivations for Faith adherence by suggesting that they were variations on familiar revivalist themes. Thus, a middle-aged woman notes: 'Then the Word of Life came and one thought oh, that's good, here comes a *living* group . . . But as the years have passed one has experienced that it has not been entirely genuine all the time.' Or again, here are comments from a man in his mid-thirties, who combined an academic job with a deep involvement in the Pentecostal Movement:

> I think that what's attracting young people is the *devotion* of the Word of Life young people, especially. The middle-aged at the Word of Life I . . . experience as [having] more of a butterfly character. They go to all kinds of conferences and they go to the Word of Life too . . . 'The Word of Life seems to have more movement so we go to the Word of Life.' And I don't take them as seriously as I take the younger people . . . they are just people who want something different in their life. I mean the basic attitude of those who go to any church and especially the Word of Life is that they want something different out of their life. They are tired of just, you know, living this ordinary 'Svensson' life, where everything is fixed.

Although he is certainly not advocating engagement in the new group, this man accepts that to some people it appears to have 'more movement' (than, we assume, other congregations), as well as offering freedom from the 'fixity' of life in Sweden. He explains here and elsewhere in the interview that he is impressed by the seriousness with which younger Faith adherents take their spiritual lives, and he mentions that this virtue can be discerned among many of the Pentecostalist youth, as well. His description of older adherents, who appear to flit between churches and are attracted to conferences, is echoed in the words of a young Pentecostalist woman when she characterises those members of her church who left to join the Word of Life as 'conference people – who went to these great big self-development[32] conferences and sought out experiences'. The invocation of the image of the 'conference

---

[32] The word she uses in Swedish for 'development' is *uppbyggelse*, literally 'building up'.

person' by these two Pentecostalists is, I think, intended to capture the sense of a revivalist attitude that is oriented towards not only major spiritual events (with associated 'experiences') but also the mass character of participation in the new revival.

SOCIALITY AND COMMITMENT

Faith discourse is distinctly totalising in its implications: ideally, the Christian should live entirely according to biblically sanctioned norms that prescribe appropriate behaviours and attitudes in relation to all areas of existence. Images of collective identity are also constructed to provide, in almost semiotic terms, systematic sets of aesthetic and ritual differences from other churches in Uppsala. Faith Christianity is described by preachers and many adherents as 'living', 'over-flowing', 'growing', 'all-conquering', as opposed to the 'dead', 'dry', 'limited' 'religion' of other people. It is true that a core of Word of Life adherents comes close to living spiritual, social and working lives entirely embraced by the myriad activities of the group. For these people, attending services on Sunday, perhaps teaching in the Word of Life High School during the week and practising in the group's choir or one of its sports teams in the evening, constitute a social, spiritual and working life made up of closely overlapping social networks of friends, family and colleagues. Yet many of those who attend Word of Life services and purchase its products are less completely committed to its operations. Such distanced participation is built into the structure of the group through its provision of relatively short-term educational opportunities, conferences, consumer goods and media communications. The services, retail outlets and conferences therefore attract a large number of Christians who often retain membership in other congregations and whose devotional lives are consequently constructed through a spiritual division of labour in which Faith theology and practice play only a part.[33] A formal ideology

---

[33] Of course, other Christians are likely to engage in (ecumenical) relations with many different churches. The point I am making here is that to combine support for a Faith church with membership in a more traditional congregation is, in the eyes of many people in Sweden, to bring together two radically different spiritual worlds.

of sectarian self-righteousness is combined with an organisational configuration in which multiple modes of affiliation are possible, from the wholehearted devotee to the distant client.

Of course, as with other mega-churches, the Word of Life's set-up enables it to reach a maximum number of potential consumers who will contribute resources vital to its continued existence. In addition, some pathways of extended participation are available – a Bible School student may stay on to take a degree at the University, for instance. However, in forthcoming chapters I shall also be attempting to show how Faith discourse and practice constantly balance a rhetorical culture of exclusivity with social structures that are far more flexible in their articulation of boundaries between insiders and outsiders. God's people are 'elect', but everybody in the world has the opportunity to be so chosen. The power of the message is indicated in part by those who demonstrate merely that they are prepared to listen to it, so that high attendance at a service or a conference, whether the audience is mostly 'Faith' or not, is itself taken as a sign of the presence of divine favour. In addition, those who have achieved election are repeatedly encouraged to extend the message and opportunity of salvation to others. The physical presence of unconverted others, or at least their evocation in linguistic or imagistic form, is not merely a challenge but is a constituting feature of the evangelical life. Faith culture is therefore oriented towards a constant extension of 'insiderhood' in the process of breaking down opposition to its assumptions and ideals. A sense of personal development comes, as we shall see, not only from practices of physical and psychological healing, but also from the constant re-enactment of the process of apparently providing salvation and self-renewal to others.

The description I gave above of the numerous sub-sections of the ministry should reinforce the point I am making here. The Word of Life congregation – the section of the group that is most dedicated to creating fellowship within a fixed population – is surrounded by other institutions dedicated to the creation of mobility, both of the message and of its human carriers: the schools, the university, the business, the media production studios. Even congregation members are constantly presented with challenges that encourage them to achieve further development and growth in

their spiritual lives – through evangelisation, the achievement of
material and physical prosperity, engagement in such projects as
Operation Jabotinsky and Prayer 2000, and so on. All spaces and
events are defined by pastors and teachers as potential missionary
fields (Stai 1993:102) – the work-place, the street, the neighbour-
hood – despite the fact that some members try to divide their congregational life off from more 'secular' activities.

Much participation in Faith activities is therefore goal-oriented.
The valorisation of stillness, calm, peace or rest in divine grace, is
far less evident in the language of Faith than it is in other Christian
discourses in Sweden. In fact, a common complaint of Christians
who leave the group is its lack of personalised systems of social and
emotional care that are so valued in other congregations (Swartling
1988). A phrase particularly characteristic of Faith circles is that
of the 'spiritual career' (Coleman 1989; Stai 1993:41), implying
advancement in personal growth but also up the hierarchy of a
given ministry. Stai notes (ibid.:67–8) that part of the establishment
of a career-path can be witnessing, so that believers learn to relate
the story of their conversion to larger and larger groups of people.
One of Stai's interviewees, a former drug-addict, actually describes himself as becoming irritated at constantly being deployed
as a 'living proof' of the powers of conversion.

There is no doubt that Faith groups provide adherents with the
opportunity to develop numerous pathways into positions of
responsibility and the development of an evangelical identity. In
the following example, Sjöberg (1988:29–32) reports the words of
a young convert, Anders, who became involved in the Word of
Life:

A group of about ten of us were saved within a few weeks of each other.
Pretty soon we formed a tremendous fellowship between us. I got to hear
that our group in particular was viewed by the congregation leadership
as pioneers who would save Uppsala first, and then Sweden and then the
whole world. My sister's circle wasn't regarded at all in the same way and
it really boosted my ego to be picked out.

Several elements of this testimony are worth highlighting since
they are expressive of common experiences at the ministry. First,
there is the sense of developing a self-reinforcing cohort, or small
fellowship, within a wider population of much more anonymous

Christians. Anders describes how members of his group developed a pattern of urging each other on through characteristic Faith practices of demonstrating charismatic commitment – casting out demons, engaging in constant prayer and being open to prophesy. Each member wished to express the ability to be a 'fearless warrior'[34] for the Lord, and implicit here is an element of mutual competition that is also evident in the reference to the supposedly less favoured circle of friends belonging to Anders's sister. The construction of an evangelical identity is bolstered by the assumption that Word of Life leaders are aware of and approving of one's identity, but also by the ambition to extend personal influence far beyond Uppsala into an unlimited realm of missionary potential.

Anders notes that he spent most of his free time involved in Word of Life activities. He therefore represents someone who gradually increases his commitment to ministry activities as his 'career' takes shape. Stai's (1993:21) account of adherence to a Faith congregation echoes that of Anders in the sense that many members of TKS come to spend most of their time with friends who are fellow members. They gradually feel less and less comfortable with friends from previous periods in their lives. My experience of Word of Life adherents is certainly that such restriction of social networks can occur, and can even be applied to family members who show themselves to be hostile to the group. However, it is equally common for believers to negotiate a more complex accommodation with non-Faith social contexts, which may involve strategies of gradual or partial revelation of one's identity as a Christian. The social distance to be travelled is usually greater for new converts to the Faith, but even people who have maintained some form of Christian identity for longer periods of time may experience hostility or incredulity from friends or family who belong to more conventional congregations.

Considerable dissonance is often felt by those Christians who choose to pay regular visits to the Word of Life whilst being members of other, usually sceptical and sometimes radically different, churches. Among these believers we see the notion of a spiritual division of labour played out most clearly. When asked,

---

[34] *Frimodig krigsman.*

they often explain their dual affiliation in terms of two, rather different, notions of identity. One's home congregation is the place to find close friends and a sense of settled fellowship; the Word of Life, however, may be seen as a context in which the person can feel empowered, both in their personal spiritual development and in their ability to evangelise. As we shall see, it is as though such Christians are able to ignore the theological differences between the separate parts of their spiritual lives in order to benefit from two sacralised environments: one where they are oriented to, and find a place within, a fixed, known locality; the other representing a more anonymous and mobile world of Faith, but incorporating the possibility of discovering new forms of potentiality for the self.

The fact that the Word of Life appears to provoke a wider range of forms of adherence and commitment than the group described by Stai (1993) is partly a function of its size. It is a mega-church rather than a medium-sized congregation, and its numerous departments create numerous avenues of participation and consumption for the believer. One thing that unites the two groups, however, is a sense of connection with wider spiritual and social realities. Stai (ibid.:54) notes that beyond the sociality of the group in Trondheim there exist local, national and global networks of contact between fellow believers. Indeed, friendship bonds are cultivated within widely ramifying frameworks of Faith activity, including Oslo Christian Centre, the Word of Life, and so on (ibid.:91). Such friendships, consolidated within the safe confines of the Faith network, indicate the apparent universality of the Word and its applications across geographical and cultural distance.

CONCLUDING REFLECTIONS

Carrying out fieldwork within the Word of Life, as well as participating in it as a member, entails the feeling of plugging into and engaging in dialogue with cultural arenas located far beyond Uppsala itself. Such engagement and constant mutual influence are not incidental to the 'real' activities of the group, but vital to its operations and self-image. The group can only be fully comprehended through an appreciation of the ways in which it is partially constituted by relations – sometimes mediated in face-to-face encounters, sometimes 'virtually' articulated through communications media, sometimes merely imagined – that are orientated to a world far beyond its own immediate environment. My argument will be that, from the perspective of the average believer, the group provides a form of ideological resource through which discourses of globalising influence and interconnection can be accessed without necessitating submission to a strictly defined and constraining set of social relations. A particular form of 'believing without belonging' (Davie 1994) is made possible that is well suited to complex, increasingly fragmented conditions of contemporary existence in Sweden.

In describing Word of Life (and Faith) ideology as making up a rhetorically totalising system, I do not mean to reify it as a static and autonomous cultural form, existing separately from other aspects of society. As Csordas (1997:51) has noted, a traditional anthropological position might be to regard any religious movement as a bounded unit of analysis, a kind of 'tribe' or 'subculture'. Such an approach ignores the fact that a movement is inevitably a reaction to, or an attempt to change conditions within, wider cultural milieux. In addition, even highly committed adherents will probably carry out their lives in many contexts; while aspects of spiritual life are likely to pervade other, apparently secular spheres, sacred norms and practices themselves must also take on the colouring of everyday existence. It is, of course, difficult in complex societies to trace the effects of religious adherence in the quotidian activities of dispersed believers, but, on the other hand, we cannot assume that behaviour in church can provide a complete picture of a person's religious activity.

Nor do I wish to discount the differing convictions of individual believers in my presentation of a Faith ministry. Stromberg cautions against the temptation to assume that a given social group like a church must also share culture in a consensual and taken-for-granted way. As he puts it (1986:9): 'The fact that it is legitimate to depict culture as consensus for purposes of description does not justify the contention that culture may be assumed to enforce consensus, and thereby constitute social order, in a group.' Analysing a nonconformist church in Stockholm, Stromberg usefully describes its culture as involving a 'system of commitment': people have chosen to accept some kind of adherence to the group, but are committed in complex and various ways to its common symbolic resources. Stromberg relies mostly on interview data to examine how believers appropriate such resources in order to construct highly personal views of who they are, with commitment entailing the development of a relationship between symbol and individual person that can transcend language. He concludes, therefore, that social cohesion, a sense of community, may be generated in processes that have nothing to do with cultural sharing *per se*.

A Faith group such as the Word of Life might appear to present the ultimate form of 'culture as consensus': believers talk very often of how the state of being born-again gives them both individual and collective access to transhistorical and transcultural truth. My description and analysis of such apparently totalising discourse does not, however, imply that I am attempting to present the Word of Life as an unproblematically consensual culture. It is important to bear in mind the varied ways in which adherents believe they appropriate religious truth – spiritually, intellectually and physically, through verbal and non-verbal cultural vehicles. Perhaps one of the particular points of interest in this study, then, is its tracing of the various ways in which idiosyncratic response is apparently removed from collective contexts of worship, and how even individuals engaging in private spiritual devotions often come to see themselves as plugging into a faith that is entirely without ambiguity. People talk in both positive and negative ways of how they feel that they are indeed being taken over by Faith language, but this admission does not imply that they are somehow turned into homogeneous automata as depicted in extreme forms of Durkheimian mechanical solidarity.

My description of a Swedish Faith ministry and its relationship to other Faith churches around the world is not therefore an attempt to describe a coherent, unified interest-group as such. It comes closer to depicting the construction of a globalised, charismatic Protestant 'public', whose boundaries of adherence may be ambiguous, but which involves the cultivation of a sense of mutual awareness and interaction among dispersed evangelicals. A Christian who plugs into the Faith network in whatever country or context does not necessarily abandon other religious commitments or even ideologies. However, Faith practices allow the believer to cultivate a sense of engagement in a wider world of religious activity that appears to transcend the cultural and geographical barriers between self and others. Such engagement can take many forms; at its most powerful, however, it permits an affirmation of the person's own commitment to faith at the very point of diffusing it to others. In such a process we can discern the development of what I call a global 'orientation', produced in accordance with the assumptions of charismatic Christianity. Throughout the remaining chapters we shall look more closely at how various media of communication, combined with embodied practices, are used to construct the framework of a charismatic world which believers create anew as they reach out to spread salvation and prosperity across the globe.

CHAPTER FIVE

Words: from narrative to embodiment

Charismatic Christianity is a religion of the Word. Powerfully charged language is read, spoken, written, memorised, prophesied, translated, pinned up on signs in houses and cars,[1] stripped of semantic meaning in glossolalia and, so it is believed, embodied not only in the flesh of Christ but also in that of his followers. Word of Life members sometimes refer to the Scriptures as their 'spiritual weapon', echoing the Pauline imagery of a sword superimposed on an open Bible that forms part of the group's logo. The sacred text is treated as an intimate possession to be taken with the person as he or she goes about their daily lives, and its margins are usually heavily scored with notes taken from sermons, classes and personal reflections. The group itself, located in an industrial zone, is akin to a verbal factory, responsible for the production of many millions of words a year in the form of taped sermons, books and magazines. Ritual practices, ranging from private devotions to collective prayers, are complemented by processes of material production in the conversion of static text into 'living', sacralised and widely broadcast words.

I shall concentrate here on some of the ways in which words relate to the formation of identity as a believer. The chapter moves from an examination of public narrative forms to an extended focus on how words appear to become embodied and materialised in the self and the environment. I endorse James Peacock's point

[1] Parallels can perhaps be drawn with other faiths, in particular those that have a bias against anthropomorphic representation. According to Starrett (1995:53), labourers and shopkeepers in Cairo attribute the protective value of displaying or carrying Koranic verses to the latter's innate power as utterances of God (cf. also Graham, 1987:61). Solomon (1994:152) notes how cabbalistic Jews have gone so far as to place cards with divine names before themselves as they prayed.

(1984:108) that, for Pentecostalists and many other conservatives, devotion to the Bible implies 'dramatization – bringing the word to life, certainly in preaching but also in one's life'. Textuality and a kind of spiritually charged physicality are not opposed in evangelical practice but are mutually constitutive. The power of Scripture and other forms of inspired language is validated through inductive strategies that seek to assess the effects of language on the self and the material environment. The application of so-called literalism and doctrines of inerrancy in relation to the Bible is as much about embodying and 'living out' the text in a self-reinforcing process of spiritual authentication as it is about the verbalised assertion that everything the Bible says is unproblematically 'true' (see also Graham 1987).

In tracing the processes of giving life to words I divide the main body of the chapter into four main parts, each corresponding to different (if obviously overlapping) ways in which language can be applied to the self. Thus 'narrative emplacement' refers to the production of *self-descriptions*, in personal or collective contexts, that locate identity in terms of a landscape of evangelical action, ideals and characters (Carrithers 1992:76). As with the notion of orientation, I am using a spatial metaphor here, but not one that implies occupation of a static position. The place that charismatics inhabit through such narrative is one that provides mythical legitimation but does not impose restrictions on personal and collective mobility in the evangelical cause. 'Dramatisation', meanwhile, implies the *acting out* of religious – and ultimately biblically derived – ideals in terms of personal conduct and behaviour. 'Internalisation' refers to the process of *incorporating* language within the self in a way that is even more embodied. It is a form of self-inscription (as opposed to description) that leads believers to understand themselves as 'words made flesh'. 'Externalisation', finally, refers to the deployment of language as a *performative* force in order to change physical, social and material circumstances.[2]

---

[2] These terms are not used by evangelicals but they do overlap, at least to some extent, with emic categories. Narrative emplacements often include but are not subsumed by sermons and testimonies; dramatisation points to the frequently articulated sense of becoming 'like Jesus' in one's behaviour and character; internalisation is expressed most strikingly in metaphors of ingestion; externalisation, an aspect of all prayer and positive confessions, may be described using the biblical imagery of sowing seeds in order to produce a harvest.

My overall aim in discussing these practices is to argue that they help produce a charismatic, Faith habitus. As believers become skilful users of sacredly charged words, they create a sense of their identity as actors within an arena of action which appears to set no limits on imagination or ambition, and which responds in controllable ways to principles that are universal in their application. In other words, believers create within and among themselves an orientation to the world that is both charismatic and global.

NARRATIVE EMPLACEMENT

Many narrative forms are deployed in Faith contexts. Part of the process of gaining identity in a congregation or Bible School is the development and constant honing of a personal account of conversion, depicting how one became born-again into a new life (Stai 1993). As Stromberg notes (1993:6), one effect of such practices is the integration of a shared religious language into the idiosyncratic details of the person's life history. The convert learns that their previous life was one of 'darkness' as opposed to present enlightenment and revelation. 'Something lacking' has been replaced by plenitude, as identity is discovered through the 'full Gospel' and 'in Christ'. God, indeed, 'has a plan' for every believer's life. Conversion narratives are used to describe the self to other Christians but also as a means of witnessing to the unsaved, and are frequently topped up by testimonies of more recent miracles that may have occurred. Thus the use of autobiography – and self-objectification as a character in such narratives – illustrates the ideal of a personal relationship with God but is also deployed as a mode of persuasive discourse.[3]

My immediate concern here is with another kind of self-definition: the ways in which the group is characterised by its members in terms of a global mission. To illustrate the point I shall focus on two complementary examples of the genre. The first concerns narratives about the head pastor and receiver of the original 'vision' for the ministry, Ulf Ekman: in effect, these constitute biography as opposed to autobiography. If the Word of Life is itself a

---

[3] On evangelising narrative as persuasive discourse, see Harding (1987:171); Carrithers and Coleman (n.d.).

product of influence from a North American centre, such a relationship of initial dependency is being transformed into a depiction of Sweden, and the group itself, as a new centre of spiritual activity of global renown. At the centre of such representations is the chief symbol of the congregation – and indeed the Faith Movement in the whole of Scandinavia – Ulf Ekman. As Ekman's reputation has grown in Sweden and beyond, he has appeared to take on some of the characteristics of US preachers, and in particular the impression they give of straddling the globe in their operations. Ekman's father-in-law, Sten Nilsson, had originally introduced Ekman to Faith teachings, and describes the result in his autobiography, *Ledd av Guds Hand* ('Led by God's Hand') (1988:281):

> Ulf was a decisive, eager runner and went at speed down the path of faith. First to the USA, just like myself, to be stimulated by the 'world record holders' in the race of faith, Kenneth Hagin, Lester Sumrall, Kenneth Copeland, Oral Roberts . . . And he learned a lot, among other things that it was more effective to run without being clad in a Lutheran uniform!

Of course one way of reading this statement is to assume that Ekman needs North American spiritual legitimation to establish his credentials, but Ekman is also represented as an independently powerful leader in his own right. The following are the words of a young pastor who describes his experience of going with Ekman on a preaching tour of the United States:

> The American pastor . . . introduced Ulf as a great man of God, an apostle who goes up and down the whole of Europe. And it just opened up in the Spirit immediately and everybody just sat there and hungrily sucked in what God had laid down in Ulf.[4]

This image not only depicts Ekman as having a particular part of the world – Europe – under his influence, but also indicates that the Swedish part of the missionary network does not merely have to receive impulses from the United States: the cultural flow (to use Hannerz's (1991) term) or the charismatic power (to use religious language) seems to be moving from a relative evangelical periphery back to an apparent centre.[5] Elsewhere in the testimony the

---

[4] Word of Life Tape ST006.
[5] Compare with my discussion of Hackett (1995) in chapter 1. Some of these points are also put forward in Coleman (1998:252).

preacher draws direct parallels between Faith activities in Sweden and the United States. He talks of visiting a congregation in Columbus, Ohio, which happens to be called the Word of Life. He emphasises that, despite the geographical separation between the groups in Uppsala and Columbus, their similarities go far beyond their names: both, he says, are currently building new auditoria with many thousands of seats; the preaching styles of their head pastors resemble each other very closely; and, most important of all, 'There's exactly the same Spirit over both [congregations]'.

Brochures advertising the Bible School note of Ekman that: 'He reaches millions of people every week through television, books, etc.', while other literature as well as adherents refer to his ability to have an influence on other nations. A Bulgarian newspaper, quoted in a Word of Life publication, describes him as 'the Swedish Messiah' who is given access to the Bulgarian Prime Minister.[6] Or again, the following is a description of Ekman's actions in Albania:[7]

In 1991 God supernaturally opened the nation to the Gospel. Before the campaign held at the National Stadium in Albania's capital, Tirana, He issued a clear command: 'Crack the nation open for the Gospel!'

It is clear, then, that Ulf Ekman's considerable reputation as a powerful evangelist, evident both at the Word of Life and in smaller Faith congregations now spreading over Scandinavia, derives in part from his ability to appear as a 'world-wide' or 'great' man of God. His charismatic qualities, as with those of other preachers in the Faith network, are enhanced by his ability to attract a following that transcends a single locality. Descriptions of him also reveal a further advantage of positioning evangelical action on a global stage: narratives of the performative effects of faith are often constructed from incidents that occur elsewhere, far from the world of the listeners. In this way, no matter what the circumstances of the audience/individual listener may be, proof of the power of the Word is presented, taken from a context the validity of which is placed beyond reasonable challenge.

[6] *Magazinet*, 1994 4:30.
[7] Albania is regarded as a particularly significant country as it lies on the dividing line between Islam and Christianity in Europe.

The practice of evoking influence over 'elsewhere' is complemented by narratives that represent the notion of the world
coming to Uppsala. To explain this point I present an extended
extract from a sermon by the North American preacher and frequent visitor to the Word of Life, Lester Sumrall. Now deceased,
Sumrall became well known in Faith circles as an indefatigable
missionary who prided himself on having travelled to well over 100
countries. The transcription is taken from a recording of a mass
service held in Uppsala in the early 1990s.[8]

*It's so beautiful to see you. We feel so much at home among you. And
we're glad to meet you that we have met in so many other countries. It's
good to have a meeting-place where we can see each other again and
where we can praise the Lord together. The greatest joy on this earth is
praising the Lord. Hallelujah. Glory be to God.*

*I am here [applause from congregation]. My wife, Louise, she is here
[applause]. We have been married for forty-eight years [applause]. We
like it so well we decided to try for forty-eight more. Hallelujah!
[applause]. My oldest son is here. Would you stand, Frank? [Frank stands;
applause]. Well, Lord have mercy on us, there are too many Sumralls!
Hallelujah!*

*How many were born in Pentecost? Let's see your hands [pause as hands
go up]. That's quite a few! How many were not born in Pentecost?
[pause] That's too bad. How many were born in the Lutheran Church?
You made a good change. Hallelujah! If Luther was here he'd be in the
front seat. Shouting and praising God and dancing in the Spirit.
Hallelujah! He had the same anointing we have. How many were born
in the Methodist Church? What's wrong with you Methodists? Come
over and get baptised in water! Hallelujah! How many were born in the
Baptist Church? How many were born in no Church? Welcome to the
Kingdom! Hallelujah!*

*I'm going to preach to you tonight about the return of the Lord Jesus and
the prophecy of the Son and the prophecy of the Holy Ghost and the
prophecy of the Father. The whole Trinity have prophesied regarding the
return of Jesus and I want to talk about all three of them.*

---

[8] The video (Word of Life Tape VLS028) comprehends almost all of a service that took place
during a Word of Life conference. The transcribed section (italics and paragraphs my
own) is from the very beginning of the sermon. Sumrall speaks in English, and Pastor Ekh
stands at his elbow and translates each sentence or short passage into Swedish. Some of
this analysis is also in Carrithers and Coleman (n.d.).

But first, I was born in Pentecost. My mother spoke in tongues every day I was there [pats stomach with right hand]. And when I arrived on the earth our house was where the women had their prayer meetings and that whole bunch of women they would scream and shout and laugh and speak in tongues. They did it so much until I wondered which language I should speak on the street. We heard as much tongues as we did English. But we grew up to know the power of God and the power of the Pentecostal. We met most of the leaders in the United States who were the *original* leaders. At the time we met them we didn't sense the importance. It never dawned on me they might die. I thought they would be just like they were forever. But now they're all gone.

The way Pentecost came to this part of the world. A Methodist pastor named T. B. Barrett, a pastor in Oslo. He went to the United States in order to raise money. And while he was there someone said 'There's a revival. Would you like to see about it?' He said 'yes'. And he told me when I visited him that they prayed for him and the next thing he knew his head was up under the piano and he was speaking a language he didn't know and he was ecstatic. He was so full of joy he forgot to raise money. And he came back to Oslo. He called the Methodist people together and he says 'I have something to tell you'. They thought he had raised a lot of money and so they were just waiting for the good news. He says 'I have it!' And they were so glad. They thought it was money. He opened the Bible till Acts chapter 2. And he says 'I have it.' 'I got it.' And the Bishop said 'You didn't get it here'! And so they turned him out of the Church. And the Church began to grow. The Pentecost Church.

Within a few minutes Sumrall has greeted the audience and invoked his family, denominational affiliations, Jesus' return, his own birth 'in Pentecost' and the origins of Pentecostalism in Scandinavia. My paragraphs thus respond to broad thematic shifts in his narrative, each of which is partially self-contained, the first three of which are concluded with 'Hallelujah'. The extract might seem to be rambling but, in common with many oral narratives that are likely to be repeated to different audiences in different contexts, it allows Sumrall to weave together a selection of elements in a way that suits the demands of the present. Much of the sermon is clearly applicable to any number of congregations in the West and beyond. When Sumrall finally says 'The way Pentecost came to this part of the world' he simply has to fit in the appropriate historical background for the occasion. Instead of saying 'If Luther was here' he might just as easily have said Calvin, and so on.

To the extent that the extract has any coherence, it is concerned with the articulation of identity. Some features are intelligible because of background knowledge shared with the audience. Thus the simple statement 'I am here' partly takes its sense, and creates its response from the audience, through the shared awareness that Uppsala is being visited by a luminary in the firmament of the Faith Movement. Similarly, the reference to meeting 'you that we have met in so many other countries' evokes the larger, unseen, global public of evangelicals and refers to the movement of preachers among them across the world. At the same time, Sumrall is presenting himself, a charismatic personality, to his audience. He actually introduces his family in person to the assembly and reveals a personal fact: forty-eight years of marriage. The preacher and Pentecost are juxtaposed and somehow co-mingled: Sumrall had tongues directed at him even as he was in the womb, and he grew up meeting those who were present at the founding of the Pentecostal Movement itself. He represents the origins of Pentecost in narrative terms but is also himself metonymically linked to such times. He clearly has the authority to bring the congregation into contact not only with its spiritual origins in the US, but also with the birth of Pentecostalism in their own part of the world. This narrative is giving Faith Christianity a distinct, if contestable, heritage. One way of interpreting Sumrall's final remark about Barrett being thrown out of 'the Church' is to see it as a reference to the rejection Faith Christians now feel from, among others, leaders of the mainstream Pentecostal Church.

The story that Sumrall is telling is therefore not only about 'me' or 'you', but also about an inclusive 'we': it introduces the listener into a social world ('Welcome to the kingdom!') that is extended in time and space but also intimate, inhabited by familiar characters. Charismatics tend to perceive events through individual action and personality, and just as we saw how Ekman stands for Swedish influence over the world, so Sumrall represents revivalist history and influence coming to Sweden. His engagement with the audience is aided by the characteristically evangelical framework of call and response, to which the audience responds eagerly with applause and the occasional 'Hallelujah!' In doing so, they begin to become participants themselves in the translocal, transhistorical account that is being presented. All this is achieved, we note, with hardly a reference to the Bible itself, but we can have no doubt that the return of Jesus, Sumrall's ostensible theme, will later be shown to have distinctly contemporary salience in Sweden and the rest of the world.

DRAMATISATION

By 'dramatisation' (drawing on Peacock (1984)) I refer to the ways in which biblical exegesis is achieved through an acting out of the text, whether in sermons themselves or in other areas of life. Believers often come to see themselves as reinvoking characters in a biblical drama whose episodes can be replayed again and again throughout history, as tokens echo an original type. Again, techniques of delivering sermons illustrate the point. When I first came to services at the Word of Life, I was struck by two aspects of preaching. Firstly, there was the way pastors spoke for such a long time, sometimes up to two hours, with no written aids except the characteristic tool of their trade, usually a large, floppy, leather-bound Bible that would rest on a perspex podium in the centre of the stage, visible and open throughout the sermon. Secondly, there was the fact that the Bible was scarcely actually consulted throughout the entire length of the sermon. Scriptures would typically be quoted at the beginning of a talk in the sense that a verse or two would be taken from one part of the Bible and juxtaposed with verses from another part to indicate that they said precisely the same thing.[9] The text itself would then mostly be ignored, having been used as the catalyst for an anecdotal, apparently effortless peroration that appeared almost Homeric in its ability to extemporise on familiar biblical themes. If the text itself remained physically static, the preacher – living embodiment of the inspired Word – would move around the podium and the stage, making rhetorical points through skilful oratory and dramatic body language.

An important aim of such sermonising is to illustrate the direct

[9] Peck (1993:123) refers to the 'text–context' form of preaching that is part of Protestant tradition. The preacher begins with a quotation from Scripture and then elaborates it by applying the passage to everyday life.

application of scriptural narrative to the present: for instance, the notion that by acting 'as' Jesus, or Moses, or Abraham we can achieve the same results as they, given the constancy of divine power and truth over time. Thus, the sermon by Lester Sumrall discussed above goes on to talk of prophecy, and in his peroration Sumrall not only refers to great biblical figures but also presents his own reflections, not least those that came to him while sitting on a hill overlooking Jerusalem. The implication is clear: we are listening to a present-day prophet who is restoring – reviving – the spirit of scriptural truth. Sumrall is not merely creating a narrative: he is also demonstrating how the characters in that narrative can come to life through the exemplary actions of contemporary people such as himself. The Bible is not only Scripture, but equivalent to the script for a play, with roles adopted by those who take its words to heart (or, perhaps more accurately, to their Spirit).

Sermons themselves are merely the most obvious of a variety of practices in which believers use the Bible in this way, as a collection of stories that can be applied directly and indexically to the self, encouraging the believer to take a particular course of action, remain firm in the faith, discover the reason for a particular event and so on. As also noted by Ammerman (1987:57) any portion of Scripture, no matter how small, can be drawn upon. Or, as she says (ibid.:52): 'The Bible . . . is not just to be believed; it is to be lived.' A striking example of this practice was provided when the Word of Life decided to put up new premises between 1986 and 1987. As the construction emerged from the ground, adherents were encouraged to believe that it represented not only the realisation of a divine injunction, but also the contemporary equivalent of an occasion described in the Old Testament, where the Prophet Elisha begins to build dwellings near the Jordan River.[10]

The insertion of the self into 'living' biblical drama takes an even more radical form in the cultivation of visions and dreams by believers. It is not uncommon for people to state that they have met Jesus or some other biblical figure through such means, and this claim is particularly true of the more important pastors. In such cases, the main protagonists of the drama are taken from

---

[10] *Word of Life Newsletter*, 1987 4:4 and 2 Kings 6:1–2.

Scripture but are inserted into new narrative contexts as they engage with and often address believers in the present. The 'truths' of Scripture are both given a new facticity and rendered creative in the sense that *unique* encounters with canonical figures are made possible.

INTERNALISATION

Faith Christians combine traditional Pentecostalism with positive-thinking.[11] Adherents are supposedly provided not only with charismatic gifts, but also with a God who is both endlessly beneficent and perfectly predictable. Access to the Holy Spirit given to the born-again believer unites such a person with the ultimate source of truth in the sense that believers do not regard themselves as *interpreting* the Bible or inspired sermons, but *receiving* them, thus gaining determinate understandings that can be shared by all who apply so-called 'spiritual' ears and eyes to sacred words. Such words are signifiers whose signifieds are supposedly assured in the context of the community of fellow believers. The symbolic, ambiguous character of language is played down, just as it is denied that mere emotions can play any part in the perception of supernatural truth since they belong to 'the natural' (*det naturliga*) – the unpredictable, idiosyncratic world of mundane humanity that incorporates the fallible flesh and mind. As Ulf Ekman puts it:[12] 'With [God's] eternal words in your Spirit you can't go wrong, because your mind is renewed. You think God's thoughts and only want what God wants.' The logic of this is that the mind and body of the believer are to be colonised by the transcendent world of the Spirit, with sacred language as the mediating vehicle between the two. A common phrase among adherents is 'I feel in my Spirit', used on occasions when non-believers would probably just say 'I think'.

Perhaps the most striking example of how the Word is invested with physical qualities is evident in the way many Faith adherents describe the process of reading the Bible as a form of ingestion akin to eating. One can 'hunger' for or 'get filled' with the Word,

---

[11] See also chapter 1. [12] *Word of Life Newsletter*, 1984 July (no issue number):1.

while the following are the comments of a youth pastor in a sermon:[13]

Jesus said 'Our daily bread' and he meant it physically . . . you can't desist from spiritual breakfast for a single day . . . You'll come in to heaven like a spiritual body-builder . . . God wants to give you spiritual nourishment, and when you're newly born you get milk . . . When you grow you get a little bread . . . But then when you've eaten for a sufficiently long time, when God knows that you can eat . . . he gives you a real ox . . . you go around like a giant . . . like a Sumo wrestler, you become the biggest when you eat God's Word.

In this view, the text is embodied in the person, who becomes a walking, talking representation of its power. Eating is an especially powerful image because it points to a notion of internalising truth directly, bypassing the distorting effects of both social context and intellect. It was also invoked in the quotation I provided above from the young pastor who noted that American Christians 'hungrily sucked in what God had laid down in Ulf'.[14] Ekman reinforces such views when he writes: 'In the same way as your outer person lives on food, so your inner person, the born-again part of you, lives off each word that comes from God's mouth . . . It means that God talks in your inner person and gives you a word or a picture of something that will come.'[15] It is

---

[13] 'Four Keys to Your Bible Reading' (Word of Life Tape LOS10). Here, as elsewhere in this chapter, we see Pauline imagery deployed and adapted (see 1 Corinthians 3:2). The imagery of eating is not exclusively invoked by Faith adherents, of course. Compare the words of a Pentecostalist (a man in his middle thirties, who had never been to the Word of Life), explaining to me why it was important to him to read the Bible: 'In what sense is it important to eat bread? It's about the same thing . . . I find it easier to preach for instance when I am *into* the Bible than when I am concentrating totally on something else . . . The other reason is just that you have to be up to date with your nutritive intake, you have to have your share of the diet.' The connections between reading and communion are again evident here, but not linked to notions of boundless personal growth. Compare also with Becker (1995:35) who talks of how the power in *refusing* to eat lies in its eventual manifestation in flesh and quotes the example of female Christian mystics.

[14] More occasionally, as we shall see in chapter 9, implicitly sexual metaphors can be used to describe this process, for instance in the idea that 'the Word' can become a seed that enters the self in order to make one pregnant with truth.

[15] *Magazinet*, 1984 7:22. Elisha (1998:15) notes that, in charismatic language, disembodied concepts such as faith, trust and surrender are often combined with sensory metaphors. Revelations are seen as illuminations: 'seeing the light'; prophecies as sacred voicing: 'hearing the Word'; intercession as nourishment: 'being filled with the Spirit'; conversion as a tactile force: 'being moved by Christ', and so on. Metaphor can be seen as the critical meeting ground between textuality and embodiment (Csordas 1994b:16).

significant that the image invoked is that of divine dictation rather than dialogue. Word of Life adherents, especially Bible School students, are often encouraged initially to consult God rather than humans when puzzled about something they have read or heard. The assumption is that they will eventually understand the essential truth behind the words once they have been given supernatural aid. Lecture notes shown to me by Bible School students also illustrate this attitude well: one person, for instance, drew arrows leading directly from the word 'God' to a depiction of a human, implying the unmediated and hierarchical relationship between the two.

From an outsider's perspective, it might be argued that what is actually being expressed is merely a metaphorical relationship to the divine: eating the Word or having an image of Christ embedded in the self appear to be powerful ways of describing religious experience, but are not to be taken literally. However, from the inside, Word of Life discourse reflects a fundamentalist mistrust of overt verbal artistry, of language as playful representation. Fernandez (1986:13–17) observes that metaphor bridges otherwise separate domains of classification, so that inchoate experiences can be linked to more concrete, easily observable realms. In the same way, Word of Life language seems to make religious experience easier to comprehend by describing it in material terms – the supposed fixity of religious language is expressed well by stating that the Word can be walked on, eaten, etc. – but it does much more than this, since such language is believed not only to describe experience, but also to constitute it and cause it to occur.

Internalisation therefore refers to an incarnational practice that goes a stage further than dramatisation. People come to regard themselves as physically assimilating and thereby actually being taken over by scripturally derived (or legitimated) words. Believers often describe Scripture as speaking to them (and their situation) through 'direct address' (see also Forstorp 1992:2). Various bodily techniques besides reading and listening are regarded as effecting such assimilation of language to the self, most notably the memorisation of verses from the Bible so that they can be conceptualised as being stored within the person, ready to be brought back into the external world through the speech of prayer or testimony. As

Graham notes (1987:160), memorisation involves a particularly intimate appropriation of the text (ibid.:165): 'It is a vastly different thing to read and revere a text as an authoritative *document* than to *internalize* it in memory and meditation until it permeates the sensual as well as the intellectual sphere of consciousness.' We see echoes here of what Thomas Csordas (1997:237), following Tambiah, calls the 'inward otherness' of language, as people come to see themselves as possessed by Scriptures but also able to utilise the 'living' and incarnated Word in new ways.

Given that the body in this charismatic culture indicates and exemplifies divine favour, illness – a state of bodily imperfection – becomes a problem of faith as well as a physical condition. Prosperity Theology thus corresponds well with conventional Pentecostal dualities in which the collectively sanctioned Spirit ideally controls the individual and egotistical flesh (Wilson and Clow 1981:242–5). As one former Bible School pupil put it to me, she came to see herself as a kind of shell, a receptacle for the divine – again evoking the imagery of salvation related to the restoration of the full image of God in the person. Thus she said: 'One has God's nature so totally, that everybody is a small Jesus, almost.' Similarly, such emptying out of the self in favour of an idealised other is expressed in the way ordinary adherents often model themselves on powerful, 'Word-filled' preachers whom they feel speak particularly to their situation. Displacing but also apparently empowering one's person can occur simultaneously. For instance, two women told me they were identified by others, and indeed perceived themselves, as being Swedish versions of a popular American preacher who regularly visited the group. They took such labelling-processes to mean that they had a calling and mission that was similar to the preacher. A striking but, so far as I know, unconscious feature of tongues-speaking at the group is the way many worshippers repeat certain phrases used by preachers, in particular Ekman. More generally, the frequent practice of 'apostolic succession', whereby a ministry is passed from father to (most often) son, is itself an expression of the replication of idealised charismatic personhood, translated into the spheres of kinship and institutional continuity: Oral Roberts passes his work on to Richard Roberts Jr, Kenneth Hagin to Kenneth Hagin Jr, and so on. Ekman himself has four sons, all active within the Word of Life.

EXTERNALISATION

Faith beliefs parallel those aspects of Austinian speech act theory that describe how discursive practice can, in performative fashion, produce that which it names (Butler 1993:13). The Word can be made to 'live' as signs of language are externalised from the speaker and turned into physical signs of the presence of sacred power. In 'positive confessions', words come to create the very reality which they purport to describe. Words of joy create happiness, and those of defeat result in despair. We begin to see why some of the opponents of Faith Christianity summarise its theology in the phrase 'Name it and Claim it'. As distinctions between the symbolic and the real, the metaphorical and the material, are collapsed, words appear to take on many of the qualities of things. People talk of 'walking on the Word', as if it were a solid foundation for physical as well as spiritual support (Forstorp 1990:161). It is said that to repeat sacred words is not to render them banal but rather to give them more potential to influence the self, as if one were accumulating quantities of a given resource.

Scriptural and other sacredly charged language can pervade ordinary discourse as well as the heightened language of testimonies, so that its deployment is certainly not confined to the liturgical framework of worship services. It allows the believer to regard him or herself as being able to alter the script of their lives through applying living words to any given situation. Verses from Scripture, if chosen correctly and spoken by someone empowered by the Holy Spirit, can ostensibly help create the health and well-being desired by the speaker, including success in the process of passing faith on to others. For instance, if Romans 5:17 refers to the possibility of the righteous reigning in life, the speaking of the verse can itself aid the believer in attaining such authority.

As Weber realised in his discussion of rather different forms of radical Protestantism, the inductive strategy of searching for evidence of one's spiritual well-being can be performed by looking without as well as searching within: the world, even if fallen, can be read as a collection of signs of the power of the Word. A Swedish woman witnesses to her being cured from hayfever:[16] 'I went round the room, and . . . I who've had such difficulties in learning Bible words, I am after all fifty-one, but just think, they came plopping out from my Spirit and I just shot them out. I went around the room and peppered Satan.' She refers here to a new-found sense of empowerment, a previously inaccessible facility with words. But it seems telling that the words she describes apparently have an autonomous life of their own; they are like objects located within her, to be brought out and used as powerful ammunition in the fight to control the material world – in this case, manifested in her own body. (The act is then itself converted into a dramatic testimony or narrative, attesting to the power of deploying anointed words.)

Such appropriation of powerful verbal forms is believed by some adherents to have clearly visible effects. Many emphasise that it is the Spirit of the person, rather than the fallible mind, emotions or flesh, which can receive, truly comprehend and activate the meanings and power of sacred language. However, through a renewed Spirit one gains the ability via the deployment of language to conquer all circumstances (whether they involve criticisms from others or poor health or finances) and convert them to charismatic purposes. Some do claim that a diligent reader of Scripture becomes better looking, while a teacher at the Word of Life Bible School talks of her recovery from a serious car crash (she had apparently been despaired of by her doctors), invoking a vernacular version of the Pauline body as temple.[17]

I was so conscious of my inner person that I saw the body as a house that needed to be repaired. And . . . I said to one part of the body after the other to begin to function: 'Leg, in the name of Jesus, walk! . . . Hand, in Jesus' name, function! You are under God's blood! You are healed in the name of Jesus . . .' We rule from the inside. We are in a position of rule over our body.

---

[16] *Word of Life Newsletter*, 1984 July (no issue number):4.
[17] *Word of Life Newsletter*, 1985 April (no issue number):6.

The healed woman in effect places her physical self under the control of supernatural authority, manifested in Jesus' name and a corporeal image of God's blood, but also activated by her own deployment of words. As with the woman who describes her cure from hayfever, collectively sanctioned language, having been internalised by the individual person, is externalised by that same person to act back on an undesired aspect of the self. A complex and recursive set of causal relationships is established between the person and the Word. The adherent learns to see her 'essential', ruling self as made up of Word-filled Spirit guiding personal will, and in the process also perceives herself as sufficiently separated from her body to view it as an object to be worked upon. Once healed, the body is no longer regarded as an alienating image of failure, but rather can be re-assimilated as a representation and, of course, experience of the power of sacred language. Deploying language becomes, according to this logic, both a loss of self and a gaining of access to a language from God that, in its bodily (and other material) effects, transcends the need for interpretation.

GLOBALISING HABITUS

Describing possible contrasts between orality and literacy, Walter Ong (1991) quotes 2 Corinthians 3:6: 'The letter kills, the spirit gives life.' He notes that spoken words engage the body (ibid.:67) and become an event in time, whereas writing tends to reduce dynamic sound to quiescent space (ibid.:82). Ong also distinguishes between the orality of non-literate peoples and a secondary orality that is rather more deliberate and self-conscious, and indeed dependent upon the written word for its operation. What I have been describing is a religious group (and Movement) for whose members the rhetoric of perfect adherence to a written text provides a powerfully charged representation of certain cultural ideals: seeing the world in black and white; perceiving the complexities of the present as anticipated by and reducible to the narratives of Scripture; understanding language as transcending semantic meaning in its effects on the world. Strategies of scriptural incarnation turn the letters of the Bible into the workings of the living Word. Appropriation of Scripture is reliant upon its existence in written form and yet acts to convert the pages of the text into the dramas of both ritual and everyday existence.

The four 'verbal' practices described in this chapter present the possibility of predictable and rational ways in which to bring the idiosyncratic self in line with idealised and universally shared incarnations of faith – the language and events of the Bible, renowned preachers (wherever they may come from), the inspiration of the Holy Spirit. States of perfect health, happiness and prosperity are supposedly achieved through becoming an embodiment and physical representation of objectified language. The believer may therefore develop a specifically evangelical habitus in which the 'textualisation' of the self is manifested in bodily dispositions and experiences. The extent to which this habitus is taken on by the believer is variable, but the presentation of self as constantly positive in demeanour and speech is often believed to echo an internal state of being filled by the Spirit as well as biblical language. Photos of preachers sometimes actually juxtapose the body of person and text in ways that implicitly parallel each other: in more formal examples the preacher often opens his or her arms towards the camera, one hand holding an open Bible towards the viewer. More informally, the preacher may be shown striding up and down the stage, expressing through mobility the power of the Word to move body as well as mind and Spirit. The general body language of services, expressing what Csordas (1997:111) calls a 'callisthenic spirituality of corporal commitment', includes apparently random movement and chaotic periods of glossolalia that demonstrate the urgency and spontaneity of the biblical message and its effects. Such occasions usually occur towards the end of a period of singing praise-songs, and just before the sermon. The disciplined evangelical body can thus constitute itself through the production of physical signs of an apparent indiscipline. On some occasions, during youth services, I have even been among a congregation that was urged to run around the room as if, filled with the Spirit and the Word, we would not have been able to contain ourselves by remaining fixed in one place.

I have already described how 'narrative emplacement' and 'dramatisation' can occur during services, but the other practices mentioned above can also be shown to take form on such occasions. Listening to an inspired preacher with 'spiritual' ears that can supposedly bypass problems of interpretation is itself a form of internalisation. A common prayer position, deployed particularly during periods of collective speaking in tongues, is that of standing up, eyes closed and head tilted slightly up towards the stage, with arms stretched out (palms up) in front of the body. When I first saw this position I labelled it the 'receive' position in my fieldnotes. It reminded me of the pose one might adopt if accepting a large box from someone. Now, I am equally likely to think of it as a stance associated with internalisation. The person appears to be filled with sacred language from a space which may be difficult to pinpoint exactly, but to judge from bodily alignment is close to that of the stage itself. The association of spiritual power with charismatic leaders is made more explicit towards the end of services, when members of the congregation are encouraged to receive intercession and sometimes exorcism from the preacher and other pastors in attendance. The pastor speaks in tongues and perhaps commands an evil spirit to depart while placing a hand on the forehead of the afflicted person (in mimesis of the healing acts of Jesus). In most cases, the person falls back – often instantly – into the arms of an usher, and may remain on the ground for a number of minutes. Here, then, internalisation involves surrendering to a power that is too strong for normal human consciousness to bear.[18]

Processes of externalisation are also enacted during services. The healing I have just described is itself a form of transfer of language from a preacher even as it involves internalisation on behalf of the normal believer. Congregations occasionally direct tongues and demands for divine assistance towards written prayer requests that are held up on stage for all to see. Such verbal utterances are accompanied by the pointing of the hand, as though words could act like arrows with magical powers, affecting the lives of those Christians mentioned in the prayer requests (Tambiah 1968;

---

[18] Csordas (1994a:233) notes that the act of falling is spontaneously co-ordinated in such a way that, following Bourdieu, it can be described as a disposition within the charismatic ritual habitus. Roelofs (1994:219–20) argues that in such actions we see an interweaving of enthusiasm and seemingly passive self-surrender.

Csordas 1997:69). In the same way, people may be encouraged to lay hands on neighbours who signal that they are in need of healing or other help. Again, tongues accompanies the physical contact of hand on shoulder or arm.

If the examples just given illustrate the focussing of language on to a specific recipient or object, externalisation can also be deployed to open up the spatial boundaries of spiritual efficacy. In both Uppsala, under the encouragement of Ulf Ekman, and London, at a meeting held by Morris Cerullo, I and thousands of other participants have been urged to turn collectively to the four points of the compass and to claim, in the name of God, the unsaved cultural territories stretching out before us. Rather than stretching out to a sacred, distant centre, as would be the case in a genuflection towards Mecca, the congregation is encouraged here to think of themselves, wherever they happen to be, as the spiritual centre of action. The area encompassed and 'claimed' by this ritual orientation is in effect placeless and universal – not limited to a fixed point in space but suggesting the desire to appropriate everything beyond the congregation itself.[19]

Csordas (1997:68) draws on the work of Bourdieu and Merleau-Ponty to emphasise the permeability of the boundaries between ritual events and the rest of existence. He thus refers to what he calls the ritualisation of life rather than to specific, set-apart ritual events in his own tracing of the creation of a (Catholic) charismatic habitus. Certainly, the Faith dispositions I have been describing take form beyond the walls of the Word of Life itself, even though at times people attempt to suppress the outwards signs of commitment for fear of being criticised. Healing of others through the laying on of hands can occur anywhere, at any time. People draw on glossolalia during their everyday lives in order to change circumstances that range from a car that will not start to feelings of unhappiness: a teacher talks of speaking in tongues to herself in preparation for controlling an unruly classroom; I have even witnessed one person talking in tongues below her breath while walking through central Uppsala, in order to protect herself from secular influences evident in the city.

---

[19] Compare David Parkin's (1992) discussion of ritual as spatial direction.

The sense that the external world is one of both opportunity and threat becomes part of everyday consciousness. Believers should be prepared to see a vision of Jesus at any moment, just as they should be on their guard against satanic attack. One young woman told me of her experience of attending a job interview in Stockholm. After a few minutes of being questioned she realised that a demonic Spirit of criticism had entered one of her inter-viewers and was visible to her, if not to anyone else in the room. For a time she engaged in an internal battle to present an untroubled, 'secular' self to her potential employers, but eventually gave in to impulses that were both spiritually and physically over-whelming. She told the presumably bemused interviewer that he was possessed and then abruptly left the room. The incident reveals the conflicts that can develop when two worlds of percep-tion and self-presentation collide.[20] It replicates some of the prob-lems that occur in more private, domestic realms when members of a family differ in their attitudes to Faith beliefs and practices. The home is a place where strict adherence to biblical principles and evangelically sanctioned behaviours can more easily be relaxed or compromised (Stai 1993). However, many Word of Life members create domestic environments that are, in material terms, mini-extensions of the physical realm they encounter in the minis-try itself. Book-shelves are filled with texts by Faith preachers; secular music is thrown out in favour of products by Christian artists; often, edifying verses from the Bible or preachers are written out and pinned up on doors and other visible places. The young woman I have just mentioned, who rushed out of a job interview on the grounds that it had become spiritually threaten-ing, was a skilful artist who put pencil drawings of Jesus around the walls of her flat so that she could feel surrounded by his presence.

The extent to which Faith assumptions and dispositions can become a part of the self is often most evident at times when the

---

[20] I remember an equally striking encounter in 1987 with a middle-aged Pentecostalist who occasionally visited the Word of Life. We were both coming out of a public meeting where Ekman had defended himself against a sometimes hostile student audience (Coleman 1989:213). The Pentecostalist remarked: 'He seemed perfectly reasonable. Why is it that he only sounds mad when he's over there?' (nodding in the direction of the Word of Life ministry).

person wishes to distance themselves from the group. The rigidity of an insistence on a Goffmanesque presentation of an omni-competent charismatic persona can become a source of consider-able inner conflict – one might say negative alienation from the iconic self-image produced for one's own and others' consump-tion. While some believers can simply tell themselves that they do not accept the rigidity of Faith principles in these matters, others feel far more trapped by their implications, especially when they feel unable to come up to ideal standards of bodily perfection or practice.[21] To a certain extent, it is possible to use rationalising arguments to explain apparent failure: perhaps the devil is attack-ing one of God's people through sending sickness; alternatively, healing or success have already occurred in the supernatural realm, but have not yet reached 'the natural' state of physical reality. Yet such explicitly articulated expressions of Faith 'logic' might prove insufficiently convincing. A middle-aged Bible School student whom I interviewed abandoned her course at the group, feeling unable to cope with the disjunction between her worsening physical condition and triumphalist Faith ideology. Other former students I spoke to had left, describing themselves as 'split' (*split-trade*) – unable to reconcile a private inner-life of failure and self-reproach with the bodily and linguistic manufacture of an exterior image of happiness and success. In these cases, the ideological division of the self into both a Spirit (colonised by sacred language) and a partially alienated body or mental state proves unsatisfac-tory, not least as the body and the mind prove persistently able to resist the supposed rule and will of the divinity within the person. One ex-Bible School student stated of Faith ideology: 'One inter-prets it so that it's only through the Spirit one communicates with God . . . And so the picture is that the Spirit is king, and the soul and the body are slaves.' Interestingly, she maintained contact with her Swedish Church congregation throughout her time as a Faith student, and never managed to harmonise the two sides of her spiritual life and practice. In describing her unease with what she

---

[21] In this context, it is significant that funerals do not take a prominent role in Word of Life literature or other forms of public discourse. Occasionally, I have heard stories of believ-ers being unable to accept the death of younger members of the group, and even sug-gesting that a Lazarus-like resurrection might be possible.

saw as the authoritarian nature of Faith discourse, she notes: 'I felt resistance against the language', highlighting in her protest the importance of assimilating such language if commitment to the Movement is to be achieved. She felt that her inner revolt led not only to theological confusions and psychological problems, but also to feelings of physical illness. Even in being rejected, Faith ideology appeared to retain, for a time, its hold on her bodily as well as cognitive state.

Faith styles of language and bodily deportment differ from a mainstream Swedish or Western habitus, involving as they do the evocation of bodily possession by powerful, externally derived and divine forces. Their distinctiveness also becomes evident in almost semiotic terms when adherents visit the services of other churches. The practices of running, hopping up and down, speaking in tongues and so on, are clearly differentiated from the generally staid character of services in the Swedish Church and most of the free churches. They come closest to the revivalist forms practised within mainstream Pentecostalism, but are subtly differentiated from them. I came to know a number of Pentecostalists in the city who also attended the Word of Life. Some of these believers, particularly the younger ones, betrayed their dual affiliation (often but not always deliberately, in my opinion) even during services in the older church. Some of the signs of Faith influence were linguistic: the use of such phrases as 'I *demand* in Jesus' name!' or 'I am a conqueror!' (*övervinnare*); or speaking in tongues with particular volume and speed. Others were more purely embodied: a kind of jumping on the spot, or swaying and waving the arms with eyes closed, on occasions when others were more likely to be standing still. Such actions, though within the bounds of possibility in more conventional charismatic churches, became Word of Life badges of identity because of their regularity, speed and force. In the context of a Pentecostal service, they indicate the adherent's continuity with, but partial separation from, more institutionalised revivalist forms where the 'fire' of enthusiasm has begun to cool. The complex relationship to the older Movement that they embody can be seen as the physical equivalent of Lester Sumrall's narrative appropriation of Pentecostal heritage quoted towards the beginning of this chapter. Self-identification with revivalist heritage is asserted even as that heritage is transformed and surpassed in the present. Habitus becomes a means of expressing both resistance and politically charged appropriation of a potentially more powerful rival.[22]

Certainly, some of the Pentecostalists I interviewed chose to 'read' Word of Life actions and deportment as transformations of their own culture. A middle-aged man describes the behaviour of Faith adherents at his wife's workplace, a hospital:

[Other workers] say they are all right but if they would just stop nagging about the Word of Life all the time, about wonderful this and wonderful that, wonderful Bible School and wonderful teaching . . . They are very concentrated on what they are doing at the moment. And I think that the Pentecostalists were just the same and I must say that there *are* quite a number of similarities.

Another Pentecostalist, a young woman, refers to her own perception of how Faith supporters can be identified in her own congregation. She feels that they parallel but also distort more usual modes of worship: 'It is partly the way they pray . . . They talk quite quickly to "The Lord", and he "has everything in his hands" . . . and they talk a more extreme language, if you understand what I mean. Those prayers where you "just give honour to" and "just praise" and "just raise on high".' In many cases, the ritual styles at the Word of Life were identified as being very American, and therefore less genuine than home-grown varieties. Thus (from a man in his late twenties): 'Americans are theatrical, I think. It is acting on stage . . . not Swedish in some way. There is a lot of "show".'[23]

The Faith habitus being described here is one that can be learnt by participation in services and classes run by the Word of Life. Preachers and those who stand closest to the stage, as well as ushers who stand at the end of each row, tend to be the most practised exponents and therefore act as exemplars for others. During the singing of praise-songs, the congregation consistently echoes the

[22] Compare Appadurai (1996:113) on cricket in countries that were once part of the British Empire: 'Cricket gives all these groups and actors the sense of having hijacked the game from its English habitus into the colonies, at the level of language, body, and agency as well as competition, finance, and spectacle.'

[23] Some Pentecostalists were aware that many of their own ritual forms were derived from the United States.

language and bodily movements of the choir, so that ample opportunity exists to pick up the rudiments of Faith deportment. Active training can also take place. The experienced Christian should go through Bible verses with converts and demonstrate the use of tongues to them, showing that such a powerful tool is subject to the will of the speaker. Novices may also go to special classes with, for instance, the youth pastor, in order to 'build themselves up' in faith. Elements of the charismatic habitus can be said to make up a global orientation in a number of ways. Narrative emplacements such as that provided by Sumrall encourage adherents to think of themselves as part of a world-wide movement. Dramatisation brings biblical characters and events into the present and illustrates the permanent saliency of a text that is shared and diffused across cultures. The apparent fact that sacred language can be internalised without distortion turns such universal applicability into a universalised bodily practice. Finally, externalisation allows believers to feel that they can spread the effects of charismatic culture, becoming powerful agents in the globalisation of the message and its benefits. Conferences and other meetings that involve visitors from abroad provide evidence of not only the widespread appeal of Faith revivalism, but also its essential similarity across the globe. Christians from abroad may speak a different language 'in the natural', but their sermons are translated in an instant. Neither glossolalia nor the body language of Faith worship requires any interpretation and demonstrate the parallel ways in which the Spirit inspires believers from all parts of the world. Faith worship even appears globalised in contrast to more staid Pentecostal ritual because of its evocation of movement and flow within and across space. Overall, a cultural system is created that is potentially more pervasive, more intimately 'appropriable' and less open to challenge than a purely verbally articulated set of ideological propositions would be (Comaroff 1985). Even as powerful missionary exemplars such as Ekman and Sumrall embody the idealisation of physical mobility in the diffusion of the message, so they demonstrate the generic qualities of being led by the Spirit: the spiritual power that they possess is – supposedly – available to all, albeit in different quantities.

The emphasis on the physical as well as spiritual state of the self, and the following of the Pauline injunction to treat oneself as a temple, fits well with Harold Turner's (1979:138) description of the New Testament Incarnation of God in Jesus as carrying with it the potential for a biblical revolution in the religious use of space. In suggesting that he is to replace the temple of Jerusalem as the focus of faith, Jesus moves the sacred centre from a place to a person, and the pioneering instance of Christ establishes a model whereby salvation is directed towards the restoration of the full image of God in man and woman. If each person becomes a 'little Jesus', the number of sacred centres that can be constructed becomes infinitely expandable. Amongst Faith Christians, the stress on the self (incorporating the body) as a vehicle for the divine results not only in a search for physical well-being, but also in a repertoire of bodily gestures that can convert any space into a context for the internalisation or externalisation of the Word. In the next chapter, we shall see how such a habitus becomes built into a globalising visual aesthetic that not only moves from the body into other realms of existence and representation, but again differentiates Faith identity from older, apparently more parochial forms of Christian adherence.

CHAPTER SIX

Aesthetics: from iconography to architecture

Social scientists as well as theologians tend to describe evangelicalism as a religion of the word in *opposition* to the object or image.[1] Harding (1987:169) emphasises how Baptist services and revivals are stripped of imagistic and sacramental material as a means of intensifying and focussing religious rhetoric. Goethals (1985:151) refers to the way the expressive power of architectural settings and material artefacts is minimised in evangelical contexts, in deference to the persuasive functions of words. Rosman (1984:159), finally, describes the evangelical tendency to depreciate human artefacts, on the grounds that physical forms cannot compete with the Word of God. These examples imply that evangelicals provide a contemporary version of the iconoclasm of original Protestant reformers who abhorred the base circumscription of the sacred on the grounds that it contaminated divine prerogative (Freedberg 1989:62). The emphasis on the inspired Word seemed to privilege direct communication with God over the mediations of a corruptible Church. Thus, Eire (1986:315) describes the aesthetic consequences of the post-Reformation concern that *finitum non est capax infiniti* – an unbounded God could not be confined to mundane objects and images: 'The stripped, whitewashed church in which the pulpit replaced the altar became the focal point of a cultural shift from visual image to language.'[2]

---

[1] Some of these arguments also appear in Coleman 1996a and 1996b.

[2] Note also Goody's description (1993:201) of early Protestants: 'Instead of visual symbols they relied on the word, the plain word, and on rational discourse.' Such aesthetic sensibilities were also exemplified by the early settlers of Puritan America, where according to Victor Turner (1982:13) the stress on the interiorisation of sacredness led to an attitude that 'The Word was to be heard, not the image or icon seen.'

In some respects, Word of Life ideology and practice appear to echo such scholarly descriptions of radical Protestantism. The members of the Swedish group commonly define themselves precisely through their attempts to achieve unmediated and inspired access to the divine. Much of Faith practice is concerned to appropriate the power of divinity through human action that is unlimited in its potential and global in its applicability. From this perspective, the cultivation of visually rich, sensuous expressions of worship – and in particular religious art – would seem to represent an idolatrous and self-defeating emphasis of fixed material form over the workings of the religious imagination. Communication with God must ideally emerge not from fixed liturgies but from means of expression that can incorporate apparently spontaneous movement: during services, dance and gesture combine with oratory and song to make up a choreography of inspiration (Coleman 1989).

Despite these initial remarks, it should already be clear that a concentration on linguistic forms provides a necessary but very far from sufficient means of understanding the articulation of a global orientation amongst Faith Christians.[3] Faith 'culture' is embodied and diffused not only in narratives, but also in a coherent system of visual, material and embodied aesthetics. Language – contained in the Bible, prayers, sermons, testimonies and tongues – fulfils its sanctified function by being converted into objects and images as well as persons, thereby permeating the total fabric of religious as well as everyday life (Forrest 1988). I want therefore to focus on certain aspects of such aesthetics that reinforce a sense of reaching out into the world, and do so in a way that resonates with deep-seated assumptions concerning the importance of constant mobility, growth and transcendence of place. Clearly, much of what I have to say will complement my analysis of language in chapter 5. In order to contextualise the argument further, I shall juxtapose the

---

[3] A parallel may be evident here with the discussion by Dewhurst et al. (1983) of the folk art of Puritan life: such material culture remained largely overlooked for some time because it was so deeply integrated into everyday life that it could be taken for granted. See also Meyer's (1997) fascinating analysis of the materiality of Protestant missionary Christianity. Generally, however, I agree with Lehmann's remark (1996:182) that one of the disappointing features of the sociology of much Christianity is the fact that it is 'aesthetically unmusical'.

Faith ethnography with brief comments on an alternative set of Christian aesthetic forms that was produced in Uppsala at almost exactly the same time as the Word of Life was emerging as a powerful force in the religious life of the city.

CHRIST AS BODY-BUILDER

The body of Christ, whether described in words, represented in icons or ingested in the Eucharist, is central to much Christian worship and identity. Not only has it been perceived as a metaphor for the Church itself (Turner 1991:12), it has also been regarded as the archetypal form of the body as temple, a sign that humans themselves have the capacity to act as microcosms for the divine.[4] The fact that Jesus is regarded as the divine Word made flesh has been linked with a variety of Protestant forms of *Imitatio Christi*, mimetic practices that associate the ideal Christian person with divinity on earth and therefore also with the Word acting ('dramatised') in the world.[5]

Despite their stress on the body and on physical metaphors, Word of Life members tend to avoid the public, pictorial display of Christ himself. Faith preachers do however talk of seeing Jesus in dreams or visions – we saw in chapter 1 that Kenneth Hagin, for instance, claims to have been granted interviews with his Saviour. The image of Jesus can also sometimes be invoked in public discourse to depict a sense of common orientation and certainty: an advertisement for the Word of Life Europe Conference of 1991 urges the visitor to 'Fix your eyes on Jesus and expect to receive everything he has planned for you this week.' Occasionally, even ordinary Word of Life members talk of receiving visions of the living Christ in their dreams or waking lives. An encounter with Christ (rendered into a narrative) can, for instance, be used to confirm the truth of a text. A ten-year-old girl states: 'When I was in the playroom Jesus came in. He shone as if a lamp had been lit . . . Only when the teacher read out the Book of Revelations in the Bible in school about how Jesus looked did I realise that it was

---

[4] See 1 Corinthians 3:16, 6:19.
[5] It is worth remembering that the phrase 'Word of Life' is a reference to Jesus in the New Testament (e.g. 1 John 1).

actually written as I had seen him.'[6] Such images represent for charismatics a form of viewing that is inspired and intensely personal. Their immediacy and evanescence illustrate how Christ has chosen to reach into the moment, into the particular situation of the individual person.

In turn, a lack of faith can be equated with a distorted image of the divine. A former student at the Bible School described how he was helped by a visiting preacher to overcome all those things that could stop him from viewing Jesus, and noted how he was urged to move in the Spirit through a tunnel to a beach, where he finally saw Jesus clearly. This event, in my terms another form of 'dramatisation', was considered by the student to be a breakthrough in both his spiritual development and his inner sight, as it implied a means of achieving an apparently unmediated relationship with a sacred figure (despite, we note, the role played by the preacher).

Pictures of Christ actually located on paper or canvas are rare. In the hall where services take place at the Word of Life, no such images, and not even a cross, are to be seen. The most significant objects are a lectern, seats and television cameras. Children's literature does sometimes illustrate biblical scenes in pictures, and may include images of a Jesus who usually possesses rather Anglo-Saxon-looking features. Depictions of sacred figures are also sometimes produced in private: in the previous chapter, I mentioned the young woman who covered the walls of her apartment with pencil drawings of Jesus, represented as a young and virile man. She saw the drawings as providing a form of protection from evil influences. Such externalisation of an image that has come from within the self has parallels with the practices of art therapy: inner consciousness is mediated and transformed through materialised symbolic forms (Shaverien 1992:4–6). As with tongues and other forms of sanctified language, the divine force located inside the person is activated through its manifestation in the world, and acts back on the agent of its mobilisation.

Only on one occasion have I seen a painting of Christ publicly displayed at the Word of Life (Figure 3), and significantly this was a temporary decoration in an office corridor. The picture certainly

---

[6] *Word of Life Newsletter*, 1987 3:12.

Figure 3 Christ represented with the physique of a body-builder, a painting put on temporary display in a corridor of the original Word of Life building.

articulates well, in its depiction of Christ's body and actions, with some of the basic elements of evangelical ideology and practice evident at the group. It recalls, indeed, the youth pastor's image of the spiritual body-builder that I quoted in chapter 5. Viewers can see the results of the ultimate in verbal nourishment, as Jesus constitutes the Word as well as illustrating the effects of its internalisation – a healthy, strong body acting as an index of faith, with boundaries that are not ill-defined but as firm and unambiguous as the objective and objectified language of sacred speech. Of course, the image depicts a specifically masculine version of spiritual perfection, though it does reinforce widely shared ideas (expressed by both women and men) concerning the inherent power associated with divinity. The painting is perhaps as close as one can get to a charismatic icon.

Like much Conservative Protestant ideology, the picture is constructed out of opposition. The artist explained in an accompanying note that he was tired of seeing depictions of a crucified Jesus, signifying an attitude of defeat. Crucifixion represents a literal if temporary fixing of divinity, but here we see instead a powerful, triumphalist Christ who embodies movement. The arms are held aloft, and the whole body seems to be emerging, perhaps into the light from darkness, or at least exalting in physical and spiritual power. Christ is breaking forth, perhaps even removing himself from the confines of the canvas rather than being placed in dialogue with other figures. In looking at the picture, I am reminded of John Berger's suggestion (1972) that images contain within themselves ways in which they should be viewed – encouragements to the onlooker to adopt a particular spatial and perhaps symbolic relationship to them. Here, we see an image that avoids the dependent visualisation of a suffering Christ looking to heaven, or a vulnerable infant Jesus gazing at his mother, and presents a Christ of power who looks straight at the viewer in direct evangelical exhortation.

Through its framing of movement, the picture displays iconographic parallels with other images (and ritual forms) produced formally and informally within the group. Its depiction of energy parallels the marginalia inscribed in notebooks of Bible School students which contain, alongside lecture notes, doodles of Bibles and crosses incorporating stylised depictions of the inherent power emerging from such objects.[7] It also parallels photographs contained in Word of Life newsletters and magazines of well-known preachers, both Swedish and foreign, women as well as men, frozen in attitudes of motion as they speak and embody the Word of God. Intriguingly, the image depicts in paint something very similar to the story told by an American preacher, Roberts Liardon, during a sermon describing a visit he paid to Jesus:[8] 'And

---

[7] On the workings of such power, see Hunt's (1998) interesting paper considering theories of magic in relation to Faith ideology.

[8] Quoted in Swartling n.d.:45; unpublished manuscript later published in modified form (1988).

there Jesus stood . . . His hair came down to about here. And one thing that I noticed; it was that he had muscles! Isn't that great!' This vision is interesting not only because it includes a minor but 'authenticating' piece of detail – the length of Jesus' hair – but also because, like the actual canvas picture, it takes the notion of spiritual strength and growth, so important to Faith teaching, to have a physical as well as a spiritual referent.

In suggesting that this image of 'muscular Christianity' embodies Faith ideology I do not wish to imply that Word of Life members are turning into a congregation of charismatic body-builders – even though a leading Faith preacher and frequent visitor to the group, Ray McCauley, is indeed a former Mr South Africa.[9] However, the parallels are more than skin-deep. If, as Harré (1989) notes, in body-building one's physical form becomes a psychologically detached art object whose individual parts can be isolated and worked on according to rational principles, many Word of Life believers display the same kind of attempt to subordinate nature, conceptualised as the flesh, the emotions and the mind, to a calculating, quantifying faith. Charismatic self-identification with Christ involves a particular form of mimesis through the appropriation of the performative force contained within biblical texts and the in-filling of the Spirit. Recall the healing process in the case of the woman who had suffered a car crash (discussed in chapter 5). In both body-building and the attitudes she displays towards her damaged limbs, apparently universally applicable principles are applied with predictable results, forcing the stubborn flesh to conform to a higher ideal. If body-builders function according to the so-called 'exaggeration principle' – the idea that in the search for eternal growth one cannot consume too much of good thing, whether it be carbohydrates or steroids – so this is also the case with Word of Life attitudes to sacred language and the power of divinity in general. As one Bible School student put it to me: 'An overdose of Jesus' love is exactly what we need.' The Word, whether contained in language or Jesus, represents a collectively sanctioned but often individually

---

[9] A view of Christ and/or the Christian as a kind of Mr Universe (in more senses than one) is not in itself new. See Moore (1994:211).

consumed principle of empowerment to which the believer has to submit, transforming the self into a living icon.

Underlying these attitudes is a technology of the self whereby inner and outer states are objectified, monitored and put on display in order to maintain a socially derived ideal (Mansfield and McGinn 1993:52). Bodily practices and disciplines amongst these charismatics call for a partial synthesis of Goffman and Foucault. 'Positive Confession' can be extended beyond the realm of spoken language into forms of self-presentation that demonstrate the empowerment of the physically and spiritually healthy person, ranging from dancing, raising the hands and even quaking during services to employing an enthusiastic demeanour in all circumstances. A self-exhortatory note written by a Bible student to herself in her lecture notes reads: 'Don't defend Jesus but let Him be seen in your life!' No matter how shabby their home circumstances may be, adherents usually try to arrive at services and classes sporting smart clothes and a positive demeanour. I remember attending one meeting when students presented Pastor Ekman with a birthday present. I had been expecting them to give him a suitably edifying text, but in fact the large packet he unwrapped contained a smart black jacket which was considered highly appropriate for a man of God who had to demonstrate signs of success to others.

The audience for presentations of a positive demeanour is made up not only of fellow charismatics or non-believers, but also the self. Just as (even personally activated) language can be applied to one's objectified body to prompt healing, so can the acting out of a joyful state produce the desired effect. Self-actualisation as well as proof of the presence of divinity are achieved through deploying a specific body language. Such language is to be understood as a form of visual, indeed corporeal, literalism, since as with sanctified words the translation from original, physical manifestation to effect in the world is ideally direct, without distortion and indicative of the presence of Truth. One former Bible School student at the Word of Life expressed well this sense of attempting to become one's own icon: 'You should have faith in your self, or you should have faith in your own faith . . . It means that if you stand sufficiently long in faith the invisible will become visible.' Forstorp (1992:96), who has studied another Faith congregation in

Sweden, talks of being told that we are a reflection of what is inside us. In a ritualised echo of this sentiment, older children at the Faith school he examined are told to chant Bible verses as they look at themselves (or one might say subject themselves to the charismatic gaze) in the mirror.

Both the deployment of visual images and the use of language illustrate some of the ambiguities surrounding individual agency and engagement in Faith practices (also discussed in subsequent chapters). It is clearly too crude to claim that members simply inscribe, in Foucauldian terms, institutional power on to the body and/or personal consciousness (Shilling 1993:75; Lyon and Barbalet 1994:49). As Turner (1994:36) puts it, Foucault's body is a conceptual object of discourse with no flesh or material activity of its own. The processual, indeterminate and potentially creative aspects of bodily practice and 'being-in-the-world' cannot be ignored (Csordas 1994; Elisha 1998). In addition, Faith supporters vary greatly in the degree to which they devote their lives to the movement, and may of course be engaged in other congregations of a very different type. Yet it is also the case that engagement involves a degree of personal as well as collective surveillance, according to which the physical body and spiritual state can be judged against ideals contained within a sacralised language that is both presented in narrative and perceived as embodied within the self. Such surveillance can be carried out in contexts far beyond the boundaries of the group itself, in self-reflexive moments during private devotions or even while carrying out everyday actions. Often, the more success the believer perceives in his or her life, the more they are likely to attribute transformed circumstances to the activation of Faith (and biblical) principles. Physical and material well-being not only become an index of successful commitment to the Faith, but also help to constitute it.

It might seem that some of these ideas and practices are likely to have particular resonances in Sweden, given that ethnologists have traced the processes whereby powerful notions of disciplining the body and the will have emerged in that country during the twentieth century. As noted in chapter 3, bourgeois culture can be shown to have marked itself off from the peasantry and working classes through the extensive control of body functions. Corporeal rituals symbolising a new, progressive life style were diffused nationally, so that ideas of order, hygiene, and efficiency became generalised even among the lower orders. While these developments have possibly reinforced Swedish Faith tendencies to see the body as a mechanical system, their significance should not be exaggerated. Equally or more important are North American influences – those which assert the virtues of youth, unlimited consumption and the power of personal will over physical matter through positive thinking.[10] In fact, the ritual evocation of spontaneity during services seems precisely to evoke a lack of decorum that would have been anathema to bourgeois ideals, and which has indeed been characterised in critical media coverage of the group as indicating a loss of self control (see chapter 9). It resonates well, however, with a religious culture that tends to orientate itself to younger members of society, and encourages sport as a means of engagement in group activity (Coleman 1999). Sport, as well as ecstatic ritual, imply for Faith members the goal-oriented use of the body for self-improving ends.

BUILDING FAITH

Ideas about the relationship between the body and language illustrate connections between two core themes in Word of Life discourse: internalisation of language as involving the unproblematic reception of the Word, and growth or healing as the automatic response to such ingestion. Faith adherents seek to materialise the sacred not only within themselves, however, but also in their immediate environments. While bodies can be treated as objects, inanimate objects can possess the same relationship to supernatural principles as living humans. One of the most striking parallels to the themes evoked by Jesus' body has been provided by Word of Life attitudes to the group's new building. As the construction

[10] Becker (1995:130) notes: 'The differentiated nature of personal experience in the West, along with the firm conviction that the individual is the personal author and agent of bodily experience, not only permits the personal cultivation of bodies in this (Western) cultural milieu, but also allows extreme objectification of bodies and fosters the body/self alienation when the myth of personal control is disrupted by an illness.' Faith ideas clearly adapt and 'exaggerate' some of these ideas.

emerged from the ground between 1986 and 1987, adherents were encouraged to believe that it represented the realisation of a divine injunction despite all adverse circumstances of weather, local political opposition, or rumoured lack of finance. After one service, members of the group also walked around its base, speaking tongues into the ground. They thus appropriated the space for charismatic purposes, and the subsequent rise of the building (Figure 1) could then be regarded as a literally concrete and collectively produced manifestation of the externalised power of sacred language. Above all, the size of the building was presented by pastors as an indication of evangelical ambition, and, in addition to numerous offices, a shop, café, classrooms and a television studio, it incorporates a hall with space for over 4,000 people. Lester Sumrall, invited to speak at the opening ceremony, stated 'The Holy Spirit has already come into this building. Our God is a big God!', indicating in effect that the construction could be seen as the architectural equivalent of the spiritual body-builder I mentioned earlier, with both striving towards a perfectionist principle of maximum exaggeration. At this ceremony, everyone present recited in unison: 'Today, the believer is God's house', again echoing Pauline imagery, as well as making the link between the body as temple and a building perceived as a manifestation of the power of sacred language.

The construction is not only very large, it is also unlike the architectural styles of conventional churches. The group's opponents, indeed, refer to it mockingly as a sports hall, and certainly it looks like a gleaming white warehouse. According to Faith adherents, the 'beauty' of the building lies both in its size and in the way it expresses ideals of maximum efficiency in the spreading of the group's message. It is a container of state-of-the-art communications technology, whose presence not only indicates material success, but also allows the Word to be broadcast to unprecedentedly large numbers of people. Yet I have also been struck by its parallels to the architecture of an earlier form of Protestant revival – that of the nineteenth-century Shakers described by Daniel Patterson (1982). Patterson talks of how Charles Dickens, while inspecting a Shaker village in New York, saw only the grim, factory-like buildings: the aesthetic sense of these revivalists favoured consciously functionalist architectural styles in opposition to the trappings of upper-class churches. Shaker art forms were created in oratory and song – such as the marching song, 'travelling towards heaven', which could express a perfectionism grounded in a belief in progressive revelation. Shakers and Faith Christians therefore share a concern for functional styles, continued self-development and a desire to differentiate themselves from established Christianity. A significant difference between Shaker and Faith forms of functionalism lies, however, in the latter's emphasis on the building and its contents as indicating the ability to command and deploy massive resources.

Aesthetic parallels can also be drawn with principles of modernist architecture – not such a huge leap given that Protestant evangelicalism and the rise of industrial society were processes roughly parallel in time and, to some extent, ideology. Modernist styles represent a modified form of aesthetic Puritanism, and express a kind of perfectionism through faith in the notion of progress linked to the rational cultivation of explicit principles. Stuart Ewen (1988) in his book *Consuming Images* talks of how Adolf Loos, a Viennese architect, published the manifesto 'Ornament and Crime' in 1908, proclaiming conquest over kitsch and unnecessary ornament since they indicated a primitive eroticism incompatible with the logic of the new world order. Le Corbusier advocated the confident modernist ideal of sustaining a single idea throughout a massive space, turning architecture into a form of engineering, working in accordance with universal laws that heralded transcultural and transhistoric truths (ibid.:137). Space could be controlled by the principles of the factory and, even in the domestic sphere, producing the celebrated house as a 'machine for living'. In the same way, the Word of Life building annexes space for evangelical purposes as the precursor of and means towards the annexation of other physical and cultural environments in the name of the principles of Faith. Ornament is shunned as mere distraction from the work of worship; indeed, form must ideally follow function in the name of evangelical efficiency.

In valuing size as a tangible, quantifiable indication of spiritual success and influence, Word of Life Christians are in good missionary company. Reinhard Bonnke, a Faith preacher currently based in Germany, claims to own the largest mobile tent in the world, while the American televangelist Robert Schuller has, in his Crystal Cathedral, the largest glass structure on earth.[11] (The Word of Life has now bought its own massive tent, obtained second-hand from a circus.) Other Faith churches in Scandinavia and beyond display variations on the 'warehouse' style evident in Uppsala.[12] Stai's (1993:1) study of Trondheim Christian Centre notes how a number of Faith groups – including some in Norway, the Word of Life in Uppsala and even Rhema Bible Church in Tulsa – are located in industrial, commercial areas and premises, in parts of the urban landscape that display considerable expansion. It appears that a global architectural aesthetic is being constructed through such ministries.

Most significantly, the ambitions represented by the Word of Life building were not perceived as being satisfied by the latter's completion: such a view would have indicated the acceptance of a fixed state or level rather than a striving for continued progress. Soon after the group moved into the new building, Ulf Ekman pointed to the empty seats in a hall that was now far too large for its normal congregation, claiming that they represented future converts. Soon, it was implied, the new building itself would become too small, outstripped by the inevitable growth of the group, just as the group's natural and supernatural growth had forced it to expand away from its old, rented buildings. A newsletter of the group explicitly links a quantified spirituality with the need for the building:[13] 'Our faith has grown and the vision of that which God has called us to do, has grown . . . we've had to adapt

---

[11] Flake (1984:57) describes Schuller's Crystal Cathedral as 'evangelical architecture . . . evolved into the American vernacular of overreaching'. Compare also Percy's (1998) description of Toronto Airport Christian Fellowship's location and building: the latter is a large conference centre, nestling among hotels, industrial estates and criss-crossing freeways.

[12] Lehmann (1996:183), describing the Prosperity-influenced Universal Church in Brazil, notes that in the early 1990s these Christians had numerous hangar-like rented buildings in outlying areas, though by 1993 the Church's services seemed to be concentrated in grandiose constructions built in more central locations. Interestingly, in the light of the argument in this and subsequent chapters, Harvey notes (1989) that architecture has become one of the aestheticised products by which global capitalism can express itself.

[13] *Word of Life Newsletter*, 1987 4:4. Miller (1997) notes that 'new paradigm' evangelical churches in the US are often rented, to allow for constant expansion. The aim, if not the method, is similar to Word of Life strategy.

the building to the reality and the growth which is happening.' The Word is made not merely flesh but also concrete and steel.

Internal features of the worship hall, meanwhile, emphasise the power of the Word and the sense that words are to be 'received' from God (often via preachers) rather than subjected to debate and multiple interpretation. Harold Turner (1979) describes how the great evangelical movements of the nineteenth century laid emphasis on the preaching of the Word at the expense of the sacraments, and constructed buildings that enabled the closest possible encounter between the congregation and the message and personality of the preacher. This typically resulted in large, open platforms, allowing the preacher frequently to leave the shelter of the pulpit in order to both dramatise his performance and interact directly with the listeners (Richardson 1990). In the main hall of the Word of Life, the most significant objects are the lectern, from which the sermon is preached, and the television cameras. Windows are very high, encouraging the congregation to concentrate on the stage without external distractions. The visual impact of the charismatic delivery, and perhaps even the seeming transparency of the message, are reinforced by the practice, evident at the Word of Life and common in Faith congregations generally, of using see-through pulpits, allowing the viewer fully to observe the preacher. The conventional celebration of communion is a rare, almost casual affair, and accordingly the sacramental table is not on permanent show in the hall. According to the logic of Faith ideology, such a communion is partially supplanted by the ingestion of the Word through preaching and reading. Union with Christ is democratised and made constantly available by being collapsed within successful communication.

Carsten and Hugh-Jones (1995:2) note that the house and the body are intimately linked in many cultures.[14] The house, as extension of the person, is also a prime agent of socialisation. Thus: 'Moving in ordered space, the body "reads" the house which serves as a mnemonic for the embodied person. Through habit and inhabiting, each person builds up a practical mastery of the fundamental schemes of their culture.' The Word of Life building is not

---

[14] See also Douglas (1970); Jacobson-Widding (1991).

a house, of course, and indeed its forms are unlikely to echo the domestic spaces of most adherents. Yet the spatial order of the construction echoes the ideal charismatic body not only in its strength and capacity for further development, but also in its attempt to remove all barriers to seeing, hearing, 'receiving' and broadcasting a single Truth with the utmost clarity.

CHRIST AS CHILD AND MAN

The Word of Life construction has parallels with those of other free church denominations in Uppsala in terms of its plain style, but not in its massive annexation of space, combination of many functions under one roof, and relative spatial peripherality. For instance, the present Pentecostal church was constructed in the centre of the city during the 1960s and contains a cross, but little other decoration. Pews are plain and wooden, and walls are white. Congregation newsletters from the time the church was built display some interesting parallels with, as well as contrasts to, the attitudes underlying Word of Life characterisations of their new building. One newsletter from 1966 exhibits a distinctly eschatological orientation in its assertion that the congregation has found its home 'until Jesus returns'.[15] However, another one, written a couple of years earlier, actually expresses the hope that the new church will not be too large as that would destroy the sense of cosiness and well-being (*trivsel*) required by the congregation.[16] It is hard to imagine such a sentiment being expressed by Ekman or his supporters.

In the following, I want to compare Faith aesthetics with another well-established free church in Uppsala and the country as a whole, the Swedish Mission Covenant (*Svenska Missionsförbundet*, or SMF).[17] If the Word of Life is the latest manifestation of Protestant nonconformity in Sweden, SMF is one of the oldest, having been founded in the late 1870s. The Covenant Church has revivalist

---

[15] *Aktuellt*, 1966 9/10:11.   [16] *Aktuellt*, 1964 5/6:2.

[17] While I have not carried out formal fieldwork in the Uppsala SMF congregation of some 750–800 people, I have interviewed a number of its members and have been interested, for reasons that will become obvious, in its attitudes to the foundation of the Word of Life in Uppsala.

roots and can be described as broadly evangelical in orientation, yet it represents a clear example of a denomination that has become accommodated to Swedish Christianity and wider social and political circles.[18] Most fittingly for our purposes, the local SMF congregation in Uppsala decided to build a new church at almost exactly the same time as Word of Life members were planning their own new building.

Some initial theological observations are necessary in order to contextualise the comparison. In his ethnography of the Mission Covenant church in Stockholm, Stromberg (1986) notes that SMF's Pietist heritage has encouraged an emphasis on an experiential, inward-looking relationship to worship in opposition to rigid, formal styles of religious life. Personal faith is seen as somehow adapted to the uniqueness of the self. The salient meaning of a symbol is thus left up to the interpretation of the individual believer, guided by the Holy Spirit. Stromberg (1986:32) sums up contemporary attitudes as follows (italics in original):

It is a *shared* outlook in this church that faith should be personally meaningful; therefore, each believer has a personal perspective on an important symbol of faith like Jesus. It is precisely the point of a personal faith that it should articulate with the most intimate and idiosyncratic details of the believer's life.

In this view, biblical interpretation is a creative act, and grace provides the experience of simultaneous self-transcendence and self-realisation. Stromberg notes how such articulation between faith and the believer's life is often perceived as a kind of physical merger, as the Christian locates him or herself within the symbolic system. Here, for instance, are some of the comments of a young man called Anders (ibid.:66; italics in original):

I listen to a sermon as God's Word *refracted through a human* . . . Exactly like you can *refract light through a prism.* It's something that's *transported via a person,*

---

[18] It was formed by secession from the Swedish Church, although some authors argue that its ideological roots can be taken back to seventeenth century, Pietist forms of worship as well as early British and American forms of evangelical Christianity. Apart from Stromberg's (1986) excellent book on the SMF church in Stockholm, I have drawn upon Lindberg (1985), Eldebo (1985) and publications produced by the Uppsala congregation itself. A recent discussion of religious art in Sweden is Arvidsson et al. (1993). Londos (1985) discusses free church art in Sweden in a brief paper.

but the person's character will play a big role in the message which is *brought forth*. I don't believe that people don't play a role, that God speaks directly, so to speak.

Evident in Anders's words here is the idea that God works *through* the world: people and configurations of events, like that of the crucifixion itself, act as mediators through which God's Word emerges. Another of Stromberg's interviewees (ibid.:69–70) expresses a roughly similar sentiment when she talks of how the figure of Jesus is a point of conjunction between the religious and the political; indeed that God can be seen as a kind of fellow freedom fighter who is far from omnipotent in the struggle for justice. This concern with the social as well as the supernatural has characterised Mission Covenant history, which over the years has combined strictly spiritual goals with aims of societal responsibility, but perhaps can be seen as on the increase as the Movement attempts to define its role within a nation generally less overtly religious than it was at the turn of the century. Now, the problem for its members seems to be less a matter of avoiding conventional sins and more a question of how to articulate a sense of solidarity and religious commitment in a society that appears to be alienated, fragmenting and increasingly secular. Certainly, over the past few years, various forums have been arranged by the Uppsala congregation to discuss such issues as immigration and peace, while SMF as a whole has over the years been a relative stronghold of the Folk Party in Swedish politics – the most socially conscious of the so-called bourgeois parties.

Another aspect of Anders's statement is the extent to which it permits freedom of interpretation and action in the exercise of faith. Again, the SMF has tended to be ecumenical over the years, and to value a certain degree of intellectual *laissez-faire*. Such tendencies have perhaps been reinforced by the fact that it has had a more middle-class membership than most other free churches in Sweden. In common with other free churches, however, the Mission Covenant has been losing members over the past three decades: in 1960, it had some 97,600 in its churches; by 1990, this figure had dropped to 77,100 (Gustafsson 1991:61). Thus, while the figures are still much greater than those of the total number of Faith adherents in Sweden, they are going in an opposite direction, and represent a population that is ageing in contrast to the youthful profile of Word of Life members.

Stromberg describes how the new church of the Stockholm Covenant congregation, dedicated in 1974, illustrates some of the ideological and social transformations undergone by the SMF itself over the past century. The original church was constructed by a congregation that was part of the first impulse of evangelical separatism, and still mindful of the laundry list of sins that seemed to be sapping the morale of the lower classes. In the old building, as Stromberg puts it (1986:33), nature is denied, 'hidden beneath careful and detailed constructions that transformed wood, stone, and glass into an intricate mass of aggressively man-made decoration'. By way of contrast, the new church, put up by a much more established denomination, deliberately creates (ibid.:33):

An open, airy feeling . . . The pews and lectern are spray-painted green with blotches of yellow and other colors. Here, then, the parishioners sit amidst the colors of the Swedish summer surrounded by soaring walls of rough brick . . . the intent is to evoke . . . the great outdoors, the highly prized forests of the nature-loving Swedes . . . the new church building has readmitted nature to its inner sanctum.

It seems as though, in a context where the boundaries of belief are self-consciously ill-defined, the boundaries of the church itself become permeable. The new construction enshrines a sense that the gaining of faith is not a binary matter of being saved or unsaved, but a process of gradual transformation and interaction with one's immediate environment.

From what I have said of SMF so far, we can begin to see some significant contrasts to the beliefs and practices of the Faith Movement. Prosperity Theology provides a religious culture designed to transcend any single place or individual circumstances in its empowerment of believers. To some extent, through its schools, university and other activities such as sports or singles clubs, it provides certain members with the possibility of shielding themselves from everyday interaction with non-Christians even as they seek to convert such people by missionary means. Adherents are encouraged to disregard the negative – indeed, when problems arise they can be interpreted as signs that 'the Devil is afraid' of a powerful Christian. In this process of appropriating the world as well as the self, converting them into ideal, iconic images and indexes of evangelical power, such Christians deploy language as if it were a material force. Christ, the Word made flesh, is depicted as an unambiguous embodiment of power, and it is the aim of the believer, in a process of self-identification with the divine, to 'see' Christ as clearly as they are able to receive the objective truths of sacred language.

Contemporary Covenant ideology has very different implications. Personal transformation involves a gradual interaction with the symbols of faith whereby the self is not believed to be turned into an icon of pure power but seeks possibly ambiguous significances in events. Faith is not a matter of conquering circumstances, but a means of interpreting them, just as sacred language itself cannot be seen as containing single truths. Engagement with society and the world, rather than appropriation of them, is to be achieved. Thus smf encourages what I wish to call a culture (and orientation) of place, of locality, whereby the meanings of faith are seen explicitly to interact with and emerge from specific contexts. If Faith ideology seeks a clear picture of Christ, the image we have seen from the smf is that of a prism, refracting meaning through the unpredictable filter of character, almost denying God a direct voice in the world.

The Mission Covenant's culture of place can be seen very clearly in its attitudes to the construction of sacred space in Uppsala. In 1983, the congregation moved from its old church into a new, purpose-built construction close to the centre of the city. Literature describing the previous church in Uppsala emphasises the dangers of isolationism, a removal from context that was inevitable in the older building: 'It was a congregation on retreat, deprived of its . . . church yard because of a widened traffic route, sheltered behind often closed doors, psychologically isolated from the heart of the town.'[19] In a number of ways, also, the congregation has regarded the process of moving the church as a means of locating itself more firmly within the context of Uppsala, making itself more open to and accessible from the town. For instance, the foyer has been made open to the city, supposedly reinforcing the

---

[19] From *En Kyrka Kommer Till*, n.d.: 4.

church's open character and accessibility to the cultural life around it. The hall in which worship takes place is constructed precisely to deny the impression that a rigid boundary exists between it and the outside world. A mural near the pulpit, depicting a 'tree of life' undergoing processes of creation and death associated with the four seasons, deliberately echoes a real tree situated outside the church, just visible from the main hall. Large windows seek to dissolve the distinction between inside and outside, as do the rough bricks visible inside and outside the church.[20]

A further striking aspect of the Uppsala SMF church is the image of Christ it displays, visible from all parts of the church. Behind the communion table a relief depicts a crucifixion scene in which Christ's identity is not solid but undergoing self-transformation, represented by an image of resurrection blended with that of a child being born. In a way, the effect is not unlike a prism, refracting a spectrum of physical states. If the Word of Life Christ expresses change through a linear principle of progressive growth combined with invulnerability, this is an image of Christ that is partially suffering, helpless and, like the tree-of-life mural, depicting through decay and growth the sense that transformation can be depicted in a way that implies circularity or at least the reconciliation of opposites. As a member of the church puts it, describing the image: 'The head of the dying Christ is at the same time the head of the child forcing its way out towards life. The humanity that suffers and dies is at the same time the humanity that struggles for life.'[21] Furthermore, as the same writer stresses, the church itself *is* 'the body of Christ, here literally carved out of the church wall'.

The Word of Life 'body-building' image was a temporary adornment, expressing the notion that the person is empowered to break through all circumstances and should act independently of

---

[20] These strategies echo some of the processes evident in the construction of the new Stockholm church, described by Stromberg. Eldebo notes (1985:61) how new SMF churches are often built as irregular rooms, with communion tables close to rather than remote from the congregation.

[21] *En Kyrka Kommer Till*, p. 15. Beckwith (1993:17) notes that images of Christ as infant and as crucified often coalesced in medieval depictions of *pietà*. She sees both of these images – reflecting birth and death respectively – as those where the claims of the body are expressed most emphatically in Christ's life.

context, but the Covenant Christ is physically embedded in place, permanently located within the context of the church as it consciously opens itself out to nature as well as the wider culture of Uppsala. Such differences echo the two churches' contrasting views of sacred language, for instance the sense one gains from Positive Confession that words are objective, autonomous, empowered means of appropriating the world and the self, and the Covenant view I have stressed that seeks a dialogue, a two-way merger, between canonical language and personal experience. They also imply a rather different relationship between Christ and the viewer: the Faith image relates to the believer as individual observer, walking down the corridor; the Covenant image, by being made a physical part of the church itself, can be collectively viewed by the congregation, perhaps even as they celebrate communion in front of it.

What I have said so far involves an attempt, through a largely semiological style of analysis of images and architecture, to juxtapose some of the different ways in which Faith and Covenant Christians might express their identity with Christ and the world.[22] One can also consider these two aesthetic systems in the light of actual social relations between the congregations (see also chapter 9). Here, the semiotics of Christ and the church take on political dimensions, since members of the Covenant church have been prominent among Christians in Uppsala, and Sweden as a whole, in condemning the practices and theology of the Faith Movement. During the 1980s, the SMF sponsored a project and book (Nilsson 1988) designed to provide as much information as possible on non-local, para-church organisations, among which it included the Faith Movement. Possibly the most visible critic of Prosperity ideas in the country has been Sigbert Axelson, a member of the Uppsala congregation and lecturer in Uppsala University's Theology Department. Along with many others, Axelson has articulated the sense that the Word of Life is a foreign import, a quasi-Fascist organisation threatening to society because of its extravagant

---

[22] Something of the contrast I am highlighting is expressed, albeit in exaggerated form, in Augé's (1995) distinction between historically constituted places and 'super-modern' non-places, such as airports and motorways, which are not designed to accommodate differentiated, organic human relations.

claims and its remoteness from free church ideals.[23] He and other SMF members favour global connections between Christians, but motivate such relationships by appealing to ideals of cultural and religious pluralism rather than control. At times, encounters between the two churches have also laid bare patently contrasting attitudes towards the body. When I attended a local meeting at which people could put questions to Ulf Ekman, a complaint was raised by a pastor from the local Covenant church. He recounted the story of how he had been approached by Word of Life pupils in the street and informed that he could transform his middle-aged, sagging features if only he possessed the correct faith. The pastor's evident outrage was aimed not so much at being singled out as a target for bodily improvement, but at what appeared to him to be an utterly unrealistic view concerning the relationship between religious devotion and the direct transformation of unwanted aspects of the physical self.

Despite their obvious differences, both Faith and Covenant Christians are noncomformist Protestants. Indeed, some former members of the Covenant church have crossed over to the new Movement. Supporters of both groups would probably agree that they are attempting to crystallise identity in a religious, cultural and political context that is changing fast. The aesthetic systems of the two churches can be seen not only as *reflective of* changing circumstances, but also as *models of* change. Both, for instance, depict a divine figure that is not static but undergoing obvious processes of self-transformation. Christ comes to represent not only a metaphor for the present, but also an emblem of future development and orientation to the world. Yet the attitudes to change and the images of Christ are very different. In one case, the church is new and linked through dense networks to similar Christians elsewhere, so that its members are still discovering how far their revival can go on local, national and even global stages; in the other, the church has had to seek a new role now that its revivalist past is distant and its accommodation to society relatively clear. Very different models of constant transformation are therefore implied: one involves the

---

[23] For more information on Axelson's attitudes to the Word of Life, see Coleman (1989) and chapter 9.

incessant, accumulative surrender of the self to canonical, universally applicable language and symbolism; the other encourages a form of constant self-exploration perceived *through* and in dialogue with such symbols.

CHAPTER SEVEN

Broadcasting the faith

Word of Life members parallel many North American televangel-
icals in their propagation of the view that the eternal truth of the
Christian message is demonstrated by its easy adaptation to
modern forms of mass media. Since at least the beginning of radio
broadcasting, conservative Protestants have regarded electronic
technologies of communication in eschatological terms as having
a vital place in their attempts to fulfil the 'Great Commission'[1]
of making disciples of all nations (Hadden 1990:166; Schultze
1996:64). Both the media and evangelical ideology encourage a
rationalised, quantitative approach to salvation alongside the presentation of belief in dramatic, experiential terms (Schultze
1990:42; Peck 1993:3). As technologies themselves have developed,
older techniques of urban revivalism have been merged with new
methods of fund-raising and self-presentation (Frankl 1987). The
activities of these Christians have therefore paralleled patterns of
growth in secular image production industries over the last two to
three decades. In an already competitive religious market, the
Faith Movement has proved to be a leader in the field. Indeed,
Schultze (1990:44) argues that the health and wealth preaching of
televangelists such as the Copelands and Hagin grew out of audience demands for an optimistic Gospel of financial prosperity and
personal health.

A number of authors locate the extensive use of media technologies in the context of specifically American cultural concerns,
such as technological optimism and expansion-mindedness.[2] In
addition, of course, the decentralised, market model of media pro-

---

[1] Matthew 28:19–20.   [2] See for instance Schultze (1991:50) and Peck (1993:3).

vision in the US has permitted those religious groups able to muster the resources and motivation to gain extensive access to the airwaves (Bruce 1990b). However, the growth in the range and availability of media technologies has also begun to be felt in other parts of the West. Shegog (1990:336) notes that the 'ecology' of broadcasting in Europe is changing, with policies of government deregulation placing public-service systems under increased threat.

Such issues are highly salient in Sweden. As noted in chapter 3, the media environment is becoming increasingly pluralistic. By the end of the 1980s, 20 per cent of the population could watch foreign programmes via satellite and cable, and the first domestic airborne commercial channel, TV 4, started regular broadcasting in 1992 (Linderman 1996). Some of the top-rated American televangelical programmes are now available on cable, while evangelical churches have generally been in the forefront of using television and local radio. None the less, the established denominations, even Pentecostalists, perceive such activity merely as complementary to the main work of the local congregation. What is striking about the use of media technology amongst many Faith adherents is the degree to which it plays a vital constitutive role in both collective and private forms of worship.

While much has been written about the impact of televangelism on dispersed audiences, less attention has been paid to the integration of media practices into the everyday functioning of a religious organisation, even one as internally differentiated as a mega-ministry.[3] The Word of Life's message does not merely express the *ideal* of universal applicability and diffusion; it is *literally* diffused by the use of modern media of communication: radio, cassettes, videos, satellite television programmes and the Internet. Neither the relic nor the conventional icon can be used as tangible, portable vehicles for sacred power and spiritually charged events; however, the video or cassette most certainly is deployed in this way. I shall therefore trace the processes whereby evangelical ideology and experience, represented and contained in electronic

[3] Linderman (1996:98) notes the findings of an Annenberg–Gallup study, to the effect there is no conflict between watching religious television and being active in a local church.

media, become objectified and commodified. Services, sermons, testimonies and so on are framed and recycled within mass-media formats and made available to unknown others as well as to the original participants. These processes echo and extend the uses of language I mentioned in chapter 5. They contribute to a Faith aesthetic that deploys visual and material forms provided they are perceived to be embodiments of power and inspired movement. In examining the use of media, we therefore revisit and extend our understanding of charismatic engagement as a means of developing a globalising orientation in relation to the self and to the world.

MEDIATED PRACTICES

Media production and consumption deal with widely available technologies, but as social practices they often take specific, subcultural forms. Alexander (1994:9) notes that televangelical viewers in the US may prepare themselves ritually before turning on a programme, perhaps by reading the Bible or praying. The media are similarly incorporated into the spiritual lives and practices of Word of Life members, both within and beyond the boundaries of the group itself. Virtually all services at the Word of Life are video- and audio-taped, and become available for sale and export soon after their occurrence in real time. Local radio is used to broadcast short devotional programmes and, on occasion, services. For a brief period in the 1990s, the group invested in its own local radio franchise before costs proved prohibitive. The group also uses satellite television to broadcast to other parts of Europe, and Bible School and university students can take courses in the uses of state-of-the-art communications media. Even membership and participation in the Word of Life congregation involves, for many, joining a monthly video or cassette club as well as physically attending services. Monthly videos include devotional material but may also incorporate documentary information on activities of the group around the world.

The arenas into which media messages are broadcast vary in their significance and construction. Satellite television programmes occupy a 'privatised' media space; occasionally, however, the group has been able to sell productions to the Swedish

Broadcasting Corporation. A recent entry to a Word of Life information web page, noting that national television will broadcast a service direct from the group in 1999, highlights the importance of gaining such recognition in the public-service arena.[4] The article states that the previous time a Word of Life service was broadcast, in 1990: 'Many people contacted us and said that God had healed them in front of the television as they listened to God's Word. Many have also said that they received Jesus after they had seen the service.' In the process, according to the article, press coverage was itself converted from a predominantly negative to a much more positive standpoint.

Media products are often expected to be incorporated into practices that imply a kind of sacralisation of domestic space, with meetings of small groups of Christians gathering round a screen.[5] Favourite videos are treasured as much as books, and repeatedly shown and scrutinised in the same way that a text might be. Ulf Ekman appears at the beginning of some tapes and provides a definition of the context of viewing:

Before you go on I suggest you switch off the tape and take a moment, whether you're on your own, with your family, in a prayer-group or with your congregation, and pray that the Holy Spirit will lead you to the truth. It's important for you to expect that God will speak to you personally through His Word, that His Spirit will reveal itself to you.

Cassettes and particularly videos provide consumers with the opportunity to engage in the spontaneity of the original event, objectified but made available to be reappropriated in the new 'ritual' arena prepared by the viewer or viewers (Coleman 1996a). A suitable context of reception is thereby created for the translation of whatever appears on the screen into a generic vehicle of empowerment, the Holy Spirit. Members of the congregation also

---

[4] Web page entry of 20 November 1998. A representative of Swedish television is quoted as saying that 'it is natural to reflect this kind of Christian service', since 'We have a duty to be inclusive in our coverage, and this deals with a large group of Christians.'

[5] Robert Ekh, the second pastor of the congregation, states in a *Word of Life Newsletter* (1987 4:5): 'Video will be something big! . . . What is today's market square? The television! . . . God . . . will come to people where they are. He will save them, heal and set them free in their living rooms! We've already received many reports about what those videos already produced have meant. Groups of up to forty people have gathered in front of the television and had a meeting!'

show videos to the unsaved during meetings or social gatherings away from the congregation.

If media are frequently used to reach people who are not physically present at a Faith service, they can even be incorporated into practices carried out at the group itself. During conferences, satellite link-ups are used to connect congregations dispersed around Europe. The back of the hall has television screens which can broadcast services as they actually occur,[6] and videos are sometimes shown to members of the congregation after a service. Media spaces are also created that are entirely 'virtual'. The group maintains an extensive set of web pages (in Swedish and English), detailing its many activities and including features from its magazines and newsletters, while individual adherents (such as Stefan, mentioned at the start of this book) often have their own sites. For Faith groups as well as private persons, the Internet demonstrates connections with other groups around the globe in literally graphic terms.[7]

Media practices are constituted not only by the deployment of technology, but also by a charismatic theory of communication that we have encountered in earlier chapters. Faith adherents stress the value of the media in reaching many people; they also emphasise the notion that such media materialise words and experience in a very particular way. Sacred words, as performative utterances capable of objective meaning, are regarded as taking on a semi-autonomous existence. Once recorded in some form, they are believed to retain their power to affect the material and spiritual world (Coleman 1996a; 1996b). The intense, physical effects that mediated communication can produce are expressed well by Morris Cerullo (a North American colleague of Ekman who has been highly active in Europe). The following is a passage taken from a video, where he is addressing the viewer directly and suggesting the correct attitude to adopt when subscribing to his video Bible School.[8]

---

[6] Schuller has a high-definition television screen in his Crystal Cathedral.

[7] Shields (1996:1) talks of how via the Internet a 'new network of virtual "sites" is being superimposed on the world of places'.

[8] Taken from Cerullo's video entitled 'Moscow 1990: Spiritual Breakthrough in Red Square!' See also Carrithers and Coleman n.d.

In this period of times, God is going to have an end time people. So I want to encourage you, open your heart, don't sit there and be a spectator. Be a participator. And let the truths and the revelation that flow from this message go deep into your Spirit until they become seed that will impregnate your being and make you pregnant with the truth that God wants to be your supernatural provision and he wants to care for you in these end times. God bless you.

As in the passage from Ulf Ekman cited above, Cerullo is commenting here on how his own evangelical discourse should be 'received'. He is attempting to control the indexical relationship between sender and receiver of biblical instruction (Jaffe 1999:136). In stressing the importance of the mediated message, he indicates belief in the power of 'anointed' language to retain its power, even when separated physically from the speaker. The imagery depicts a form of internalisation through bodily incorporation, not in this case through eating (see chapters 5 and 6) but instead by becoming open to a form of impregnation. In effect, Cerullo is presenting himself as a vehicle, via the Holy Spirit, for the verbal insemination of his dispersed congregation. This variant of the idea of the Word made flesh (and, indeed, 'living') is not to be taken as pure metaphor by believers, since it can be seen as producing real physical changes, including healing and self-renewal. 'End Time people' are therefore created through processes that involve active and passive orientations simultaneously. The ideal viewer participates and does not just spectate; but a key aspect of such participation appears to be a direct and unambiguous acceptance of the message that is sown into the person's Spirit. Although it is impossible to chart the presumably varied reactions of viewers to Cerullo's words, one can note that Faith practices do include ritualised means of signalling assent to and reception of such messages. Preachers of sermons require responses from congregations in the form of an 'Amen' or 'Hallelujah!', and these expressions may also be used during domestic viewings of videos; in addition, many Faith textbooks urge the reader, converted or not, to conclude their perusal of a passage not by merely closing the book, but with a prayer or promise – sometimes a repetition of a phrase used by the preacher/writer – declaimed aloud. In acting by speaking, the believer converts a message from words heard or read (internalised) to words spoken (externalised). The message is therefore both bodily appropriated by the self and activated anew in a novel context.[9]

FRAMING CONSCIOUSNESS

Words and actions are, of course, framed by the constraints of the material forms that contain them. If revivalist ritual is ultimately about the dissemination of a message, videos and tapes extract the spiritually significant elements of the original event (praise-songs, the sermon, selected audience reactions and unambiguous signs of healing or conversion), thus editing out unnecessary distractions (cf. Harding 1987:169). Following Sontag (1977:3), one can remark that such technology renders experience into a mental object to be worked upon as well as owned, although, of course, media products are also incorporated into ritual practice. The use of videos even opens up the possibility for ordinary participants to turn themselves into iconic objects of contemplation by allowing themselves to be 'inscribed' into the official framing of a service. As participation is converted by the camera into the depiction of inspired worship (members of the audience, when filmed, are often speaking in tongues, praying, being healed, etc.), adherents are enabled to see themselves as embodying idealised, generic images of enthusiasm. Personal experience becomes collective representation, and, moreover, one that can be reconsumed by individuals as they buy and watch a service in which they have taken part. Furthermore, the taping of services facilitates their classification as objects of spiritual power: when they are marketed, different videos or cassettes are often presented as being particularly efficacious for specific social, spiritual or physical problems, depending on the contents of the sermon. I have even known Word of Life members 'prescribe' tapes on a particular topic for a friend or relative who has concerns related to that issue.

[9] Even the material vehicles for disseminating the Word can themselves be made subject to its powers. After the collapse of the communist bloc, the Word of Life placed 100 video players in the larger towns of the Soviet Union. These machines were 'blessed' at the group's 1989 conference by the laying on of hands, much as one would bless a person.

Such media therefore objectify and commodify experience, but they do so in a way that corresponds with (morally charged) charismatic aesthetics. They provide a powerful means of resolving a potential tension between fixed states of being and processes of becoming as mutually contradictory embodiments of the divine (recall the 'icon' of Jesus as body-builder). Videos record the Word in physical, predictable, repeatable form, yet also reproduce the appearance of inspired spontaneity. They provide a new way, complementary to that of sacred texts, of storing, transporting and scrutinising language (Goody 1977; Ong 1991:75), but unlike writing retain a visual record of the original 'event' of verbal creation in time and space. The easy diffusion of divinely inspired messages in a video becomes a televisual counterpart to, but also an extension of, the original Protestant reformers' concern to democratise sacred language and render it into the vernacular. The sacred words of the sermon and the service keep their place within the flux of charismatic experience while also offering the distant viewer or listener the opportunity vicariously to sample such experience. The excitement and sensuous quality of the oral and the visual are retained, yet they are also objectified, made portable and removed from their original context of production but still regarded as capable of producing powerful responses in their consumers.[10] The workings of such media have affinities with a religion whose roots, despite its stress on the centrality of the biblical text, lie in an oral, participatory culture. In adapting to the cassette and the video, such charismatics provide a potent combination of the pre- and the post-literate; a sort of mixture, as David Martin (1990:165) puts it, of Lévy-Bruhl and Marshall McLuhan.

Central to these practices is the assumption that inspired events and, indeed, culture can be removed from one context and re-embedded anew somewhere else. The recorded event is not only a perfect replica of the original, it also has a metonymic relationship

[10] One advantage of the televised image is that it allows the audience to feel themselves closer to the preacher than they would have done in the back row of a mass rally, particularly when the preacher overcomes the potential limitations of the medium by using direct and/or dialogic modes of address in relation to his or her remote audience. See also Ellis (1982:162); Goethals (1985:151); Bruce (1990b:131); Ang (1996); Coleman (1996a).

with it through the retention of charismatic power.[11] Watching a service is not considered to be necessarily inferior to actual participation. Televangelists in North America may urge audiences to place their hands on the television screen, as if they could literally touch the preacher whose healing image is projected in front of them. A similar implication is evident in Sweden. One Word of Life pastor, Svante Rumar, describes an occasion when the main hall was too crowded to accommodate all of the congregation: 'God's Word was powerfully present even in the side-room – where over a quarter were forced to watch the service on screen.'[12] Following Baudrillard (1981), one might perceive this as the substitution of signs of the real for the real itself, as words spoken by a preacher directly to the congregation are transformed into a sermon simultaneously reproduced in a contiguous space. However, the charismatic theory of language claims that the essential power and therefore 'reality' of the Word are retained.

Walter Benjamin (1970) famously claimed that the mass reproduction and democratisation of a work of art removed its sacred aura, an aura derived not least from being firmly located in time, space and ritualised tradition.[13] More recently, Alfred Gell (1992:49–51) has argued that the photographer is typically less valued than the artist in the West, not least because processes of artistic production are so much more mysterious for the viewer to

[11] These evangelical vehicles for the sacred can in certain respects be compared with objects drawn from very different ethnographic contexts. Tambiah (1984) describes how Thai amulets are seen as containing the sedimented presence and power of Buddhist saints. The process of sanctifying such objects involves them being impregnated with the sacred words of a holy figure. By circulating around the country, spreading the efficacious and protective energy of saints, amulets also help to bridge the gap between parochial and national traditions, thus apparently reducing differences between religious centres and peripheries.

[12] *Word of Life Newsletter*, 1987 4:7. Another Word of Life publication, *Magazinet* 1994 7:14–18, includes a report of the summer conference of that year. It talks of how a meeting was broadcast via satellite to twenty countries in Europe, and quotes a missionary in Albania as saying 'It was like being in Uppsala.' The Albanian TV-technician who was facilitating the broadcast was said to have been healed in his arm.

[13] Compare John Berger (1972:10): 'When the camera reproduces a painting, it destroys the uniqueness of its image.' Or Susan Sontag (1977:179): 'The powers of photography have in effect de-Platonized our understanding of reality, making it less and less plausible to reflect upon our experience according to the distinction between images and things, between copies and originals.' Cox (1984:68) also invokes Benjamin in his discussion of the use of media by Pentecostals.

imagine. In this charismatic culture, however, the photo has more power than the portrait precisely because of the nature of photographic representation. Tapes and, indeed, satellite programmes can provide apparently direct access to sacralised reality to a potentially unlimited audience. In a sense, sacred aura is augmented through the possibility of creating a globally diffused and endlessly reproducible message. The notion that spirituality mediated through technology can have a 'value-added' dimension is expressed by Ekman in the following claim, taken from a 1987 brochure advertising audio-cassettes:

I had personally memorised hundreds of Bible verses, of which most weren't living for me, till one day I received a cassette with Bible teaching in the Holy Spirit's power. I became entirely free! The words I memorised earlier suddenly gained life within me and the life I had longed for, a life in victory and harmony, began to be realised for me.

Here, the words of a cassette are made effective through the inspired quality of the Holy Spirit, and, in turn, are able to animate those contained within the preacher.

On the whole, such products do not draw attention to their social relations of production. Lists of credits on videos, for instance, tend not to be extensive, and techniques of representation are unobtrusive. At the Word of Life, the camera focusses mainly on the stage, although reaction shots of the audience are often included. The sense that the dissemination of the message should involve a minimum of distortion unites views on witnessing, face-to-face sermonising and recorded services. These observations are reinforced by the comments of employees of Kenneth Copeland. A member of his stage crew argues that extraneous noise from the sound equipment used on preaching crusades is to be avoided at all costs; indeed, it is a moral issue: 'Our objective is to provide the (right) kind of atmosphere . . . so that the Word can flow unhindered . . . All it takes is just a small thing to disrupt the flow . . . a buzz or a hiss, a little feedback – that's all the devil is looking for.'[14] A producer of cassette tapes for Copeland, meanwhile, thinks of his work as a calling: 'When we have anything to do with a cassette tape – from duplicating it to putting it in the

---

[14] Interview in *Copeland Ministries Newsletter*, 1986 6:5.

binder – in God's eyes, it's just as if we taught that message our-selves.'[15] The worker will not glean the celebrity of a preacher, but he expresses here the evangelical idea of being able to appropriate or 'receive' fully the message of another person so that it can then be reproduced without error. Intriguingly, something similar even can occur during translations of live sermons. Since so many of the visiting preachers who come to the Word of Life only speak English, local preachers and teachers often become very skilful at standing next to a foreign speaker, immediately rendering their words into Swedish. At a New Year Conference in 1986, I observed an American pastor swaying around, both describing in words and embodying the notion of being 'drunk' in the Spirit. Repeating the (translated) words and actions of his American counterpart, the Swedish interpreter made himself a vehicle for both the inspired language of the sermon and its performative effects. His behaviour implied a transcendence of mere mimesis of another person in favour of actual possession by a common 'Truth'. Like a video, he 'faithfully' attempted to absorb and render available to others, in translated but otherwise unchanged form, the words and move-ments of the foreign preacher. A clearer demonstration of the sup-posed transferability of a globalising charismatic habitus can scarcely be imagined.

In practice, the everyday use of videos of course varies, and some less-committed consumers treat them as casually as one would a Hollywood film. Yet their reintegration into ritual prac-tice at the domestic level is frequently believed to have powerful effects. Among the testimonies I have seen or heard, one adherent compares home-viewing with the experience of participating at the Bible School itself. To another person, a film involving inter-cession and healing has proved useful in promoting healing in their own living-room, so that the timing of the domestic attempt to apply spiritual power coincides not with the real event at the group but with its image reproduced on the television screen. More broadly, the watching of videos has become the subject of a form of miracle discourse, ranging from personal self-realisation, 'The video led [me] from defeat to victory', to an appreciation of the

[15] Interview in ibid., 1986 4:7.

transformation of language into images, 'Fine to see God's word in pictures.' On some occasions, the repeated focus on a particular passage in a video can almost equal in intensity the scrutiny of verses in the Bible.

Alongside the focussing of the evangelical gaze on to spiritually charged events, the use of such technology by charismatics can be seen as expanding self-identification with a wider Christian world. Mass media are used to give viewers/listeners access to the various and wide-reaching activities of the transdenominational parachurch. A brochure advertising the group states: 'Through cassettes, videos and books God's Word goes out powerfully over the whole of our country, the rest of Scandinavia and wider out in the world.' Hoover suggests (1988) that programming can promote 'translocalism' in the sense that a new consciousness is promoted, typified by an ever-widening circle of perceived contacts and inputs. Wuthnow (1990:98) similarly argues that religious television not only provides personal religious gratifications, but also creates a sense that one is participating in a broader project. Whether the cassette or videos involve a documentary of what God is doing in the world or a programme of prayers, witness and Bible reading, these media illustrate an ability to reach out into the world, appropriating profane technology and, with God's help, saving souls as well. After all, the very identity of such Christians is constituted precisely by the action of spreading the message to others. The virtual, media world into which Christian culture can be projected is a symbolically rich one because it is unconfined and expansionary, having no borders or, indeed, direct response from those who prove resistant to witness and testimony (Coleman 1991; Schultze 1991:173). The sense of a lack of borders can be conceptualised in terms not only of culture, but also of time and space. Driessen (1992), discussing Roman Catholic festivals in Spain, argues that the selling of rituals on tape desacralises them by removing them from their weekly and daily cycles. At the Word of Life, however, the use of videos and cassettes is explicitly incorporated into a revivalist ritual framework that does not depend on links to the changing rhythms of the ecclesiastical year or the passing seasons (see chapter 6), but acknowledges rather the importance of present enthusiasm. Fenn (1982), meanwhile, argues that the language of liturgy can provide a last resort for problems of authority posed by ambiguities of human speech. Although much depends on the relationship between speaker and hearer, the temporal and spatial boundaries of a church can create a closed 'linguistic garden of paradise' (ibid.:ix–xv). Word of Life ideology again contradicts such a view, since speaker and hearer are frequently separated in time, space and even culture, and yet linguistic paradise as opposed to babel is supposedly created through taking objective meanings beyond the boundaries of the church into the everyday life of the believer. Horsfield (1984; see also Goethals 1985:149–53) comes close to accusing such Christians of producing a form of fetishised Protestant sacramentality in which idolatry is transformed into 'technolatry'. Horsfield's judgement is a product of his own denominational preferences, but the point is still valid that videos and cassettes act like relics from other, older traditions, transcending spatial divisions by diffusing the sacred from centres to peripheries (Geary 1986:183). As with many relics, we see how tapes are sanctified through their contact with a charismatic personality, retaining a kind of social substance in the form of their inspired words.

These attitudes to the use of media and language help to articulate a faith wherein believing does not appear to depend on immediate, first-hand belonging (Davie 1994). Both the participants at and the locations of services are rendered generic and usually easily able to be accommodated within the assumptions of the charismatic consumer, since watching a service on tape frames and focusses attention on the stage and stereotyped responses from the congregation. Recordings of Word of Life services are 'exported' to other parts of the Faith network, and many Swedish believers are accustomed to viewing videos and listening to cassettes from foreign preachers. When they do so, they observe styles of worship or even architecture with which they feel familiar from their experiences in Sweden – just as the logos of Faith ministries tend to incorporate variations on the imagery of a sword, often in association with a globe or a Bible (cf. Gustafsson 1987). Even if one were not to understand the language being spoken, the images could possibly 'speak' for themselves. Furthermore, sometimes the language broadcast is not that of conventional speech but is rather

glossolalia – a 'universal' means of representing inspired spontaneity without overt semantic meaning (Csordas 1995:8). Electronic
media can therefore help adherents to articulate a sense of place
or belonging within a potentially infinite community of believers.
Not only can they regard the whole world as a potential market
for their products, but they can also come to regard their own
actions as having far more than parochial significance. Every
'receiver' of the evangelical message is also a potential 'sender' of
it elsewhere.

At the same time, Faith claims that media reproductions retain
the performative efficacy of the original event have ironic consequences. The ideology of direct reception is akin to hypodermic
models of media communication and helps believers equate size of
potential audience with number of souls assumed to be saved or
renewed (Hoover 1988; Peck 1993:103). A notion of injecting faith
into consumers is clearly an image of power (Schultze 1991:196),
and moreover one that cannot easily be tested in the sense of accurately measuring responses to media output. Yet it also plays into
the hands of opponents who subscribe to a brainwashing thesis,
which assumes that helpless victims of religious ideology are
deprived of their critical faculties once they have been exposed to
the charismatic powers of Ekman or some other preacher. Neither
adherents nor their critics always acknowledge the fact that, at least
viewed sociologically, conversion processes tend to involve long-
term, face-to-face contact between individuals.[16] In Sweden and
elsewhere, the vast majority of consumers of evangelical programming and videos have already been converted.[17] Any witnessing
that appears on such programming is literally, in most cases,
preaching to the converted, and this tendency is particularly true
of videos and cassettes as they tend to be purchased and exchanged
within Christian circles, without having to be broadcast on public-
access channels. However, in contexts where identity is constituted
partly by the action of reaching out to others, a re-enactment of

---

[16] Indeed, it is standard Faith practice to make contact with a person who has expressed
interest in conversion and try to bring them to the group as soon as possible.

[17] See for instance Bruce (1990b:134); Hoover (1990); Linderman (1996:97). Alexander
(1994:33) notes that the number of viewers who regularly watch some form of religious
television in the US is 13,300,000, comprising only 5 per cent of the American population.

the process of conversion on screen and in words can be a powerful restatement of purpose for people who are already born-again (Stromberg 1993). Much Faith worship is itself centred around notions of transformation: towards the end of a service, members of the audience are urged to come up to the front either to be saved or, if they are already saved, to be healed and renewed in body and spirit. The processes of conversion to and restoration of faith are liturgically and rhetorically very similar, and broadcasting the Word to others can be a way of reinvoking and reconstituting one's own commitment. As we shall see in the next chapter, the question of who precisely makes up the audience for conversionist rhetoric is an important one to answer if we are to understand how a geographically global yet anti-pluralist world of charismatic influence is constructed.

Most importantly, the Faith notion that sacred words are signifiers whose meanings are fixed is served well by objectifying practices through which the possibility is removed of challenging 'official', collectively articulated depictions of sacred experience by means of idiosyncratic responses. I am certainly not arguing that the ideal of creating a translocal communion of Christians through the unproblematic, hypodermic-like broadcasting and reception of images and words is anything other than an evangelical ideal. However, Word of Life beliefs and social arrangements undoubtedly lessen the possibility of mounting public challenges to such a model from within the system. The Faith ideology of perfect consensus is reinforced by the perceived need to present an external, iconic image of the self. To participate in a service at the group itself is an experience not dissimilar to viewing it as a spectacle on the television screen in the sense that the responses of the congregation-cum-audience are mostly limited to conventional words of assent. Beyond the group, in the living-rooms of far-flung individual consumers, varieties of response are often uncontrolled, but are given no voice, no representation in collective contexts unless they witness to the power of the mediated word and image. The creation of a distanced 'congregation', vicariously sampling its services, allows the Word of Life to maintain its reflexive presentation of a unified body of believers, whose sense of affiliation is extended to a community of the imagination located far beyond the borders of Uppsala.

TECHNOLOGISING THE SELF

Much of what I have said so far centres around the relationship that appears to be established between the mediated word and the charismatic self. Faith ideology asserts the presence of an affinity between sanctified language and a renewed Spirit – indeed, the two are constituted by the same substance, the same divine force. My own analysis of Faith uses of language invokes a rather more prosaic account of, among other things, internalisation and externalisation of verbal forms. I wish now to suggest that both of these accounts can be rephrased in terms of a third schema of interpretation (albeit one that is already close to my own): that of social scientific theories of objectification.[18] Influenced by Hegel's *Phenomenology of Spirit*, Miller (1987:12) sees objectification as involving 'a series of processes of externalization (self-alienation) and sublation (reabsorption) through which the subject of such a process is created and developed'. Miller therefore argues that consumption or sublation can act in positive ways, helping society to reappropriate its own external forms in a mutually constitutive process of development. In Tilley's words (1991:155), objectification involves 'a process of externalization, whereby individuals or groups consciously or unconsciously are in a state of "becoming". Through their material praxis and cultural representations people project themselves.' By way of contrast, the purely Marxist view sees objectification as a process whereby a product under conditions of estrangement becomes alien to its maker, taking on a reified external reality divorced from its origins of production (Miller 1987:39–44).

Both Hegelian (as described by Miller) and Marxist senses of 'objectification' are relevant in describing the different ways in which individual charismatics respond to the assimilation of verbal forms to the self. Positive and negative forms of self-alienation and

---

[18] See also Coleman 1996a and 1996b.

objectification can be shown to be evident, and I shall illustrate what I mean by reference to practices relating to the media. The juxtaposition of two contrasting case-studies (both of which echo the experiences of other adherents) should make the point.

A former student at the Bible school explained to me how, as she fell asleep in bed, she would regularly play tapes of her own prayers and readings back to herself. She thus indicated the ability both to exteriorise her own inspired words on tape and to reconsume these words – 'living' yet also objectified – as she listened to them again and again. The taping of a personally constructed 'ritual event' was carried out by this believer because she valued the possibility of preserving and replicating sacred experience and then rendering it into an easily accessible form. The technique worked for her because each playing of the tape recontextualised a fixed passage of powerfully charged speech within her own experience of the moment, giving it new or at least equal significance every time it was used.[19]

By way of contrast, a former follower described how, whenever he attempted to pray, set phrases would appear in his mind as if a motor had been put in motion (Swartling 1988:33–9). Here, the image of an independently running machine seemed to have invaded his internal consciousness, and instead of providing access to a predictable source of inspiration was perceived as a form of disturbing self-alienation. Unable to reappropriate the phrases by applying them to his present circumstances, he felt that they were appropriating him instead. His sentiments are similar to those of adherents, mentioned in chapter 5, who described themselves as 'split': the iconic, object-like nature of sacred language is perceived in such cases as a threat to the self, rather than helping to constitute it in a new way. We recall, for instance, the woman who talked of her struggle to articulate 'resistance' to a language that appeared to be attempting to control her.

---

[19] Schieffelin (1996:82) notes how ritual participants often work creatively to adapt ritual performances to the contingencies of the present: 'Texts and genres must be accommodated to historical situations . . . they are submitted to some determination by history. Otherwise rituals could be effectively enacted simply by playing recordings of them on video-tape.' The creativity mentioned by Schieffelin emerges here not via novel ritual performance but through the way the fixed words on the tape retain a dynamic sense of 'becoming' by being shown to 'speak' to all situations.

These contrasting approaches to the objectification of sacred language express, in microcosm, positive and negative forms of alienation offered by group practices. Adherents may come to view their lives as positively transformed by the externalisation and reabsorption of the performative effects of sacred language, not least as such language is brought to bear upon a range of different situations and therefore helps to reconstitute their surroundings, no matter what or where those surroundings might be. In Faith argot, the person learns to 'overcome all circumstances' in achieving a desired goal. On the other hand, the adherent may be unable to see how circumstances are transformed in this way. Instead, the words and iconic images produced cannot be reabsorbed into a unified sense of self, and remain external to the desires of the conscious person. In the process of, in Marxist terms, a fetishised attribution of life to language, the disillusioned Christian feels not that they have augmented the self, but rather have rendered an aspect of it inaccessible to the will (cf. Keane 1998:13). The result is not so much language that is truly 'living', but rather a mechanised stream of words that have lost any connection to the inner being.

We see played out here variations on a broader problematic in the articulation of many strands of Protestant tradition. As Keane (1998:24) puts it, speech is often seen as mediating between the material and immaterial, visible and invisible, interior and exterior realms. Words, which rise from the true, spiritual locus of the will, are the Spirit made manifest in the world. Yet language is also social in origin and therefore exterior to the speaker, threatening the autonomy of the subject. In certain contexts, it can be taken to reveal the incipient insincerity that (in common with material objects) threatens to intervene between speaker and divine addressee. The articulation of Pentecostal tongues, or indeed Quaker silence, provides ways to overcome such insincerity, since they appear to deconstruct or bypass fixed social convention. In the eastern Indonesian case Keane describes (ibid.: 26), the shutting of eyes during prayer is a bodily expression of marking off the boundary between interior and exterior and aiding concentration on the former. In Faith contexts, sincerity of will and fear of a stultifying idolatry are also stressed, and yet the social, shared aspects of language are not abhorred in the same way. Ideally, the appropriation of inspired language (in both glossolalia and conventional words) is a means of gaining access to universal sources of power. Admittedly, as we saw in the example above, the appropriation of linguistic forms becomes disturbing when all that remains are those forms, and not a sense of how verbal force can be integrated into a developing sense of the charismatic self.

Examples of how a charismatic persona may be constructed with the aid of technologies of mediation are given a further dimension when we consider the role of charismatic leaders, 'great men and women of God', in the Faith network. Famous preachers are people who not only travel physically round the globe, but also consolidate their reputation and charisma through their endless self-reproduction and dissemination in mediated images and sounds. Such figures encapsulate and even transcend geographical and cultural distance in their physical and virtual appearances in group and domestic contexts. For instance, Morris Cerullo's web pages describe how 'a world-wide network of National . . . Directors have literally taken "Morris Cerullo in a suitcase" to bring the message of the resurrected Messiah to hundreds of sites – to some of the most remote areas of the world!' Video is regarded as being able to spread an anointing throughout the world in order to fulfil Cerullo's plan (and, according to him, God's command) to reach a billion people with the Gospel message within a few years.[20] Another publication notes that: 'Morris Cerullo knows that there is no distance with God . . . and He [God] will honor prayers through the TV airwaves into your home just the same as He honored the needs of the hurting when He physically walked the face of the earth!'[21] Such claims reconstitute Cerullo's charismatic authority even as that authority is represented to the potentially infinite numbers of readers of his web pages.

Thus in one sense charismatic power is democratised in Faith practice because any given believer can render their own words into mediated and replicable form; however, the absorption of the spiritual power from a leader such as Cerullo (or Sumrall, or Ekman and so on) involves internalisation of language from someone whose spiritual persona is reproduced and diffused, one

---

[20] Web page available during 1997.   [21] *Victory*, 1995 Autumn:13.

might say globalised, to an endlessly greater degree than that of an ordinary adherent. Charismatic authority is frequently assessed in quantified terms – size of congregation attracted, number of countries visited, money raised, sinners converted – and in this context mediated messages are of particular value because they can reach so many people across such great distances. In a sense, we see another dimension here of the 'exaggeration principle' discussed in the previous chapter. The successful preacher is not usually a body-builder, but the spiritual force contained in his body can be multiplied in unlimited ways. When a sermon is preached in front of an eager congregation, it can have great power and impact within the four walls of a church; when it is recorded and broadcast to others, it extends the reach of the speaker to a far greater constituency and makes the message itself appear more powerful. Electronic media therefore replicate face-to-face processes of externalisation and internalisation, but they also distanciate such processes, stretching them out over space and time and therefore providing them with particular significance in a charismatic culture that values extension into unconfined social and spiritual space (cf. Jaffe 1999:136). In the language of Bourdieu, a charismatic personality gains symbolic capital out of being appropriated – in texts, cassettes, videos and so on. Electronically mediated communion becomes a means of self-sacralisation and, one might say, self-sacramentalisation as the substance of the speaking body of the charismatic preacher dissolves boundaries in space and time when it is subjected to ritualised processes of media consumption. Power is thereby mediated through the personality of the preacher, but personal idiosyncrasy in this context is valued less than the ability to make available a charismatic force that is sought after precisely because it is demonstrably diffused to so many contexts and people.

There are echoes here of Bauman's (1998:19) comments on the non-terrestriality of power in a globalised world. In contexts where mobility is prized, he says, power-holders become de-physicalised. He even cites an analogy between cyberspace and the Christian conception of heaven (the human soul freed from the frailties and failings of the flesh) to make his point. I am not, of course, implying that Faith leaders are freed from embodiment as such – indeed, as we have seen, embodiment plays a key part in charismatic expressions of commitment to their beliefs. What is striking, however, is that Faith practices involve the dissemination of an aspect of the born-again person – the Spirit – that can be detached from one person and re-embedded in another. In one sense, the Spirit is generic, able to be absorbed by anybody who has been made receptive through processes of salvation. Yet it is also clear that some people's spiritual power has greater currency and exchange value than others. In the next chapter, we explore further the issues of charismatic personhood and agency and relate them to a central medium of power and exchange that has so far been little explored in this book: money.

CHAPTER EIGHT

Expansive agency

If a single image defines the Word of Life to sceptical outsiders, it is that of the accumulation of money. A television documentary, broadcast nationally in 1985 and repeated the next year, focussed on the ministry's practice of taking collections in large white buckets. It closed with the words: 'From nought to twenty million kronor in two years, and turnover growing all the time – when Ulf Ekman preaches the Word of Life.'[1] Critical books by Swedish clergymen, with titles such as *God and Money: On Prosperity Theology in the USA and Sweden* (Hellberg 1987) or *Para-churches: On Business and Prayer in Sweden* (Nilsson 1988), highlight similar concerns in their promotion of the view that spiritual authenticity is inevitably compromised by material rewards.

Money does have an all-pervading and multivalent significance in the lives of many Word of Life adherents.[2] Of course, it could simply be argued that considerable finance is needed to maintain ambitious and technologically driven programmes of expansion (Barron 1987). Such a view, while partially justified, cannot provide a complete understanding of the extent to which imagery related to wealth, finance and business is constitutive of identity: it promotes a limited, 'top-down' perspective on Prosperity beliefs, according to which ordinary members are viewed as mere suppliers of material resources for a growing religious organisation. A more subtle approach might argue that Faith Christians are invoking but also transforming an older Protestant Ethic, in line with

[1] See Coleman 1989:169–70.
[2] See also my comments on the Health and Wealth Gospel in chapter 1. John Wesley, of course, argued that wealth put to proper use was sanctified (cf. Comaroff 1985:132; Kramer 1998b:1).

wider societal trends. Faith convictions can be interpreted as shifting assumptions concerning the material manifestations of divine favour away from personal asceticism and towards a mainstream, secularised spirit of modern consumerism.[3] Thus, Brouwer et al. characterise Prosperity Theology as presenting principles that are accommodated to a therapeutic ethos (1996:241): 'The new theology is devoted to a form of hyperindividualism, a transformation of one's personal relationship with Jesus into regular concentration on one's own piety, one's own feelings, one's own health, and one's own financial security.' This emphasis on the cultivation of the self is certainly evident among Swedish believers. For instance, I am reminded of a remark made by a retired Pentecostalist missionary who regularly visited the Word of Life. When I asked him why he went to both groups, he replied: 'I go to the Pentecostal church to help others; I go to the Word of Life to help myself.'

None the less, I want to shift focus away from a concentration on mere material accumulation and immediate self-gratification in the analysis of Faith attitudes to wealth.[4] I argue that these practices are complemented by another method of deploying financial and other resources: one that I describe as the 'charismatic gift'. We shall see how 'gifting' by Faith Christians, in common with practices we have already examined relating to the body, language and the mass media, is linked to the promotion of not only personal growth, but also a sense of projecting a mobile and inspired self into the world. I therefore survey Faith attitudes to giving before juxtaposing them with social scientific perspectives.

PRACTISING PROSPERITY

Faith teachings are underpinned by the assertion that the same spiritual laws govern all spheres of existence (Hunt 1998:275).[5] One such sphere is that of wealth. In his book *Financial Prosperity*, Ulf

---

[3] On modern consumerism and transformations of the Protestant Ethic, see Bell (1978); Lears (1983:4); Campbell (1987); Gifford (1998:336–7).
[4] As far as I can tell, Faith Christians in Sweden do not appear to be markedly wealthier than average.
[5] Marsden (1991:133–4) has shown how nineteenth-century evangelicals adopted inductive, Baconian models of understanding in seeking to find harmonies between spiritual and physical realms of existence.

Ekman (1989:11) argues that the issue is key to a Christian understanding of divinity: 'Financial prosperity is not just another
subject. It is a part of the character of God.' A true appreciation
of God's beneficence is created not only through successful and
productive work, but also through redistributing resources in
certain ways. Practices of giving performed by humans can be seen
as earthly replicas, even instantiations, of divine action. As Ekman
puts it (ibid.:12), prompted by John 3:16: 'Just as you enjoy giving
gifts to others, God enjoys giving to you. God is a cheerful giver.'[6]
The believer should therefore follow divine example and maintain
a 'positive attitude' in the process of divesting the self of resources.
Furthermore, such action will receive a certain reward.

The American preacher Kenneth Copeland, who has gained a
considerable reputation in world-wide Faith circles for his teachings on material prosperity, also emphasises the close connections
between human and divine action in relation to the deployment of
assets: 'Did you ever stop to think that in giving, Almighty God also
received? In fact, that is why He gave His Son, so that He could
receive many more sons! Hallelujah!'[7] In these terms, Jesus' death
was both a sacrifice and a gift (Kramer 1998a; 1998b), leading to a
new covenant that has made prosperity available to all believers.
The idea of giving can therefore refer to the investment of many
different kinds of 'resource', ranging from money to other material
goods to, in God's case, his son. Cheerful acceptance of the resul-
tant benefits then becomes a duty. Copeland continues: 'You
wouldn't think well of a farmer who planted seeds, then let his crop
rot in the field while people are starving. It's just as irresponsible to
give financial seeds and not to receive a harvest from them, while
there are people starving to hear the gospel.' However, wealth
should ideally be put back into circulation: 'The world has the idea
that if you get rich, you have to keep everything. But you can give
it all away if you want to. Just keep the flow going.'
Copeland's words draw a conventional evangelical distinction

---

[6] There are echoes here of Pat Robertson's 'Kingdom Principles' according to which the
person can give themselves out of need, since, as Robertson says, 'You know you can't
outgive God' (quoted in Peck 1993:155).

[7] These and the other citations in this paragraph come from *Believer's Voice of Victory* 1985
12:4.

between 'the world' and the realm of the believer, but also show how apparently secular resources should be appropriated for Christian ends, thus transforming their significance and removing them from the clutches of a Devil who is sometimes described as a 'thief' (cf. Kiernan 1988:456). Ekman states (1989:58): 'Wealthy people who are not saved are reservoirs for the Devil. They pile up possessions and gather wealth to themselves, thus restricting resources which could be put to much better, active use.' In Faith language and imagery, secularised actions and attitudes are associated not only with stasis, but also with sterile forms of limitation.[8] Constant circulation of resources therefore becomes akin to a test of faith. Christians are encouraged to think big, to consider investing in sowing out financial 'seeds' that appear on a profane level of understanding to be unwise. Thus Ekman exhorts his readers (ibid.:67): 'If you want to get somewhere with God, you need to reach beyond your present financial limitations.' Or note the words of a staff member of the Word of Life, explaining the rationale for risk-taking ambition in the following appeal for money to fund missionary work:[9]

You can give – money! Lack of money should not be allowed to be a barrier to reaching out. When it comes to giving, let's be like the congregation in 2 Cor. 8:1–2 . . . They gave 'more than they could'. They gave when in the natural they 'couldn't afford to'. They put pressure on circumstances instead of going under them. When we do that, we break through on the economic plane and don't remain hedged around by monthly pay or bank-balances. We become unbounded in God and can become an enormous blessing for these people.

The idea of being 'unbounded in God' again evokes the imagery of the evangelical body-builder (see chapter 6), freed from the limitations of the cross and bursting out of the picture-frame. In this instance, such self-development is created not through accumulation ('internalisation') of resources, however, but by a form of charismatic donation that both 'externalises' resources in the act of giving and 'dramatises' (brings into the present through mimesis) the actions of a biblical congregation. The fact that the writer is

---

[8] See, for instance, Mark 10:30; Luke 6:38; John 3:16; Galatians 3:13–14; Ephesians 3:20. See also Taussig (1997:132) on Marx's view of hoarding money.
[9] Curt Lahti in *Word of Life Newsletter*, 1990 1:15.

appealing for resources to aid missionary work in the former Soviet Union indicates further how a sense of urgency in reaching out is often given an eschatological dimension. The importance of spreading the Gospel in these 'Last Days' cannot be denied, particularly when it involves missionising a previously communist region.

Numerous ways exist for narrative depictions of the production and redistribution of prosperity to be put into practice. As we saw in chapter 6, the group's building is itself a mixture of worship hall and extensive offices, incorporating various branches of a media business. Courses on business and finance are taught at both the University and the Bible School. More broadly, faith is not seen as relegated to the periphery of society. The head of a computer company argues the following in a talk given to Christian Student Front: 'Preaching the Gospel . . . is a profession, it's a kind of work . . . it's as serious as being president, or more serious . . . if you were prime minister of Sweden that's less serious than being Ulf Ekman, and having his job.'[10] This outward-oriented[11] view of the Christian's calling is reinforced by a lawyer, talking to the same group of students: 'One is accused [by one's colleagues] of being out for a career and being out to earn money . . . It's very simple . . . God loves people who have careers . . . God loves people who have success. God wants you to have success, wants you to have a career.' Thus: 'Instead of travelling to India . . . [one should] take a job . . . be a Christian at one's workplace . . . be a light, a witness for one's workmates . . . When they meet such a Christian, they are encountering the Holy Spirit.'[12] In this latter example, the Christian is evangelising not through preaching, but through a form of embodied witness that illustrates the generic foundations of the exemplary life. The power of the Spirit is mediated through the actions and demeanour of the born-again worker.

Activities of work and of worship are often conflated by Faith adherents, and encapsulated in the phrase 'spiritual career'. The idea is that Christians should develop themselves in a goal-directed way, thus ascending in a hierarchy of charismatic influence. Such

---

[10] Christian Student Front meeting, Tape 2, 1987.
[11] Compare Wilson (1973) on religious movements' responses to the world.
[12] Christian Student Front meeting, Tape 4, 1987.

influence can be exercised through ministry itself, but can be expressed in multiple other ways that actively appropriate the secular world and its resources for Christian purposes (Coleman 1995). One man, who combines his work as the pastor of a small Faith church in Stockholm with a job as a financial consultant, argues:[13]

> We need businesses in Sweden which are steered by the Holy Spirit. It's frightening to look at the Swedish business world – the most ungodly category in the whole of Swedish society. Sweden is one of the world's richest countries . . . and there sit a load of ungodly old men who keep hold of all that money . . . Think if God could take over Volvo, for example. . . . That would be wonderful, wouldn't it? . . . [With] spiritually anointed people who led Volvo, and all their billions . . . we could send out Volvo missionaries to the whole world.

The Spirit is not seen here as an irrational alternative to the relentless logic of the secular world of business, but rather as an invaluable aid in the correct deployment of Swedish economic influence on a global scale. The sense that spiritual, material and rational realms are complementary – even, at times, co-extensive – is reinforced by an extract from a manual describing the Word of Life Bible School. Beside a picture of a young, suited computer specialist, who is shown standing in front of a technical exhibition, the caption reads:

> Back to work after Bible school, Lennart Pedersen, with a leading position in an international company, risked his career when he took a sabbatical career to come here. 'The Bible school taught me many spiritual principles which I have applied in my work', he says. 'Now, my job is going better than ever.'

Some believers start up businesses as a means of building a career combining spiritual and material development. For instance, I interviewed a number of people who worked for a telephone sales company staffed entirely by Faith adherents, which had been founded by a member of the congregation. The nature of the business, appropriately enough, involved the deployment of words in order to achieve success. At times during the work-day, secular

---

[13] Christian Student Front meeting, Tape 3, 1987.

language was replaced by spiritually charged speech. As one worker put it: 'You could sit and pray and rattle off tongues as you wanted', while she often told herself: 'And now I demand in Jesus' name that I'll get ten things sold this hour so I'll get a good commission, kind of thing.' Even the language used to describe entrepreneurial action must be carefully deployed. When two brothers bought a small fast-food kiosk, one of them asked Johan, an interviewee of mine, what he thought of the venture. Johan told me that when he said he felt the brothers had paid too much for the business, 'they reacted to that and thought that I gave "negative confession" over the kiosk'.

Engagement with the group can itself involve an act of financial faith.[14] Bible School students have told me how many of them worked part-time to support their studies, but others trusted in God's beneficence. One student said: '[You] should have faith in yourself, or you should have faith in your own faith, so faith becomes like an assurance of things one cannot see. It means that if you stand sufficiently long in faith the invisible will become visible.' She adds: 'People say "I stood in faith for a car or suit and I got that and that and that".' Another person who, in fact, left the Bible School before finishing her studies stated, with much irritation, that she had shared a house with a fellow student who was always short of money, and that: 'Each time I gave her money or asked her to share a meal she said "God you are good, you answered my prayer" . . . She never accepted that it was I who gave her money out of sympathy – it was always God who had sent me.' Taking risks is itself akin to a form of positive confession, expressed in action, and indicative of ambition as well as faith. A member of the congregation told me how he had decided to move into a larger house, even though he knew he could not really afford it, since a bigger home would represent a measure of his aspirations for himself and his family. He showed similar drive in his work life, converting a training in both theology and advertising into a career running a newspaper devoted to publicising developments in the Faith Movement.

[14] Of course, Christian missionary history is full of examples of believers who have trusted in God's beneficence (see, for instance, Sundstedt 1972).

This lack of embarrassment about money can be felt in many dealings at the Word of Life itself. Shortly before a sermon, a member of the group may spend some minutes explaining the importance of giving as much money as possible to a project before donations are given. Sermons themselves occasionally deal exclusively with money. One Sunday morning, for instance,[15] a pastor outlined the expansion plans of the group, reminded the congregation of its obligation to tithe, and instructed each person to turn to their neighbour (a common practice during sermons) and affirm: 'You and I are stewards.' Outside the hall where services take place is a large shop in which videos, audio-cassettes, books and specific consumer items, such as jacket pins carrying the Word of Life logo, are for sale. The extensive literature the group produces in the form of newsletters and magazines is full of adverts giving reduced prices on goods, and includes testimonies of the economic (and other) miracles members have experienced in the past month. For instance, the following appeared in a *Word of Life Newsletter* under the title 'Hundred-fold Harvest':[16]

At a meeting there was a sermon about God as the God of plenty. Two collections were taken up. On the second one I felt that I should give my last money. I needed it. In any case I put 50 crowns [about 4 pounds sterling] in and thought I had 10 left. When I came out I had the 50-crown note left and must have put the tenner in instead. But in my heart I had given the 50-crown note away. The same day I went into a video shop. As I stood there a man came in and said: 'Lucky that you're here. You see my wife and I decided this morning to give you 5000 crowns!!!' I was so happy at this 100-fold harvest that I witnessed about Jesus to everybody standing around me and on the way out. God is good!

We see here how a sermon leads to inner conviction, followed by action. The motivation of the person is not only tested, it is also measured – and found to be worth '50' rather than '10'. Giving is rewarded by receiving, not from the original recipient (in this case, the group itself) but from two people who may or may not be strangers to the narrator but who themselves feel an urge to give to him. The reward is an impressive return on the original

---

[15] Sunday-morning meeting, 11 September 1994.   [16] *Word of Life Newsletter,* 1987 3:12.

investment, and the event as a whole is converted into immediate testimony (in the shop) and subsequently a narrative reproduced in the newsletter.

Quite early on during my first fieldwork period at the group, I experienced an example of such giving in a way that, at the time, I found rather puzzling. I had turned up as usual one evening to a mid-week service. I was a few minutes early, and along with others in the crowded hall I sat down, looking round for people I knew while listening to the background piano music being played on stage. At first, I hardly noticed the elderly woman sitting next to me but then she touched me on the shoulder and smiled. She explained that she was very short of money, at which point I wondered if she was going to ask me for some. In fact, the opposite was the case. She explained that God had blessed her by giving her the equivalent of a little under £20 the day before. God had also told her, apparently, that she should give half of the money to someone else whom she would meet at the service. That person was me – not somebody she had ever met previously, but the person who happened to sit next to her. She opened a purse containing two notes and handed me one of them. After considerable internal debate, I decided to accept the money. I felt I could not oppose what she clearly believed was a divinely instituted act, so I rather sheepishly put the note into my back pocket and tried for some time to forget that it was there.

Many of the personal investment decisions detailed above echo those made by leaders of the group. The decision to build new, privately owned premises in the mid-1980s undoubtedly provided a test of the ministry's ability to gather resources. A woman who worked in a hotel located near to the Word of Life and who regularly went to its meetings told me proudly in 1994 that the ministry was 'unique': it had had no money when the foundations of the building were laid, and yet the project had been completed. Here, she said, as in other tasks, Faith Christians showed their capacity to 'believe forward' sufficient money to accomplish vital goals, both by prayer and by taking the decision to spend resources that would surely appear. The impression of risk-taking in the name of constant progression appears also to be confirmed by the work of a local economist, Lars Fälting.[17] Fälting argues that the Word of Life has often appeared to be lacking in money and yet has continued to invest in large-scale projects. Taxes due in April 1990 were paid a number of months late, and a year later the group was taken to court because of unpaid bills. Indeed, in July 1991 the Word of Life apparently paid no wages to its staff.[18] Similar evidence of financial difficulties came in 1994 when the group sold its local radio station. At the same time, the rhetoric and reality of expansion have continued throughout the group's short history, and as yet show few signs of abating.

THE CHARISMATIC GIFT

How, then, are we to interpret Faith practices of investment in the light of a wider argument about the creation of a globalised, charismatic identity? Let me begin by restating the point that money clearly acts as one among a number of 'measures' of faith and associated agency. The numbers of souls saved, bodies healed, resources collected, countries visited and churches started in this evangelical economy are the subject of constant appraisal, and are located within narratives of inexorable progress and growth. An example is provided by the collection that is taken up at every meeting. A report on the 1986 Faith conference talks of how, one evening, 100,000 crowns were raised for a big television project run by Lester Sumrall.[19] Then Sumrall himself spoke in support of an offering to the Word of Life's new building. The next day, the amount collected for the building was announced – well over a million crowns – to considerable acclaim from the congregation. On such occasions, a double-edged form of assessment seems to be going on: the amount gathered represents a collective achievement of the group in support of a shared project, and is spoken of as demonstrating what can be done if enough faith is present. In addition, it acts as a measure of the charismatic drawing power of Sumrall himself, who can be shown to have marshalled such resources from those who have come to hear him speak. Sumrall

[17] See the front page of *Upsala Nya Tidning*, 29 February 1992.
[18] Fälting's claims that no wages were paid were denied by Ulf Ekman in a letter to *Upsala Nya Tidning* on 2 March 1992.   [19] Reported in *Word of Life Newsletter*, 1986 4:10–11.

can then be compared with other 'world-wide' Faith preachers in terms of the size of collections he attracts.[20] These 'spontaneous' forms of giving oriented to a specific project or person have rather more symbolic resonance than the practice of tithing, which is recommended to congregation members but not enforced. As an interviewee said of tithing: 'We've never done it. They teach about it, but we've given so much anyway.'

Key to such a system is that people – whether ordinary members or internationally known preachers – cannot rest on their laurels: the presence of the Spirit in the self should be monitored all the time. Believers are supposed both to guard against doubt and to seek evidence of continuous personal growth in God, the source of all prosperity. Money cannot be stored and rendered immobile, just as in a sense Sumrall is only as good as his last collection or the Christian entrepreneur is only as good as his or her last deal. In this context, giving more than one can afford – to the congregation, to a friend, to an unknown other – makes perfect sense: it keeps money in circulation through a form of sacrifice that is oriented towards future, potentially unlimited reward; it permits assessment of the effects of one's action on the world; and it helps to render material one's inner state of faith. Money is both an index of internal spiritual power and a medium for gaining the resources needed not only to lead a comfortable life but also to disperse faith among numerous recipients.

Ideas concerning the workings of money link with other attempts to seek systematic principles that both describe and control divine force immanent within the self.[21] For instance, practices associated with money resonate remarkably well with linguistic strategies and forms of verbal self-objectification employed by believers. We recall that Faith adherents frequently regard sacred

[20] In the light of later discussion, it is worthwhile noting here David Harvey's (1989:100) discussion of Marx's view of money in *Capital*: 'Money lubricates exchange but above all it becomes the means by which we typically compare and assess, both before and after the fact of exchange, the value of all commodities.'

[21] Heelas (1999) notes that some New Age ideas also stress empowerment and prosperity. He sees Norman Vincent Peale's positive thinking as mediating between a characteristically New Age search for what lies within, and a more commonly Christian, theistic emphasis on what lies beyond the person. His argument draws partly on two texts that are particularly relevant to Faith ideas: Biggart (1989); Bromley and Shupe (1991).

words as 'thing-like' in their autonomous force and their production of tangible results. Keane (1994), referring to his work on Sumba in eastern Indonesia, similarly describes the object-like qualities of ritual words and their ability to become detached from the particularities of speakers and events. In the Indonesian context, the power of ritual speaking derives from appearing to repeat verbal types grounded in an ancestral past, so that ancestral agency is echoed and evoked. Word of Life sacred language is also object-like, but derives its power and protection against the contingencies of the present not from ancestors but from a notion of the living and active influence of God, embodied within and rendered active by the believer's practices of reading, listening and speaking. And, just as words atrophy if they remain stored in a text or lodged only in the memory, so money is made (re-)productive by being removed from a bank account and sent out into the world.

Keane's piece argues that the successful conjoining of words and things on Sumba helps portray transactors of exchange as bearing an agency that transcends physical individuals. He states this in the context of arguing that assumptions concerning the boundaries between persons and things have, since Marcel Mauss (1990), been challenged by theories of exchange. It is this last issue I wish to discuss in detail – and more specifically the notion that the use of both language and money in a charismatic context can be reconsidered in the light of Maussian analysis.[22] In developing my argument, I am not suggesting that direct parallels can be drawn between contemporary Swedish charismatics and the 'archaic' contexts described by Mauss (for instance Melanesia, Polynesia and the Pacific Northwest). Such an approach would hardly do justice to ethnographically contrasting notions of sociality, identity and material culture. However, a Maussian perspective can be used to encourage reflection not only on processes of circulation in any given context, but also on the nature of the relationships that might exist between human participants in relations of exchange. A particular feature of the approach, of course, is a focus on objects which mediate between people engaged in such transactions (Carrier 1995:viii, 9).[23]

---

[22] For some of this argument, see also Coleman in Cannell and Green (forthcoming).
[23] Some of the following uses Carrier's (1995) excellent summary of Mauss.

Mauss's underlying thesis is that archaic societies differ greatly from industrial, commercial ones in defining persons, objects and groups as well as their mutual connections. Economic and other social relations are closely meshed at the more archaic end of the societal scale, just as people are largely indistinct from the groups to which they belong. Objects themselves are not considered to be entities independent from people. In such contexts, a gift cannot be truly alienated from the donor since it retains some part of their spiritual essence or identity. The recipient is therefore under moral obligation not only to receive a present but also to make a return (Parry 1986:453–8). Indeed, the giver acquires a kind of superiority over receiver, since a form of indebtedness is established (see also Gregory 1982; Thomas 1991:14). As a consequence, the participation of the person in the object creates an enduring bond between transactors who are reciprocally dependent.

By way of contrast, industrial and commercial societies encourage the spread of alienated, mass-produced objects and transient, impersonal transactions. Various reasons can be put forward to explain such a shift. A view of the autonomous self has emerged in the West over the past few centuries. At the same time, economic relations have become increasingly differentiated from other kinds of sociality. Exchanges which previously contained aesthetic, religious, moral, legal and economic elements have been stripped down to their purely economic aspects, and so unique ceremonial valuables have, in effect, been transformed into depersonalised money (Parry 1986:457; see also Keane 1996:72). Just as people are seen as having an identity distinct from social groups, so objects are not regarded as having any substantial relationship with their owners.

As writers subsequent to Mauss have pointed out, such developments do not mean that gift-giving as a means of cementing social relations has lost its significance in contemporary societies. Carrier (1995:14) remarks, for instance, that people have tended to construct two putative spheres of existence in their lives; impersonal, utilitarian 'work' versus personal, affective 'home' (and leisure). When commodities are appropriated as gifts they cross the boundaries between these two spheres and must be subordinated to the individual emotions of the giver. The ideology of the purely disinterested gift, one that does *not* entail overt compulsion to make a return on behalf of the recipient, has developed in symbolic opposition to the overtly interested relations evident in commercial and market contexts (Parry 1986).

The validity of Mauss's evolutionary perspective can be debated, but here I am more interested in using some of his analytical categories to reconsider my material on Faith Christians, and in particular the connections that are evident between charismatic identity, objects (or object-like substances) and exchange. By invoking the Maussian framework, we are immediately forced to consider the fact that Faith principles do not emphasise strong boundaries between economic and other realms of existence; if anything, these realms are self-consciously reintegrated as a means of asserting the universality of spiritual laws, just as the distinction between 'persons' and 'things' is not always clear. In contrast to the 'archaic' examples discussed by Mauss, such integration derives special significance from its challenge to a powerful mainstream model (or at least ideology) of differentiation between spheres of economics, religion, kinship and so on.

Let me apply aspects of the Maussian framework to Faith uses of language before I return to the uses of money. We have seen that charismatic words, like objects of exchange, are activated – put into a kind of verbal circulation – to take effect. They have a quality unusual in Western contexts in that they are regarded as possessing object-like characteristics that allow them to be removed from the person whilst retaining a semi-autonomous existence. Such existence is *semi*-autonomous not only because words are directed at recipients, but also because they retain an objectified element of the charismatic identity of the speaker or writer. Clearly, the recipient of language is not expected to reply with an equal or greater number of words, and is not 'in debt' to the speaker in an obvious way. However, one who deploys sacred language expects a return on his or her linguistic investment. That return involves a belief that the words have taken effect, made a difference to the world in a way that can be assessed and thus attributed to the spiritual agency of the speaker (recall, for instance, Morris Cerullo's description of his words as fertile seeds which produce people pregnant with truth, quoted in chapter 7). To externalise sacred words that have been stored internally is not merely to communicate in semantic terms; it is also to re-create and extend one's persona through offering an aspect of the self to others – an aspect that is never truly separated from the giver.[24] It is therefore notable that those who pronounce most effectively at meetings tend to be leading pastors or evangelists, and it is they who attract the most narratives subsequently detailing the effects of their words. Sermons are in certain respects akin to gifts that, in a Maussian sense, illustrate the mutual constitution of the born-again person and 'thing-like' words. They are not 'pure' gifts, of course, because they do expect a return. Overt or assumed approbation contributes to the further development of a reputation as a powerful charismatic personality. Verbalised spiritual agency is therefore 'expansive' in two interrelated ways. It not only has the potential to travel vast distances, it also reinforces and builds up the charismatic persona of both donors and recipients.

In a similar way, the giving of money by Faith Christians is an externalisation of the self – not in words but in financial resources – and the sign and measure of money's inspiration is usually the interest it has acquired in the process. Ekman enhances his reputation not only by sermonising, but also by showing that he can take risks in spending considerable resources to build up his ministry, or even in donating money to projects run by other Faith groups.[25] At times, of course, we see how one medium of exchange (the words of a preacher) is effortlessly converted into another medium (money) as congregations respond to requests for donations. On a much smaller scale, the elderly woman's decision to hand me half of the contents of her purse was not, I came to realise, a disinterested gift to a young man who possibly looked a little underfed. In fact, she was practising a form of giving that *did* expect a very specific return, and I was a somewhat unwitting vehicle towards achieving the payback that she desired.[26] Mauss's 'archaic' gift suggests a model whereby participation of the giver in the object creates an enduring bond between donor and recipient.

---

[24] Occasionally, as we have seen, the self is both donor and recipient of the verbal gift.

[25] In a sermon at the Word of Life, Lahti (3 April 1987) talked of how Ekman 'sowed' 10,000 dollars into Sumrall's television work, partly in order to gain benefit for similar operations run by the Word of Life.

[26] Compare Ekman's statement in a *Word of Life Newsletter* (1995 3:2): 'Pray for Russia! Pray for our Missionaries! Help us help Russia, and God will help you!' The aid to Russia is rewarded not by Russia, but by God.

The woman, however, was not expressing or creating a permanent tie between me and her; rather, she was extending her divinely charged gift into a world where an *unknown* other could be the apparent recipient of her donation, and where the primary beneficiary would be herself. She, after all, would gain interest on the original investment according to the laws of spiritual increase. A commodification of the spiritual self (embodied in a banknote) in one respect was an attempt to reappropriate her objectified, augmented spiritual force in another. God, a joyful giver, would recognise her own divinely inspired act and reward it accordingly. In practice, I do not know whether she subsequently received a suitable financial recompense from her investment. However, as an English visitor to her church, I was perhaps a fitting recipient of a gift aimed at extending the donor's spiritual persona into a much wider sphere, that of an unbounded, potentially global, sphere of influence.[27]

The speaking out of words and the giving away of money are therefore akin to each other in the way they provide means of reaching into a world of opportunity as well as threat. Both actions pervade many arenas of human action – overtly ritualised and apparently everyday, carried out in solitude as well as in public, engaging fellow believers as well as those as yet unsaved. Just as money is to be kept flowing, so words can only become living and gain power when spoken and thereby tested against the contingencies of the present. An aesthetic of constant movement combined with growth is common to both, just as the giving of money as well as the broadcasting of the self in language extract the charismatic 'essence' of the person and render it available to others. That which is most sacred and transcendent within the person, spiritual power, is also that which can be made most accessible to outside

---

[27] Compare Kramer (1998a; 1998b), whose analysis of a Faith church in Brazil indicates considerable similarities of practice with the Word of Life. Comaroff (1985:235) shows that African Zionist understandings of collection implies an accumulation to the self – a means of regaining control of the self in the gift – rather than an alienation from the self implied by conventional Christian ideals (see also Kiernan 1988). Yet, if the Zionists described by Comaroff provide personalised contributions to the fund of power of the collectivity (akin to Word of Life collections during services), the gift-giving I describe here is much more oriented towards a form of self-realisation through donation, often to individual and unknown others.

appropriation. At the same time, the manner in which the self is externalised and reabsorbed tells us much about the nature of social relations articulated in this evangelical culture. An ideology of uninterrupted flow and reception is reinforced by the global charismatic habitus in combination with particular ways of structuring linguistic and financial 'transactions'. The demeanour of adherents, at least in public contexts, usually corresponds with idealised forms of positive self-presentation and mutual comprehension. In addition, the constant flow of people through conferences, workshops or even ordinary services encourages social encounters that are governed by generic modes of charismatic etiquette and maintained between people who often remain relative strangers to each other. My own intense but anonymous and short-lived encounter with the elderly woman was hardly unusual. It is surely also significant that Faith evangelism is one that is designed to use communications technology. Electronic media contain and transmit objectified words of speakers (or writers), but divorce the 'giver' from immediate interaction or dialogue with the 'receiver'. At times, of course, the believer can even imagine an audience or set of 'receivers' where none may exist.[28]

The beauty of such a system, then, is that the recipients of charismatic gifts are frequently constructed as merely passive, generic others: the idea of a recipient is necessary to the system, but such a person often does not need to be interacted with on an intimate level. Ekman (1989:106) describes them as 'channels' through which God provides bounty to the believer. In 'broadcasting' words and money, the charismatics I describe are opening themselves up to criticism from a secular world that regards such actions as both aggressive and needlessly upsetting to the evangelised, but various means exist to insulate the viewpoint of the speaker/writer/donor. An attempt to convert the other or transform the world through such means is not merely aimed at saving a soul or benefiting another believer; it is also an attempt to convince, or even reconstitute, the charismatic persona of the self. Yet such reconstitution

---

[28] As Alfred Gell (1988) has remarked in a different context, 'magical' thinking in our society can be efficacious not only because it is imaginatively compelling, but also because it opens up ideal realms of possibility towards which people can strive using prescribed action.

does not depend upon the existence of stable social relations. Donors and recipients are not bound by the need to maintain repeated acts of reciprocity, while rewards for gifts are often perceived to come from third parties. Indeed, the fact that the group and the Movement as a whole are mobile and dispersed lends a kind of enchantment to such 'stretched' social action because it can appear to extend agency into distant spheres of influence.

In circumstances where personalised objects and objectified persons are being constructed, the specific qualities of money as both 'matter and sign' (Keane 1996) frequently come to the fore. The money which accumulates in white buckets during collection provides tangible proof of financial clout. At the same time, money can move easily from 'concrete particularity' to 'abstract universalism' (Taussig 1997:131). Both Simmel and Marx associate money with the growth of individualism and potential destruction of community. Harris (1989:234) also notes, however, that liberal philosophy sees in money the advent of rationality in human behaviour and the freeing of humans from the shackles of dependency. Such a view is echoed by Simmel's notion that money can promote a wider and more diffuse sort of social integration – an enormously expanded social universe. Anonymous and impersonal, money for him measures everything by the same yardstick and so can act as a condition for the extension of the individual personality and expansion of the circle of trust (Bloch and Parry 1989).

The parallels with the Faith Movement are clear: in the putative global charismatic economy, the deployment of both language and material resources such as money ideally provides individual members, no matter what their circumstances or culture, with the means to assess themselves according to apparently neutral, universal criteria (cf. Harvey 1989:102). The investment of positive confession and/or money in acts of faith provides the route to rational and measurable possibilities of self-transcendence. The sacred and the material become not antithetical but mutually dependent in the sense that the religious 'community' of faith is also an internal market of striving individuals, each keen to further their 'spiritual careers', and each keen to use whatever resources are available to extend into an anonymous world whose transformation implies that investments of the self in the world are never truly alienated. Money, like words, provides the possibility of self-abstraction and circulation away from a sharply defined, limiting social fabric (Comaroff 1985:144). Both, of course, can easily be translated into meanings or values appropriate to different parts of the world, and in this sense speaking in tongues is the most generic verbal medium, equivalent to the unfettered flow of global finance. Both are infused with an even more abstract vehicle of power, the Holy Spirit, that is located in but not bound by the physical person and thus allows an unhindered extension of the evangelical will (Johannesen 1994; Austin-Broos 1997:121). Thus the charismatic gift is one that appears to combine elements from two ideal–typical worlds. A generic aspect of the person – the power of the Spirit – is transferred into such mobile media as words and money, and made available for appropriation even by unknown others, consumers in the global charismatic market. Yet such action is located within a social and cultural framework that encourages the donor to seek, even imagine, divinely derived signs that indicate the influence of such expansive but never entirely alienable agency.[29]

AGENCY, POWER AND PERSONHOOD

In this and previous chapters, we have seen how, in Faith ideology, a bounded, uncreative, idiosyncratic, fleshly self exists alongside an apparently limitless, reproductive, universally shared persona. Believers often describe being born again as a process of self-empowerment, as they learn to draw on internalised spiritual forces to 'conquer circumstances' and gain a sense of control over near and distant events. However, from a social scientific perspective, the apparently dual nature of charismatic identity brings different questions of agency into stark relief: to what extent, one might ask, can the believer claim the authorship of externalised actions and language that are perceived to derive their power from

---

[29] In fact, Appadurai (1986:12–13) argues that the social scientific tendency to oppose materialism and religion, market exchange and reciprocity, 'objectification of persons' and 'personification of things', exaggerates and reifies boundaries between gifts associated with small-scale solidarities, on the one hand, and commodities combined with expansive capitalist economies, on the other.

a transcendent, generic source?[30] After all, believers often see themselves as becoming mini-versions of powerful preachers or of biblical figures, so that successful leaders create others in their own spiritual image; open books and open gestures convey the same message – that of complete accessibility in the transference of truth and power (cf. Forstorp 1992:135). Given the rhetorical dislike of mediation (or at least mediation that distorts its message), leaders are seen as important vehicles for divine power, which they should convey in abundance to others without interferences from bounded flesh or confused intellect.

Keane (1997:7) talks of the Western inclination to locate agency in biologically distinct individuals. He goes on (ibid.:24) to discuss some of the analytical problems associated with adopting such an attitude on Sumba. In eastern Indonesia, ritual speech illustrates the uncertainty of attributing agency because of the way it indicates the ambiguous authorship of spoken words: they are associated at once with the speaker and with the ancestors. Other ethnography from non-Western contexts – much of it written, of course, with Mauss at least partly in mind – questions the universality of mainstream, Western ideologies of autonomous agency and personhood. Busby (1997), for instance, compares 'permeable' persons in South India with 'partible' persons in Melanesia. Despite obvious ethnographic differences between the two models, both might loosely be characterised as describing non-bounded 'dividuals' in contrast to the individuals of the West (Marriott and Inden 1977; Strathern 1988).[31]

My point in mentioning such work is not to compare it directly with charismatic ethnography but to address the questions that it poses in the light of Faith experience. The construction of charismatic personhood clearly involves a sub-cultural model somewhat at odds with mainstream Western ideology. Of course, believers

---

[30] Austin-Broos (1997:265) raises a related issue in arguing that Pentecostal notions of divinity inhering in the person provide an ironic equivalent to Marx's demand that people reclaim the transcendental God and make his powers immanent in them all: 'Just as Marx proposed that workers should reown the alienated God through reowning the state, so Pentecostalism has asserted that saints embrace the immanence of God by dissolving structures of church organization within an egalitarian community of saints.' Of course, ideologies of egalitarianism do not guarantee their realisation in practice.

[31] Compare also Küchler (1988); Gell (1998).

often think of themselves as individuals. However, much evangelical practice encourages the externalisation of aspects of the self in linguistic, material and even gestural forms that are regarded as extending the person and associated agency into wider realms than would normally seem possible. To appropriate a phrase from Gell (1998:229), the charismatic actor is a spatio-temporally extended person. Significantly, also, spiritual power is an unlimited good: the Christian does not lose such force from within the self in transferring it to others, and even if money runs out, words never can.

However, in the global exchanges that make up the market of Faith ideas, actions and consumer goods, some people possess more widely diffused agency than others. If charismatic reputation can be seen as a form of evangelical symbolic capital, it gains value not through exclusivity and limited availability but rather the precise opposite. Ekman, Cerullo, Copeland and others are powerful because their words and actions are demonstrably appropriated by consumers separated by vast territorial and cultural distances, often in the form of electronic media designed to mass produce the image and the power of the charismatic leader (see also chapter 7).[32] The value of the charismatic person is created through the transferability and exchange-value of communications which contain metonymic contact with the original speaker/writer.[33] The Faith Movement provides a context where such leaders do not hold fixed places in a hierarchy of redistribution, but must constantly prove and recreate themselves within a global market of accumulation, redistribution and consumption of charismatic resources.

---

[32] A recent work edited by Werbner and Basu (1998:21) on Sufi cults also explores the connections between embodied charisma and the creation of wider-reaching sacred topographies.

[33] Percy (1998:10) reiterates the Weberian point that charismatic leaders can act as obligatory passages through which the best blessings flow. Certain people become key points or agents in a distributive power circuit (ibid.:12). Compare also (ibid.:13) his statement that: 'Charisma is a dominating nodal point in a circuit of power, which is also a place of limited exchange for believers. They must be willing to shed material or ideological baggage and suspend belief above reality, but in return for this they receive power themselves, and feel blessed. The more you give, the more you get.'

CHAPTER NINE

Contesting the nation

In a country where religious matters do not customarily make front-page news, the Word of Life has attracted extensive and dramatic coverage in the Swedish media. Attention was particularly focussed on the group during the 1980s, when Ekman became a nationally known, even notorious figure. He was described in the press as, among other things, a 'shaman', 'God's capitalist' and the leader of a 'hidden Religious Right' (see Coleman 1989:166–212). Faith adherents are regularly depicted as either passive, brainwashed victims or active aggressors against those deemed to have insufficient faith, particularly the poor and the sick. In chapter 3, I noted that at one point the Movement was even linked to a suspect in the Palme murder trial: a more potent metaphor of threat to national security and values could hardly have been presented to the Swedish public.

During the 1980s, the Archbishop of Sweden released two 'Statements Concerning the Word of Life' which captured something of the tone of the wider moral panic surrounding the group.[1] He referred to spiritual movements 'born in foreign environments . . . often foreign to our own Christian interpretation and tradition of faith. Among these movements there is one which is closer to our own Church than others. I refer to the tendency which is often called Prosperity Theology and which describes itself as the Word of Life or Faith preaching.' This tendency is described as causing 'splits, confusion and arguments' in the Church's congregations,

---

[1] Publicised in the press in March 1986 and July 1987. Reproduced in Wikström (1988:13–15).

just as it encourages 'fanaticism' and possibly leads to individual depression. The notion that 'correct faith is always rewarded with economic success, bodily health and earthly happiness' is regarded as unbiblical. These comments express concern over the psychological as well as theological dangers represented by the group, invoking a desire to protect the integrity of both country and Church.

Although many Word of Life members claim to avoid the secular press and are sometimes enjoined by pastors to do so, most are well aware of the presence of unfavourable media attention in local and national contexts. Yet the effects of widespread criticism cannot be regarded as entirely destructive or disheartening. External condemnation of Faith practices permits believers to see themselves as fighting against a powerful and ultimately demonic 'Other'. I have often been told that 'Satan is scared' of the power of the group; that he is focussing his attacks specifically on those who have spiritual power in the country. Furthermore, by answering critics through writing articles and letters in the national press, appearing on television and speaking at public meetings, Ekman has been able to place his agenda before an audience much wider than those likely to go to church or purchase Faith products. Ironically, he has increased his reputation among adherents as a man of influence precisely through the opportunities presented by hostile media.

In the process of justifying the group either to outsiders or his own supporters, Ekman frequently takes the opportunity to contextualise Word of Life practice specifically within Swedish tradition and culture. The Faith Movement is presented as a means not only to transform the country, but also to restore it to its proper role as a nation blessed by God. Such narrative emplacements, which celebrate the virtues of locality and patriotic attachment, may appear to contradict much of what I have said so far concerning the creation of a globalising orientation. I shall argue, however, that Faith rhetoric appropriates symbols of nationhood in a way that is entirely appropriate to an imaginative construction of the possibility of translocal influence and empowerment. In effect, the evangelical idea of 'the nation' is seen to constitute a framework of action and identity that gives meaning to but does not undermine otherwise placeless and generic principles of Faith. I consider Robertson (1992:58) to be correct in his assertion that the prevalence of national society can be taken as an aspect of globalisation. We must also realise, however, that ideological constructions of global activity and of nationhood not only change over time, but also are likely to have sub-cultural dimensions such as those we see in specifically charismatic understandings of the connections between the national and the global.

We begin by looking at how the Word of Life has been labelled by outsiders as a threat to many aspects of society, not least those associated with the 'Swedish Model' discussed in chapter 3. The focus then shifts to Faith responses to such criticism, including a consideration of charismatic constructions of nationhood. Two important points should emerge from the analysis. First, that the ideology, organisation and rhetoric of the Word of Life can easily be made to look anomalous in the Swedish context. Second, that the group may at the same time embody many of the forces of change and transformation that are evident in other spheres of society. Faith practice and ideology can therefore be seen as threatening to so many people in Sweden not only because they represent 'matter out of place' in the context of powerful mainstream representations of the nation and its institutions, but also because they point to a distinctly possible future – one where previous understandings of nationhood and identity can no longer be sustained in recognisable form.

CONTROVERSY

Journalists, theologians, doctors and worried relatives of adherents have found common cause in condemning the Word of Life. At a meeting arranged in 1986 by the Uppsala Mission Covenant church, designed to bring together political and religious constituencies, the Communist Party representative even remarked on the similarity between her own views and those of the Christians who were present: 'It's a question of the same morality, the same understanding of democracy.'[2] Press coverage has ranged from the

---

[2] See Coleman (1989:174): extract taken from unpublished minutes of the meeting.

Figure 4 A sample of the graffiti placed on the exterior wall of one of the
Word of Life buildings, in 1986–7. Between the inverted cross and the
666 sign is the phrase 'Word of Death Rules!'

often sober reflections of broadsheet newspapers to the humorous
depiction of Ekman in satirical magazines. Sermons have been
preached on the dangers of focussing on God as a source of prosperity, while academic studies have attempted to understand the
theology, psychology and politics of adherents.[3] The controversy
surrounding the group made its literal mark on Uppsala when, one
morning in October, 1987, people woke up to find such slogans as
'Word of Death', the 666 sign and 'Hang Ekman' daubed on
walls around the town, including those of the group's premises
(Figure 4). Insulting graffiti have even been introduced into virtual
space: the web pages of the group are frequently penetrated by
hackers who overlay the text with alternative imagery. One recent

---

[3] Perhaps thirty or so academic or semi-academic reports have appeared so far. The best-
known are probably the following: Hambre et al. (1983); Bjuvsjö et al. (1985); da Silva
(1985); Lindholm and Brosché (1986); Brandell et al. (1986); Nilsson (1988). Forstorp's
excellent work on Faith language (which is analytical without being condemnatory) is
available in English in a contribution to Hansson (1990).

're-writing' added references to 'the Word of Death', a number of links called 'Paradise Lost' and an inverted cross labelled 'Satan'. Besides referring to the 'brainwashing' activity of the group around Europe, the modified text characterised the Word of Life as a sect, equating it with Scientology.[4]

Criticism of the group has generally clustered around a number of recurring themes. Engagement in services has often been seen as potentially threatening to psychological stability. Here, for instance, are the words of a journalist working for *Kyrkans Tidning*, the national paper of the Swedish Church:[5]

> The meeting began when a young guy went on in a fanatic tone about Jesus and His works. Then the meeting continued with group songs, which were very simple so everybody could join in . . . I didn't take part, but just looked on and was somewhat surprised when they began to praise Jesus in tongues or to music. It was what one might call mass-psychosis, difficult to avoid being pulled into.

The charismatic habitus evident in group worship clearly does not resonate with that of the reporter.[6] We see here and in similar depictions a common trope in 'cult controversies', invoking the discourse of the powerless adherent (Beckford 1985; Robbins 1988). The group's influence is assumed to be so strong that it can break down the resistance of the autonomous individual as conceived in mainstream Western discourse (Barker 1984:1). The adherent becomes a 'victim', absolved of responsibility for joining a sect or cult whose attractions would not otherwise be evident to a reasonable, rational person. Thus Sigbert Axelson, an academic in the Theology Department in Uppsala University, notes in a widely read local paper: 'I have not criticised the congregation and its members, since they are . . . entirely guiltless and, besides, powerless.'[7] An academic thesis (Sjöberg 1988), focussing on the psychological problems of people who had left the group, reinforced the sense that contact with Faith ideas might result in the need for

---

[4] This version of the web page was visible at various times during 1998.
[5] Issue dated 8 March 1985.
[6] Daun (1988:326) refers to what he regards as the Swedish characteristic of hiding emotions in public, associated with a lack of gesticulation.
[7] *Upsala Nya Tidning*, 24 October 1986.

therapy. Indeed, it was supported by a project set up in Uppsala by the Swedish Church in order to aid such people (Wikström 1988).[8] Often, the theme of victimage has been applied not to adherents but to those whom they encounter. A television programme broadcast in the mid-1980s juxtaposed scenes from the group with those of a severely disabled woman who stated that she had been mocked for her sin by Bible School students.[9] In such depictions, Word of Life belief in faith-healing is perceived not only to be a naïve alternative to medical science, but also to contain an authoritarian dimension hardly appropriate to the treatment of vulnerable members of society. If the imagery of mass psychosis implies that religious engagement threatens the independent agency and autonomy of the individual, that which describes adherents as attacking the weak presents them as exhibiting a 'surfeit' of agency in subjecting innocent others to their views.

More broadly, the Faith Movement has also been accused of exceeding the boundaries of social propriety by engaging in political advocacy under religious guise. Although group members have tended not to become directly involved in party politics, Ekman has sometimes appeared to advocate right-wing governments before general elections. His book *Gud, Staten och Individen* ('God, The State and the Individual') (1988) encourages the reader to vote, but not to support any party that appears to be anti-Christian in policy, or indeed one that 'oversteps certain boundaries' (ibid.:48) in controlling its people through restricting private ownership or increasing taxes.[10] Although such a point of view does not specify any particular political faction, it clearly cannot be taken to support socialism in the Swedish context. In addition, Faith opposition to abortion and homosexuality, combined with preachers'

---

[8] The project was started in 1987 and originally called RI: 'R' standing for *rådgivning* ('advice') and 'I' for *information*. As Lester Wikström, the leader of the project, put it (1988:5), when Word of Life people met Unification Church or Scientology people 'they had had basically similar experiences and could therefore help and support each other'. Members of the project participated in an anti-cult network established across Europe (Melton 1999).   [9] See Coleman (1989:191).

[10] Thus Ekman (1988:50): 'God is and remains a protector of private property. He is not a supporter of egoism, but he supports the right to own, and egoism can be found in the state as well as the individual. When a government has an ideology which weakens or attacks or is suspicious of or prevents the right to private ownership, God reacts.'

frequent deployment of military metaphors in describing the power of faith, makes up a powerful package that has clear political implications. The sense that Faith adherence might be linked to 'extreme' political forces emerged strongly in 1987, when the group's decision to invite the South African preacher, Ray McCauley, to preach in Uppsala led to considerable press speculation as to McCauley's views on apartheid.

Critical media representations of the group paralleled, and probably also influenced, attitudes expressed more informally to me during interviews I conducted with inhabitants of Uppsala who were not members of the group.[11] Roughly half of the twenty-five people I contacted were active Christians, while the other half professed no particular religious affiliation or interest. Two features of these interviews stand out as relevant here. First, I was struck by the considerable awareness of the Word of Life apparent even among those people who had no other interest in religion. All but one of my interviewees claimed to have heard of the group; in contrast, only one of the non-believers knew, for instance, that a Methodist church was located in the town.[12] Second, I found that particular stereotypical expressions were commonly invoked in response to questions relating to the group. When I asked why people thought that the Word of Life appeared to be flourishing in Sweden, many of the Christians identified faults in their own congregation, as if the appearance of the new ministry could only be seen in negative terms. In addition, both believers and non-believers frequently stated: 'It's a sign of the times',[13] implying usually that the Word of Life was a manifestation of a self-seeking attitude that was pervading all sectors of society. In reply to my asking whether the Word of Life seemed to be a Swedish phenomenon, almost all informants replied with disapproval that it was 'American' or 'Americanised',

---

[11] The 13 interviews with non-believers (7 male, 6 female) were obtained by snowball sampling from non-religious friends in Uppsala. Their ages ranged from early 20s to 50s and they covered a range of occupations. Twelve interviews focussed on local priests and pastors of various denominations (though 1 was based in Stockholm and 1 had moved to the south of Sweden). Ages of the clergy (all but one male) ranged from 25 to 55.

[12] Twelve mentioned the Word of Life, 10 the Pentecostalists, and then knowledge of other denominations fell away quite dramatically. All who knew of the Word of Life said that they had read about it in the papers; 2 had visited a service out of curiosity; 3 had encountered members of the group at work.   [13] In Swedish: *Det ligger i tiden*.

and many added that it contradicted 'typically Swedish' ways of acting. If the American way was to promote aggressive forms of individualism, the Swedish attitude was to avoid either putting oneself forward or claiming particular virtues at the expense of others. The significance of such widespread invocation of a common stock of stereotypes is difficult to assess. Views are clearly constructed out of the rhetorical desire to emphasise cultural contrasts, but also express in personalised, vernacular form a political discourse of equality through redistribution of resources.[14] Similar trends are noted by Hambre et al. (1983:24) in their discussion of why positive thinking might actually be attractive to some minority sections of the population:

Many in Sweden feel that we have a view of the person that is too negative, where one constantly stresses human weaknesses and failings rather than abilities. They also say that Swedes begrudge people's success, that behaviour is governed by an unwritten law: 'You shouldn't believe that you amount to anything.'

The majority of critical reactions to the Word of Life echo those frequently invoked in Western contexts in relation to New Religious Movements (Beckford 1985): authoritarianism is contrasted to democracy; true spirituality, contained within a religious sphere divorced from commerce and politics, is seen as antithetical to business-orientated and politically loaded missionising; medicalised methods of healing are regarded as more trustworthy than irrational faith in divine powers. As we saw in chapter 1, Prosperity preaching has also attracted some censure in the United States, especially from fellow Christians. However, a number of features relating to the controversy have taken particular form and significance in the Swedish context. Compared to the US or other European countries such as the UK, Sweden's population is extremely small and its degree of religious pluralism is still relatively low. The model of the mega-ministry has counterparts in the US but none in Sweden, not even within the Pentecostal

---

[14] Ingvar Carlsson, a former Social Democratic prime minister, expressed this aim of equality through economic and social solidarity in a speech given in 1987 to his party Congress: 'There is no winner unless we are all winners.' See Coleman (1995:163); also quoted in Milner (1990:228).

Movement. Independent or private education, although present in Sweden, is still a rarity. The creation of an autonomous and multi-functional organisation based on evangelical principles may be protected by important principles of religious freedom, but it can also be interpreted as an overt challenge to a relatively centralised and mutually reinforcing religio-political order. The extent to which the group presents an organisational novelty has clearly been expressed in some of its dealings with political authorities, for instance in disputes as to whether it should be granted charitable status or regarded as too 'profit-oriented' to qualify as a properly religious entity.[15]

We saw earlier how North American and Swedish concepts of the person were sometimes juxtaposed by people in a way that emphasised differences in self-regard and orientation to others. Similarly, models of social organisation are contrasted in significant ways by critics. If the Word of Life appears to embody an aggressive, market-driven spirituality, it can be seen as the converse of the ecumenical, locally based and socially conscious body of mainstream Christianity. A widely publicised book by Fred Nilsson (1988), a minister in the Swedish Mission Covenant, examined the group as a para-church phenomenon, unrooted in local contexts and yet with extensive links to similar organisations in other parts of the world. Nilsson also noted in a later article (1990:35): 'The climate for popular movements and knowledge production in Sweden is increasingly influenced by American religious businesses.' As an SMF pastor accusing Faith Christians of lacking local roots, Nilsson expresses in words the sense I tried to convey in chapter 6 of the aesthetic differences between the older and newer groups: the contrasts between a culture of 'place' and a culture that explicitly attempts to transcend context in its application and influence.

A colleague of Nilsson, and a particularly significant figure in the context of national debates concerning the Word of Life, has been Sigbert Axelson. When I first came to Uppsala in the mid-1980s, I was told by university friends that he was the obvious person to meet for anybody interested in the group. As was evident

---

[15] Discussed more fully in Coleman (1989). Considerable controversy also attended the group's first attempts to obtain state support for its schooling programmes.

from my first encounter with him, he rivals Ulf Ekman in his energy and drive, and he has come close to becoming a moral entrepreneur in acting as a catalyst for opposition to the ministry. Axelson has combined lecturing in Mission Studies at Uppsala University with membership of the Swedish Mission Covenant and public support of Social Democratic ideals. He is the author of numerous newspaper and academic articles condemning the supposedly right-wing politics, heretical theology and overpositive psychology of the Word of Life. In addition, he has supervised a number of academic works on Faith-related issues and participated in Nilsson's project to investigate para-church movements. In 1986, he was one of the speakers at a government-run workshop on the political and global role of religion, where he chose to speak on the Word of Life in the context of a talk entitled 'The New Religious Right as an International Phenomenon' (Axelson 1987a). After a visit with academic colleagues to the US to examine the roots of the religious right, Axelson felt moved to ask (1990:10): 'What kind of organisations are these that are flooding the world? Have they outflanked the old churches . . . as mission organisations?' Axelson names Ulf Ekman with Ray McCauley, Reinhard Bonnke and Yonggi Cho as influential leaders of the new movement, along with their North American colleagues. He goes on (ibid.:17) to identify what he sees as the contrast between American missionary practices and those considered normative in Sweden:

In New York I bought a handbook for Christian youth who want to work abroad, help others or gain international experience, The Overseas List. It recommends as pretty much equal alternatives 'Private Development Assistance, Church Mission, Study and Tourism, Teaching and Journalism, International Organizations, The US Government – including the Navy, the Army, the Air Force, the Defense Intelligence Agency and the National Security Agency . . .' The book was published with the help of the National Council of Churches. Could one imagine the Swedish Ecumenical Committee, for example, supporting such a book and such an idea for *Swedish* Christian youth?'

In reply to his own question, Axelson notes (ibid.:18) that 'Whatever else they are, such people in the US see it as their main mission to be Americans in the world.'

Axelson occupies a fascinating place in debates concerning the significance of the Word of Life.[16] His involvement in both the Mission Covenant Church and Social Democratic politics means that he represents two important 'popular movements' (*folkrörelser*) which emerged in the late nineteenth century in Sweden and which have since become part of the mainstream religio-political framework. In a report he prepared on the future of the Swedish popular movements, he explicitly juxtaposes their ideals with those of the Word of Life. For instance, in a discussion of the potential for Christian schooling in Sweden, he notes (1987b:52):

Consciously authoritarian movements are stealthily emerging in the name of democracy, and the National School Board seems to be allowing it to happen so long as applications for independent schools look blameless, which they naturally do. That is how Södermalm Church in Stockholm has managed to get its application approved . . . despite the fact that it is clearly a supporter of the Word of Life Foundation in Uppsala. The latter's view on knowledge and humanity reveals clearly anti-democratic and authoritarian tendencies within an abstruse religious language. Many such schools will be founded in the country as a whole. One must ask . . . whether this is directly opposed to the early, pioneering work of the popular movements.

Axelson is not recommending here a form of Swedish isolationism; in fact, his defence of the popular movements and their future role is located within an explicitly global vision of international co-operation. However, it is clear that his aspirations for global influence contrast sharply with those presented by the Word of Life. For him, the traditional movements have the potential to encourage pluralistic impulses, and are also rooted in models of solidarity through local action that he regards as constituting a vital part of Swedish civic culture. His juxtaposition of social models is echoed by Nilsson (1988:379) in the latter's report on para-church impulses in Sweden:

The para-church movements are to some degree lay movements, but often entirely lack the character of a popular movement. They are as a rule more professionalised and more dependent on technology than the congregations . . . The Swedish Mission Covenant should work on a strategy to strengthen its character both as a lay movement and as a democratic popular movement.

---

[16] Axelson also contributed to a project in the late 1970s that was critical of a visit by Billy Graham to Gothenburg (Coleman 1989).

If Axelson and Nilsson's views express a highly critical view of the Word of Life from a standpoint that purports to defend the original spirit of the Swedish popular movements, their sharp profile in the debate contrasts significantly to that expressed by representatives of another popular movement in Sweden: Pentecostalists. The boundaries between the Swedish Mission Covenant and the Word of Life have been drawn fairly clearly in public discourse; however, the relationship between traditional Pentecostalism and the new charismatic Movement has been difficult to establish. The national Pentecostalist newspaper, *Dagen*, has been much more wary of condemning the Faith Movement than other parts of the secular or indeed religious media.[17] In an interview conducted in 1987, the chief pastor of the local Pentecostal church in Uppsala told me he had spent the past three or four years being besieged by phone calls from members of his church as well as other believers, asking for his position on the Word of Life. He himself had decided not to condemn the group: he had not joined in the Mission Covenant's 'discussion day' on the Word of Life, and although in his sermons he had referred to certain salient issues such as 'spiritual leadership' and healing, direct reference to Faith churches was avoided.

In fact, the pastor had not been able to avoid one event that involved a significant marking of boundaries in his church. After much discussion, he and the elders decided that they had to respond to the disquiet and questioning evident among many congregation members. In October 1986, after a Sunday-morning service, the pastor read a statement from the elders. Clearly moved, and in a voice of considerable solemnity, he stated that they had come to the decision that those who wished to remain involved with the new group should leave the Pentecostal church. He explained that it was not a matter of persecuting individuals, but of protecting a certain view of the Bible. Then, one of the elders came to the podium and announced that he could not endorse this negative response to the new revival. Using a phrase that certainly would not have been appropriate in a Faith context, he begged the congregation to forgive him for his 'weakness' in the matter.

---

[17] See Coleman (1989) for an extended analysis of media coverage of the Word of Life.

As we have seen, the poignancy of the situation for Pentecostalists lies in the fact that many of them see in the Word of Life a mirror of their own ideals and past history, albeit one that appears at times to be distorted and exaggerated.[18] The older Movement grew out of Anglo-American holiness origins, and in Sweden was effectively formed after a dispute among Baptists over an interpretation of who qualified to take communion in church. Although Pentecostalism is now a largely respected member of the body of Swedish free churches, it was widely criticised in its early years, with its putative effects on the 'weak nerves' of supposedly susceptible victims functioning as the rhetorical equivalent of the brainwashing metaphor commonly applied, some seventy years later, to Faith churches (Coleman 1989:272). Many Pentecostalists react negatively to what they see as the overpositive, materialistically oriented message of the new revival, yet they see in it signs of the 'life' that often appears to be lacking in a revival that is now showing signs of its age. Thus Bror Spetz, the pastor of a Pentecostal church in Stockholm that a few years later was effectively to be ejected from the older Movement, defended his support of Faith ideals to fellow pastors in a speech that was reported in *Dagen*. He compared the current situation to that evident when the great leader of Swedish Pentecostalism, Lewi Pethrus, was removed from fellowship with Baptists early in the century. If Pentecostalism had now become an organised institution, true revival was 'something indefinable, it's a force, it's life in indeterminate form'.[19] Spetz's implicit message was one that Pentecostalists could not themselves dispute: God's power cannot be confined to limiting human institutions, no matter how venerable or rich in historical significance. By opposing Faith activities, Pentecostalists might be denying the revivalist message at the very heart of their own Movement.

---

[18] Besides fieldwork in the Pentecostal church in Uppsala, in 1987 I conducted thirteen interviews with members of its congregation. Ages of interviewees ranged from 15 to early 80s.

[19] In *Dagen*, 23 December 1986. The four pastors of Södermalm congregation had the right to hold weddings withdrawn from them in 1988. According to the Pentecostal Yearbook of 1989, the reason was that they 'in word and deed did not demonstrate that they were willing to consider themselves as united with the Pentecostal Movement's other congregations' (in Skog 1993:90).

RESPONSES AND REDEFINITIONS

On occasion, Word of Life responses to criticism have appeared defensive and sectarian. Soon after the opening of its Bible School in the early 1980s, non-students were banned from attending classes, although monthly conferences remained open to anybody interested. Literature given to students at the time told them to expect attacks from 'the Devil'; when going out to missionise they were instructed not to engage in discussion if they were criticised by members of the public. Even in more recent years, some adherents have chosen not to reveal their identity to 'secular' others, particularly when seeking work in Uppsala.

Ekman has often spoken and written of the need for believers to understand the origins and motivation of criticism. In sermons, he has suggested that people should not become nervous by reading newspapers but instead should 'listen to Jesus' and be 'fanatics in faith'. He has also attempted rhetorically to interpret negative comments in accordance with the tenets of positive confession: 'We believers have different standards from the world. Where the world criticises and judges, we set free. Where the world nags and complains, we speak well and build up.'[20] This depiction of stark contrasts between opposing sides was certainly echoed by one member of Christian Student Front after a public meeting that had involved Ekman speaking to a large audience of sometimes hostile people. When I asked the student how he thought the meeting had gone, he replied with one word: 'War!'

Responses to criticism expressed in binary terms of good versus evil are usually intended for internal consumption and are delivered either in private conversation or in sermons and 'in-house' literature. When addressing critics in public arenas, Faith leaders tend to display a more obviously civic self, locating Faith principles and practices in the context of ideals of good citizenship. Ekman and other leaders have often referred in press articles to members' respect for democracy, sense of duty, support for the family and responsible attitude to the work-place. One way to interpret such behaviour is obviously to see it as involving the presentation of an

[20] *Word of Life Newsletter*, 1986 7:3.

unthreatening image to outsiders. As Wallis (1976) has remarked in relation to Scientology, religious adherents may often choose not to expose unconventional beliefs in conventional domains. It is also the case, however, that Faith discourse as a whole is concerned to present evangelical action as supportive of the nation and its institutions. While critical commentators characterise the Movement as profoundly 'foreign', Faith leaders promote (both internally and externally) a counter-discourse of spiritualised patriotism whereby conservative Protestant values are presented as essentially Swedish, as opposed to either secularised churches or repressive political forces. Sunday-morning services include prayers for the government. Sermons and literature frequently stress that Sweden has a divine vocation, and such claims appear to involve a conscious 're-territorialisation' of the group's activities. At the end of Ekman's *God, the State and the Individual* (1988:95–6) he includes a prayer for the country called 'God Bless Sweden!' It contains the words:

We proclaim freedom for Sweden and for God's plans and thoughts for our country. We demand that God's angels protect the borders of the country and protect what God wishes to carry out in the country. We lay claim to purification in the blood of Jesus for Sweden, to forgiveness, purity, protection and freedom for the whole nation.

We see here, as in other statements made by Ekman (such as a taped lecture series entitled *Faith for the Nation*), the implication that Sweden, a country with divinely appointed borders, must be prepared to facilitate the carrying out of God's specific intentions for the country. *God, the State and the Individual* goes further in asserting that moral and political revival can only be achieved by protecting such God-given 'building-blocks' of the nation as the law-abiding individual citizen, the nuclear family and the congregation. In formal and informal contexts, other Faith adherents also stress their patriotism and support for the Swedish nation, even if they cannot approve of the fact that it is ruled by a secular state (and, moreover, one that has been prepared to join the 'super-state' represented by the European Union).[21] Faith Christians are also

---

[21] One member of the congregation, a lawyer, talks of the need for Christians to 'sit in parliament in the name of Jesus', and at least some members have expressed an interest in becoming involved in KDS, a small Christian Democratic party.

engaging in ritualised demonstrations in order to gain a national voice, such as a yearly anti-abortion rally in Stockholm entitled 'Yes to Life', in which abortion is explicitly associated with the nation's spiritual, moral and cultural decline. A form of 'dominion theology' (Percy 1998:188) is being constructed, which emphasises the need to exercise influence on national government.

In stressing the need to guide Sweden so that the country can fulfil its divine calling, Faith adherents appropriate a form of civil religious imagery inherited from North American colleagues (Peck 1993:12; Brouwer et al. 1996:15) and also deployed in other Faith contexts (Gifford 1998; see chapter 1). As with the US, Sweden is described as a country with a manifest destiny, especially blessed by God, which can be realised through evangelical action. However, an irony of deploying such imagery in the Swedish context as opposed to the American is that it has few resonances with wider political and cultural discourse. Brandell et al. (1986:7) note that the historical and social–structural conditions for the development of strong civil religious sentiments (revolution, struggle for independence, widespread religious discourse) have not hitherto existed in the modern Swedish state (see also Therborn 1988:34). Even the death of Palme did not prompt sustained attempts to 'spiritualise' his significance in relation to national identity. In such a context, the combining of political and religious imagery not only appears anomalous, it comes close to appearing to advocate an irrational form of nationalism. Indeed, one of Ekman's most notorious sermons according to the press's standards of assessment was preached in the mid-1980s, just before a general election, when he stated: 'True nationalism . . . is . . . gratefulness to God for the country and the borders He's given us. It's willingness to take responsibility for the country, to look after it, to defend it from everything that aims at breaking it down and destroying it.'[22] Ekman's sentiments could be interpreted as combining an attack on the prevailing Social Democratic government with an assumption that nationalism was divinely instituted.

It might seem as though these attitudes imply a desire for a fixing and delimiting of identity and influence. Yet Faith ideology in

---

[22] Quoted in *Word of Life Newsletter*, 1985 August:1. (No issue number given.)

general, including that propounded in Sweden, talks not only of single nations, but also of the existence of a world-wide division of labour between divinely appointed nation-states. The image invoked is that of a kind of spiritual totemism, whereby each country has the God-given vocation to seek both internal revival and external spiritual influence. As Ekman puts it (1988:7): 'Like every nation Sweden has a calling. That calling is to return to God and become His means to spread His glory over the whole world.' Or, even more forcefully (ibid.):

> God's grace is, thank goodness, greater than all of Sweden's sins and transgressions, and I am convinced that God has the ability to change the spiritual atmosphere in the country and move Sweden to the position he wants it to have – to be a beacon for God's power and life, whose beams reach out over the whole world. It is not surprising that there is so much spiritual strife over this country. Does that mean Sweden is more special than other countries? No. But it is important for us to take our place in God's global plan, so that we do what we should to hasten the Lord's return: preach the Gospel of Jesus, confirmed by signs and wonders the whole world over.

Contact between territorial communities is given a specific meaning and also located within a linear, eschatological concept of time, since it is argued that efficient and effective evangelism will lead all the more quickly to Jesus' return. National identity is thus simultaneously recognised and, in a sense, flattened, as *all* countries are seen as 'New Israels' (Hadden 1989:230), having essentially the same spiritual mission to perform and being threatened by the same prospect that moral decline brings with it economic and political failure. At times, explicit parallels between the spiritual needs of different countries are made in order to reinforce such comparisons. Thus, an advertisement for a book called *The Christians' Fight for America's Future*, written by one of the group's members, reads: 'This unique and highly interesting book deals with the USA, but it could equally well have dealt with Sweden.' In the late 1980s, a Word of Life missionary wrote a personal letter to group members who would accompany him on an evangelisa-tion tour of Finland, and echoed the words of a song commonly sung at the group: 'All of Finland's people will see God's glory!'

The recipients of the letter would have recognised the words immediately and have been aware that they would usually have referred to Sweden rather than Finland. More recently, a newsletter from 1995 talks of how Ekman and a Swedish colleague marched around Red Square in 1990, 'binding the spirits' over the city, just after God had told Ekman to concentrate efforts on Russia.[23] The article stresses: 'The vision in Moscow is the same as in Uppsala', emphasising the need to 'Equip God's people with the word of faith, show them their spiritual weapons, and teach them to use them in victorious battle for the Lord'. The leader for the Word of Life's work in Moscow adds: 'There is a strong sense of solidarity in the Bible School with what is happening in Uppsala. It feels like we have one Bible School in two different areas.' The importance of nationhood as a paradoxically homogenised badge of personal and collective identity is nowhere more evident than at Word of Life conferences. Much of the power of these occasions is said to derive from the fact that so many countries are represented by delegates under one roof (along with their national flags) thus indicating the diffusion as well as influence of charismatic communities.

In their articulation of a sense of global consciousness, these christians therefore retain the idea of the nation-state as a conveniently bounded moral community but do not allow this to affect their promotion of global activities – after all, every member of the world-wide Faith network shares essentially the same Spirit and access to objective charismatic knowledge. Thus, while Smart (1991) has implied that, in a globalising world, those who hark back to quasi-civil religions will run the danger of celebrating something essentially obsolete, the experience of the Word of Life suggests that the image of the nation-state can retain some importance within a wider system of transnational practices. Besides Sweden, two nation-states in particular have significance in the sacralised landscape of Word of Life Christians: the United States is not only the source of many powerful ministries, it is also a country that does not appear to be oppressed by overcentralised government

---

[23] *Word of Life Newsletter* (English version) 1995 3:3.

(Ekman 1989). In addition, of course, Israel is a sacred territory that plays a central role in eschatological thinking. Here, for instance, is Ekman's geo-political characterisation of the connection between revival activity and the Last Days, taken from a conference at the Word of Life to which the South African preacher Ray McCauley had been invited to speak (quoted in Gustafsson 1987:56):

The Lord's glory will come from the north, south, east and west. North is here. The Lord's glory will come from the north. It will run down like syrup into Europe. South is South Africa. We have representatives from the revival that is happening there . . . Preachers from the West . . . have come here from the USA. East – you know what's happening in Korea. The Scriptures say the Lord's glory will come from the east, west, south and north and flood together in the middle, in Jerusalem. Then Jesus will return.

These words are of particular significance because they provide the current configuration of Faith ministries with a role in fulfilling the divine plan for the world. Biblical truth is not only being echoed and dramatised, it is actually being effected by global evangelical activity. The conference itself is a physical enactment of the coming together of nations, just as Faith activity frequently involves making its adherents view, and even visit, other nations within a framework of evangelical action and imagination. Missionary visits abroad, 'pilgrimage' tours of Israel or the US in the company of famous Faith preachers, even the sponsoring of Russian Jews to 'go back' to Israel – all provide physical mobility with spiritual significance. In addition, as we have seen, the electronic media can help enrich a translocal charismatic imaginary. Perhaps appropriately, Ekman's words quoted above were followed by a plea to his audience to 'sow into' Lester Sumrall's television work as a further means of filling the world with God's glory.

A MICROCOSM OF GLOBALISATION?

Faith beliefs and practices form a powerful package that presents charismatic Christianity as a paradigm for anti-institutionalisation on personal, religious and political levels in contemporary Sweden.

Although the Word of Life is not supported by a powerful evangelical lobby or a coalition of right-wing political activists, as it might be in the US, its message acquires a strong profile from its clear opposition to the established religio-political framework in the country. The notions of empowering the self, as well as exercising personal responsibility for one's physical and financial state, can easily be read as foreign-derived criticisms of paternalist forms of Social Democracy that have been dominant in the country over the past sixty years.

Hannerz has written (1996:153–4) of the process of Americanisation as involving not so much a direct importation of American values as the provision of a cultural resource to be adapted for local purposes. In the case of the Faith Movement, clearly some direct importation is going on, but impulses from the US are also manipulated in more ambiguous ways. In one sense, North American evangelicalism provides a model for action, yet it cannot be allowed to supplant the notion of a divinely sanctioned role for Sweden in the world order. These Swedish charismatics can admire developments in the US but hold up their own achievements as equally valid in terms of a global divine plan. It is as though they have adopted Olof Rudbeck's triumphalist vision of the centrality of Sweden (mentioned in chapter 3) but given it a charismatic Protestant twist. The Holy Spirit, rather than Swedish civilisation, is being diffused across the globe, while the Christians of *every* nation should aspire to make their own country a source of world-wide influence.

It is perhaps not surprising that the radicalism of the group appeals particularly to younger believers on personal and political levels. The globalising charismatic habitus incorporates the imagery and practices of youth – physical movement, deployment of contemporary musical forms, technology – and locates them within a context of protest against an established religio-political order. However, Faith ideology is more likely to convince the uncommitted or downright hostile of the justifications for their scepticism than it is to convert them to the Faith. This new form of revivalist Christianity has become a widespread trope for an irrational assault on the autonomous and self-controlled individual, and moreover one that is un-rooted in local institutional structures. The group ironically plays into the hands of its critics by promulgating hypodermic models of the influence of language and media that reinforce opponents' representations of the dangers of brainwashing by powerful preachers.

Certain images of North America have come to exemplify and give direction to the threat apparently posed by the group. The US, after all, is not only the source of much cultural influence in the country anyway, it is also an immensely powerful actor on the global stage. Faith adherents appear to swallow a sanctified version of the American Dream even as they adopt 'showy' and 'unSwedish' forms of body language. Certainly, the transatlantic credentials of the group cannot be denied. Yet there is a sense in which the Word of Life merely exemplifies 'disruptive' influences which cannot be associated with any single nation-state, no matter how powerful. In the 1980s and 1990s, Sweden has undergone some considerable transformations: the political situation has become more volatile, with the Social Democrats no longer being the automatic governing party; immigration from within and beyond Europe has promoted cultural diversity; the media have become increasingly plural and international in orientation; and, of course, the country has recently decided that its future lies in membership of the European Union rather than in splendid and prosperous isolation. While apparently constituting a somewhat 'extreme' movement in both religious and political senses, Faith Christianity manages to touch many of the frayed cultural nerves that exist in contemporary Sweden. It may not point the way forward for mainstream political and religious impulses in the country, but, in raising such issues as the role of government in an economic climate dominated by transnational corporations, the relationship between the nation and the rest of the world, even the place of material consumption in defining identity, it has located itself (temporarily) at the centre of current debate over the future of society.

The Word of Life embodies the power of global processes as much as it does North American imperialism, and here it is appropriate to recall another image of Sweden presented at the beginning of chapter 3: that of the death of Olof Palme. The last fifteen years have seen Swedes attempting to understand Palme's death by searching for his murderer as well the specific reasons for his brutal assassination. So far, no definitive answers have been found, and the event remains both inexplicable and resonant of unpredictable danger. The emergence of the Word of Life has also been seen as deeply threatening, but in this case the culprit appears to be easily identifiable as North American evangelical Protestantism. There is some truth in such a claim. But the presence and activities of the group also illustrate the power of global forces that are far more difficult to identify and control: the constant movement of people, images and capital; the reflexive and mutual awareness of others that is a constitutive part of global 'orientation', whether evangelical or secular; the sense that any national territory is only a small part of an infinitely wider whole. Of course, many in Sweden see globalisation in positive terms, as providing new opportunities for human contacts and influences. Charismatics may, however, embody the 'wrong' kind of transnationalism as far as most people are concerned. The death of Palme and the rise of the Word of Life both point to an uncomfortable thought: that national agency, consensus and (benign) surveillance are unsustainable in a new world disorder.

There is, of course, a further dimension to the controversy roused by the group. Faith Christianity has now been a visible force in Sweden for almost two decades. Even during the 1990s, the group has roused its fair share of controversy, and in 1998 it was termed one of the most dangerous 'sects' in the country.[24] Supporters' revivalist spirit and universalising imagination can partially be sustained through the creation of constant flows of enthusiasm at conferences and the perpetual influx of people to the Word of Life Bible School and University. None the less, adherents are themselves becoming more established within the Swedish religious and cultural landscape. Skog (1993:100–2) estimates that the moral panic surrounding the group is losing some of its intensity. Ulf Ekman's book *The Jews: People of the Future*[25] has achieved the respectability of being put on sale at the Pentecostal bookshop in Uppsala. As Word of Life members age and gain more of a

---

[24] The Word of Life web pages now include descriptions of criticisms made of the group. The one quoted here is from *ICA-kuriren*, reproduced in a Word of Life news item of 21 October 1998.   [25] *Judarna, Framtidens Folk* (1992).

voice in mainstream contexts they must allow themselves to be labelled in terms of familiar Swedish categories: as comprising just one free church congregation among many. Of course, Swedish society and its institutions will continue to bear the marks of global influence and action; at the same time, Faith Christianity is likely to become relatively more assimilated to aspects of an ecumenical, even an explicitly 'localising', consciousness.

CHAPTER TEN

The Word and the world

Some years ago, at a college dinner, I found myself sitting next to a distinguished scientist. On hearing that I was an anthropologist, he asked: 'And what is your tribe?' In reply, I explained that I did not study a tribe. I pointed out that my research was based on a group of Protestant, charismatic Christians located in Sweden; that I studied their rituals, language and material culture. My companion listened carefully before commenting, in a polite if conclusive manner: 'So you *do* have a tribe.'

Of course, he had a point. Parts of this book have been based on the study of a specific social group – a Christian ministry located in Uppsala – with its own conventions of behaviour, cultural ideals and social boundaries. Affiliation to the Word of Life has, at first glance, the look of membership in a totalising and self-enclosed institution. Work, leisure and religious worship can all be carried out within the same set of buildings. God provides a 'plan' for each person's life, complete with 'spiritual career'.[1] On closer inspection, however, the lives of most adherents entail much more complex and precariously balanced negotiations between conflicting forms of identity and belonging. Involvement in the group is often regarded with scorn or suspicion by neighbours, colleagues and even family members. Many believers combine support of the Word of Life with attachments to more conventional congregations.[2] Most intriguingly, participation in the group

---

[1] In effect, the Faith term for a 'calling'.

[2] In their somewhat schizophrenic modes of attachment to religious groups (one might almost say modes of semi-detachment), these Christians perhaps provide a conservative Protestant variation of the 'de-traditionalisation' of religion (Heelas 1996). Consumer choice and authority are given some priority over long-term and taken-for-granted affiliation to a specific group.

involves a process of constantly reaching out beyond the self, articulating a globalising orientation not only in word and conscious thought, but also in action and experience.

It is the nature of this reaching out that has been at the heart of this book. I have tried to show that in certain respects it echoes many of the wider themes of globalisation that have been discussed in the burgeoning literature on the subject. In organisational terms, the Word of Life is akin to a transnational corporation in its development of connections between a 'head office' in Uppsala and satellite groups elsewhere. The ministry takes full advantage of the technologies of electronic communications, and trains adherents to be expert users of such media. Members of the group learn that 'the world' can refer not only to unsaved sinners, but also to the expanding realm of the Faith Movement, stretching across national borders and criss-crossed by the preaching tours of great men and women of Faith. Charismatics in Sweden and elsewhere are therefore constructing a form of awareness that echoes, but, in addition, lends a sub-cultural dimension to, the various levels mentioned in Robertson's (1992) formulation of global consciousness.[3] Robertson refers to the individual, national society, systematic connections between national societies and humankind as a whole. When describing the intimately connected arenas that frame action and self-understanding, charismatics are more likely to invoke the born-again believer, sacralised nationhood, the division of labour between countries and the totality of human souls in need of salvation.

Much work on globalisation refers to technological, organisational and cognitive matters, but not to issues of ritualisation and embodiment. I have tried to show that the actions of these charismatics prompt us to examine how a globalising habitus can emerge, comprising particular forms of language and physical engagement with the material environment. In my argument, 'habitus' and 'orientation' are virtually synonymous. However, I retain the metaphor of orientation because it adds to habitus a more explicit notion of adopting a stance *in relation to* others or to the external environment.[4] The Word is projected into the world

---

[3] Discussed in chapter 1.
[4] See my descriptions of habitus and orientation in chapters 2, 5 and 6.

through speech and writing, but also through less obviously discursive means. Experiencing the self as both a receptacle for and transmitter of generic power; perceiving congruences between an aesthetic of spiritual self-development and the constant growth inherent in divinely ordained language and money; constructing social action not only as 'dramatised' exemplification of biblical precedent, but also as a resource to be commodified, replicated and reconsumed in electronic media; all of these elements of evangelical practice contribute to globalising processes that can only be understood through an appreciation of the ritual forms and ideological assumptions of charismatic Christianity.

Faith Christianity in Sweden therefore displays a Janus-face to the forces of globalisation. Certain features of contemporary life, as it is experienced in many parts of the world, are wholeheartedly encouraged. These features include: extensive contact with people from other nations; an appreciation of the extent to which events in any given context can be influenced by developments occurring elsewhere; the increasing replacement of face-to-face contacts by mediated events; the incorporation of consumption practices into daily existence. As a result, Word of Life members travel physically, virtually or imaginatively to other parts of the globe, and do so as a daily, constitutive part of their spiritual lives. At the same time, Faith appropriation of global imagery is also a conversion of it to Christian ends. The orientation cultivated among believers is one that encourages the evangelical gaze to interpret translocal contacts in specific, self-limiting ways. European Union, involving the formation of an overarching framework of international action that constrains the powers of individual states, is seen as the work of Satan; but the global division of labour among divinely instituted and essentially equivalent nations is regarded as blessed, indeed a necessary part of global salvation.[5] In addition, Faith channels of reaching out involve doing so in a manner that restricts the possibility of encountering challenging responses from an unpredictable world. At conferences and workshops, believers meet fellow Christians from other nations who act in familiar ways, employing an evangelical etiquette and presentation of self learned from a common stock of Faith literature, widely dispersed

[5] Although the particular importance of the US and Israel is discussed in chapter 9.

images and travelling preachers. Missionising through electronic media allows the imaginative construction of an unbounded and endlessly responsive constituency of consumers. Ridicule from those who refuse to be evangelised, or criticism from representatives of religious, journalistic and medical authorities, can be interpreted as originating from a common source: a satanic figure who is the converse of God not only in his evil intent, but also because he represents the forces of stasis and lack of ambition. The world of Faith gives an impression of unlimited scope if viewed through charismatic eyes; from another perspective it represents an ideologically charged 'reality' that is constructed to reinforce sub-cultural assumptions while apparently extending believers' agency into new arenas of action and influence.[6] This book has therefore described the 'charismatisation' of the global as much as it has charted the globalisation of charisma.

In arguing that participation in the Word of Life involves engagement in globalising cultural forms, I am not suggesting that believers are necessarily attracted to the group with this explicit aim in mind. The factors underlying religious conviction and adherence are far more complex than any single cause can comprehend; furthermore, the reasons people have (consciously or unconsciously) for joining a group may differ from those that keep them within the religious community. I do suggest that the development of a globalising habitus is one of the keys to developing a rewarding – and rewarded – engagement with Faith activities. It is unlikely that many adherents would say that they had joined the group *in order to* gain access to global sociality and empowerment; they are more likely to say that the Holy Spirit gave them no choice, that they recognised aspects of themselves in Ulf Ekman, or that its members seemed so 'joyful' and 'full of life' compared to other Christians. However, they would probably agree that any evangelical group worthy of the name must cultivate a desire to

---

[6] Of course, more secular modes of engaging in globalising processes will also involve culturally determined appropriations of technology and even habitus. For instance, a study of how McDonald's constructs and diffuses its operations on a world-wide scale might even be able to discern the incipient creation of a globalising orientation among, say, students at Hamburger University (see e.g. Leidner 1993). Furthermore, as I have pointed out, Faith adherents may bring their own evangelical orientation to bear on their business lives, even when they are working within ostensibly secular contexts.

'take the world for God', using the bountiful resources provided by divine favour. Through participation in Faith activities most people are encouraged to locate their identity and agency within a wider yet more controllable frame of reference than before. Engagement with forces of globalisation becomes comprehensible within the motivational paradigms, spiritualised experiences and sacralised language of evangelicalism. The person ideally gains benefits from God, but can then become a divine tool in providing blessings for myriad others. A charismatic group based in Sweden, a country hardly known as a hot-bed of spiritual action, appears to take on world-wide significance, and its credentials are constantly confirmed by the presence of preachers, students and images from other parts of the globe.[7] These Christians worship a God who is both within the self and a permanently moving force on the earth as a whole. Self-transcendence through reaching out is expressive of the divine, unconfined part of the person. The godly and the global are, it seems, united in this charismatic habitus.

Of course, Faith groups in Sweden have not emerged *de novo* into a blank spiritual environment. Believers' styles of appropriating the rhetoric and rituals of nonconformist faith can partially be attributed to their attempts to take over the mantle of missionisation from more arthritic forms of evangelicalism. To 'globalise' revivalist forms in this way becomes, to some extent, the mere injection of enthusiasm and new ambition into already established practices. In effect, it becomes a quality of action that extends the aims of religious agency. I am not suggesting, however, that the specific features of Faith Christianity can *only* be explained in terms of protest against Christians whose worship appears moribund and static. In more positive terms, members of the Movement in Sweden and elsewhere emphasise and recast in contemporary light certain evangelical concerns regarding the restoration of well-being through the grace of God. An evangelical package is constructed that encourages believers not to retreat

---

[7] In discussing the place of locality in contexts of cultural flow, Appadurai (1996:178) notes that it is 'constituted by a series of links between the sense of social immediacy, the technologies of interactivity, and the relativity of contexts'. We see his point illustrated at the Word of Life.

from the world, but to appropriate its institutions and assets; not to deny national identity, but to give it new meaning in the context of a world system of sacralised societies;[8] not to avoid consumerism, but to incorporate it within expansive modes of religious attachment. In the eyes of sceptical outsiders, these Christians have made a fatal mistake: they have become both in the world *and* of it. To Faith Christians, however, the only way to reconstruct human society at a global level is to promote divine influence without concern for boundaries between the material, the social and the spiritual.

A GLOBAL LANDSCAPE OF FAITH?

I have provided an ethnographic account of globalisation by juxtaposing a detailed study of a single Christian ministry with a broader overview of the Movement to which it expresses allegiance. My approach illustrates how a translocal orientation is constructed at a particular point in the extensive network of Faith churches.[9] But I also imply that the moving, global landscape of Faith ministries is not made up of purely discrete landmarks. The boundaries between groups, despite their self-identification as independent units, are permanently breached by flows of people, consumer goods, resources and images. Part of my point is that we cannot view such flows as somehow 'additions' to essentially Swedish, or North American, or Nigerian, organisations. When Kenneth Copeland preaches in Uppsala, or Ulf Ekman in Texas, they are contributing to a culture that simply cannot be confined to societal or sectarian borders. The Word of Life has emerged in a national context that, notwithstanding the presence of a large Pentecostal Movement, does not appear to encourage extensive religious missionising. Undaunted, group members do not confine their ambitions or reference points to Sweden alone. Ideological and material resources are obtained from elsewhere in the world, as are many Bible School students and preachers. In a sense, the

---

[8] In this sense, the Word of Life actually contributes an evangelical perspective on the 'Swedification of Sweden' (see both chapter 3 and Ehn et al. 1993).

[9] An alternative approach would be to juxtapose several equivalent accounts of Faith ministries in the same volume.

presence of the Word of Life in an apparently 'anomalous' national context is a further indication of the power of globalising forces: without support from outside, the ministry simply would not survive in its current form.

Connections between ministries across the world are obviously reinforced by the marketing of videos, cassette tapes and books, which are exported widely and translated into local languages. American products have achieved leading positions within the internal evangelical economy, but they do not entirely monopolise the market. Mutual influences between widely dispersed Christians are also expressed in the diffusion of a broader religious aesthetic. Metaphors of growth, movement and sowing out are very common in Faith contexts. Numerous churches around the world are filled with smartly dressed adherents, clutching well-thumbed, heavily noted Bibles and eagerly drinking in the words of a preacher who circles the (often transparent) podium. The metaphor of the sword of the Spirit is incorporated into the logos of many ministries, rendering a biblical image into material form and converting it into a global trademark.[10]

As I have described in chapter 1, certain ideological themes tend to recur in world-wide expressions of Faith theology. Faith Christians often appropriate civil religious imagery in seeking local legitimacy, sometimes prompting heated debates over the boundaries between secular and religious authority. The spiritually empowered believer, frequently young, preaches freedom from financial constraint alongside the need to break the bounds of tradition, represented by such limiting factors as ethnic identity, political institutions or ossified revivalist movements.[11] Describing the impact of charismatic, prosperity-oriented Christians in Nigeria

[10] Referring to a very different ethnographic context, Carrithers (1996) has examined the creation of a pan-Indian sense of Jain ethnicity and community during the first two decades of the twentieth century. He notes how religious leaders created a palpable sense of a Jain public – a sense of mutual recognition and consciousness amongst disparate Jain interlocutors. Public meetings, publications, and rhetorics and rituals of inclusion enabled leaders to speak both to and for a translocal community of interaction. Carrithers characterises such a process as a form of 'concrete imagining', in which a community of kin became a community of civil society. The parallels and contrasts between Jain and evangelical 'concrete imagining' are explored in Carrithers and Coleman (n.d.).

[11] We see here an example of the combined destructive and creative sides of charisma, as understood by Weber (Eisenstadt 1968:xx).

and Ghana, Hackett (1998:258–9) refers to the way electronic media become tools of evangelical aspiration, operating at the intersection of public and private life and mediating differences between selves and others.[12] She talks (ibid.:269–71) of how media provide consumers with the impression that they are part of a global system of Christian unity, and asks whether the emphasis on distant sources of religious power makes such divine force appear more appealing and effective. She is providing an ethnographic account of Christians far removed from Uppsala: yet the issues she raises are as salient in Scandinavia as they are in West Africa. Faith churches reflect and reinforce current trends within neo-Pentecostal churches around the world, giving spiritual legitimation to practices of consumption and downplaying an older Protestant ethic associated more with work and production. As the imagery of the sword of the Spirit displaces that of suffering on the cross, so the valorisation of self-sacrifice through labour and self-abnegation has been challenged by an emphasis on entrepreneurship and risk-taking in order to discern God's actions in the world.[13]

It is nevertheless clear that Faith practices, ideologies and preaching styles encompass numerous parochial nuances and influences. In Sweden, the Word of Life's identity and self-presentation is partially constructed out of the need to highlight contrasts to well-established and ecumenically oriented free churches. Its members must negotiate a legitimate place within a politico-religious framework marked by a relative Social Democratic hegemony and an assumption of secularity in the public sphere. The globalising charismatic habitus is readily labelled fanatical and self-deluding in a cultural context where much more restrained uses of the body and presentations of the self are normative. The very meanings of money, youth culture, agency and prosperity clearly take on different resonances in different parts of the Faith network. Searching for health or wealth in Nigeria or Ghana is not quite the same as seeking a better life in Sweden or the US. A recurring theme in Swedish Faith discourse is the sense that spiritual and cultural

---

[12] Compare van der Veer (1996:2).
[13] In the context of Sweden, at least, the risk-taking occasioned by such means of self-assessment is rendered relatively safe given the existence of a still extensive welfare state, although it might have different implications elsewhere.

peripherality is being overcome by believers; in the US, such concerns over the place of the nation in the world are not salient in the same way. Some powerful political leaders in Africa and Latin America have expressed overt support for prosperity ideas; similar statements would be electoral suicide in Sweden and many other European countries.[14] We see how Word of Life Christians are constructing a global orientation that derives many of its impulses from a charismatic culture that is diffused around the world. However, specific circumstances have an effect on both expressions of Faith and the likely repercussions of adherence. The various members of the global Faith Movement may inhabit differently constituted worlds even as they interact with each other in ways that give the impression of mutual comprehensibility.

Thus the charismatic Christians who attend church in the 'sports hall' on the outskirts of Uppsala are neither isolated in a sectarian enclave nor participants in a fully universalised or homogeneous culture of Faith. Their lives are much more complex than that, involving constant interplays between representations of generic religious belonging, the articulation of national identity and the embodied appropriation of spiritual power whose origins are often traced to contexts far distant in both space and time. They may not succeed in their aim of convincing all other members of humanity that their particular version of global fellowship is the one to which everybody on this earth should subscribe. Other, more cosmopolitan manifestations of globalisation are on offer in Sweden and elsewhere. In a more modest way, however, they express cultural themes whose significance extends beyond any transnational religious ghetto.[15] Many social commentators have argued that we inhabit a world where social structures

---

[14] At the same time, as Gifford (1998:333) points out, Western concepts of nationalism are not necessarily replicated in many parts of Africa.

[15] Of course, to some extent Faith Christians express wider trends in religious practice. Babb (1995:3–4), for instance, notes that contemporary media technologies have greatly increased the mobility of religious symbols in South Asia, breaking down social as well as physical distance in a process of disembedding religious traditions. In the same volume, Little (1995:254) studies the Swadhyaya Movement and focusses on the use of videotaped discourses of its leader, Athavale. He argues that the technology 'allows what was previously impossible – namely, a global religious movement organised around participation in a sacred group experience that traditionally depends on the physical presence of a sacred figure'. Wilson (1999:5), meanwhile, refers to the need for religious movements to construct clienteles in the context of consumer-oriented societies.

are increasingly being challenged by mobile structures of communication; where the rationally arranged spaces of modernity are blurring into the shifting and mediated images of post-modernity; where the increasing 'disorganisation' of capitalism has involved the movement of subjects and objects whose flows cannot easily be synchronised with national boundaries.[16] The Word of Life and the Faith Movement as a whole illustrate just a few of the ways in which such developments can be acknowledged and sometimes even embraced. These Christians promote views that will probably seem remote from the assumptions of many readers of this book; yet they are addressing social and cultural transformations central to the world in which all of us live.

[16] Discussed in the Introduction and chapter 2. See also the discussion in Lash and Urry (1994:10).

References

Ahmed, A. and Donnan, H. (eds.) 1994, *Islam, Globalization and Postmodernity*, London: Routledge.

Albrow, M. 1990, 'Globalization, Knowledge and Society', in M. Albrow and E. King (eds.), *Globalization, Knowledge and Society*, London: Sage, pp. 3–13.

1996, *The Global Age: State and Society beyond Modernity*, Cambridge: Polity.

Alexander, B. 1994, *Televangelism Reconsidered: Ritual in the Search for Human Community*, Atlanta, Georgia: Scholars Press.

Ammerman, N. 1987, *Bible Believers: Fundamentalists in the Modern World*, New Brunswick: Rutgers University Press.

1991, 'North American Protestant Fundamentalism', in M. Marty and R. S. Appleby (eds.), *Fundamentalisms Observed*, University of Chicago Press, pp. 1–65.

Anderson, B. 1983, *Imagined Communities*, London: Verso.

Andström, B. 1966, *Lewi Pethrus*, Malmö: Bengt Forsbergs Förlag.

Ang, I. 1996, *Living Room Wars: Rethinking Media Audiences for a Postmodern World*, London: Routledge.

Appadurai, A. 1986, 'Introduction: Toward an Anthropology of Things', in A. Appadurai (ed.), *The Social Life of Things: Commodities in Cultural Perspective*, Cambridge University Press, pp. 3–63.

1996, *Modernity at Large: Cultural Dimensions of Globalization*, Minneapolis: University of Minnesota Press.

Arvidsson, B., Hartman, L., Hellström, J., Holte, R., Kieffer, R., Sundin, M., Nilsson, N.-H. and Stengård, E. 1993, *Bildligt: Om Gudstjänst och Bild*, Uppsala: Svenska Kyrkans Forskningsråd.

Asad, T. 1983, 'Notes on Body, Pain and Truth in Medieval Christian Rituals', *Economy and Society* 12:285–327.

Asp, S. (ed.) 1986, *Pingströrelsens Årsbok*, Stockholm: Förlaget Filadelfia.

Augé, M. 1995, *Non-Places: Introduction to an Anthropology of Supermodernity*, London: Verso.

Austin-Broos, D. 1997, *J'A'maica Genesis: Religion and the Politics of Moral Orders*, University of Chicago Press.

Axelson, S. 1987a, 'Den Nya Kristna Högern som Internationellt Fenomen', in A. Jeffner (ed.), *Religionen som Samhällsfaktor i ett Internationellt Perspektiv*, Stockholm: Regeringskansliets Offsetcentral.

1987b, *I Rörelse? En Problematisering i Stället för en Definition av Folkrörelse*, Stockholm: Institutet för Framtidsstudier.

1990, 'Varför USA för Missionsvetenskapliga Fältstudier och Hur? Till Studiet om the New Religious Political Right', in *Kristen Högervåg i Amerikansk Mission?* (Mission Report, Theology Department), Uppsala University, pp. 9–34.

Babb, L. 1995, 'Introduction', in L. Babb and S. Wadley (eds.), *Media and the Transformation of Religion in South Asia*, Philadelphia: University of Pennsylvania Press.

Barker, E. 1984, *The Making of a Moonie: Choice or Brainwashing?*, Oxford: Blackwell.

1989, *New Religious Movements: A Practical Introduction*, London: Her Majesty's Stationery Office.

Barron, B. 1987, *The Health and Wealth Gospel*, Downers Grove, Illinois: InterVarsity Press.

Baudrillard, J. 1981, *For a Critique of the Economy of the Sign*, St Louis: Telos.

Bauman, Z. 1998, *Globalization: The Human Consequences*, Cambridge: Polity.

Becker, A. 1995, *Body, Self, and Society: The View from Fiji*, Philadelphia: University of Pennsylvania Press.

Beckford, J. 1985, *Cult Controversies: The Societal Response to the New Religious Movements*, London: Tavistock.

Beckwith, S. 1993, *Christ's Body: Identity, Culture and Society in Late Medieval Writings*, London: Routledge.

Bell, D. 1978, *The Cultural Contradictions of Capitalism*, New York: Basic.

Benjamin, W. 1970, 'The Work of Art in the Age of Mechanical Reproduction', *Illuminations*, London: Cape, pp. 219–53.

Berger, J. 1972, *Ways of Seeing*, Harmondsworth: Penguin.

Berger, P. 1990, 'Foreword', in D. Martin (ed.), *Tongues of Fire*, Oxford: Blackwell, pp. vii–x.

Berger, P. and Luckmann, T. 1966, *The Social Construction of Reality: A Treatise in the Sociology of Knowledge*, Harmondsworth: Penguin.

Bergesen, A. 1990, 'Turning World-System Theory on its Head', in M. Featherstone (ed.), *Global Culture*, London: Sage, pp. 67–81.

Beyer, P. 1990, 'Privatization and the Public Influence of Religion in Global Society', in M. Featherstone (ed.), *Global Culture*, London: Sage, pp. 373–96.

1994, *Religion and Globalization*, London: Sage.

Biggart, N. 1989, *Charismatic Capitalism*, University of Chicago Press.

Bjuvsjö, S., Carlsson, G., Cedergren, S., Dahlén, R. and Hansson, A.-C.

1985, *Framgångsteologi I Sverige: Lundarapporten om den Nya Trosförkunnelsen*, Stockholm: EFS-Förlaget.

Bloch, M. and Parry, J. (eds.), 1989, *Money and the Morality of Exchange*, Cambridge University Press.

Bloch-Hoell, N. 1964, *The Pentecostal Movement*, London: Allen and Unwin.

Bourdieu, P. 1977, *Outline of a Theory of Practice*, Cambridge University Press.

Brandell, C., Bådagård, T., Härnvi, S., Morhed, S.-E., Olofsson, I., Sultán, M., Tigerschiöld, A. and Wahlqvist, K. 1986, *Kristen höger I Sverige?*, Stockholm: Religionssociologiska Institutet.

Brandon, A. 1987, *Health and Wealth*, Eastbourne: Kingsway.

Bromley, D. and Shupe, A. 1991, 'Rebottling the Elixir: The Gospel of Prosperity in American Religioeconomic Corporations', in T. Robbins and D. Anthony (eds.), *In Gods We Trust*, London: Transaction, pp. 233–54.

Brouwer, S., Gifford, P. and Rose, S. 1996, *Exporting the American Gospel: Global Christian Fundamentalism*, London: Routledge.

Bruce, S. 1990a, *The Rise and Fall of the New Christian Right: Conservative Protestant Politics in America 1978–1988*, Oxford: Clarendon.

1990b, *Pray TV: Televangelism in America*, London: Routledge.

1998, 'The Charismatic Movement and the Secularization Thesis', *Religion* 28:223–32.

Busby, C. 1997, 'Permeable and Partible Persons: A Comparative Analysis of Gender and Body in South India and Melanesia', *Journal of the Royal Anthropological Institute* 3:261–78.

Butler, J. 1993, *Bodies that Matter: On the Discursive Limits of 'Sex'*, London: Routledge.

Campbell, C. 1987, *The Romantic Ethic and the Spirit of Modern Consumerism*, Oxford: Blackwell.

Caplan, L. 1995, 'Certain Knowledge: The Encounter of Global Fundamentalism and Local Christianity in Urban South India', in W. James (ed.), *The Pursuit of Certainty*, London: Routledge, pp. 92–111.

Capps, C. 1980, *Why Tragedy Happens to Christians*, Tulsa: Faith Library.

Carrier, J. 1995, *Gifts and Commodities: Exchange and Western Capitalism since 1700*, London: Routledge.

Carrithers, M. 1992, *Why Humans Have Cultures: Explaining Anthropology and Social Diversity*, Oxford University Press.

1996, 'Concretely Imagining the Southern Digambar Jain Community, 1899–1920', *Modern Asian Studies* 30:523–49.

Carrithers, M. and Coleman, S. n.d., 'Making a Public and Making History: Evangelical Witnessing and Video Use as Exploded Interaction', in preparation.

Carsten, J. and Hugh-Jones, S. (eds.) 1995, 'Introduction', in *About the House: Lévi-Strauss and Beyond*, Cambridge University Press, pp. 1–46.

Chaney, D. 1994, *The Cultural Turn: Scene-Setting Essays on Contemporary Cultural History*, London: Routledge.

Chesnut, R. 1997, *Born Again in Brazil: The Pentecostal Boom and the Pathogens of Poverty*, New Brunswick: Rutgers University Press.

Childs, M. 1936, *Sweden: The Middle Way*, New Haven: Yale University Press.

    1980, *Sweden – The Middle Way on Trial*, New Haven: Yale University Press.

Coleman, S. 1989, 'Controversy and the Social Order: Responses to a Religious Group in Sweden', Ph.D. thesis, University of Cambridge.

    1991, ' "Faith which Conquers the World": Swedish Fundamentalism and the Globalization of Culture', *Ethnos* 56:6–18.

    1993, 'Conservative Protestantism and the World Order: The Faith Movement in the United States and Sweden', *Sociology of Religion* 54:353–73.

    1995, 'America Loves Sweden: Prosperity Theology and the Cultures of Capitalism', in R. Roberts (ed.), *Religion and the Transformations of Capitalism*, London: Routledge, pp. 161–79.

    1996a, 'Words as Things: Language, Aesthetics and the Objectification of Protestant Evangelicalism', *Journal of Material Culture* 1:107–28.

    1996b, 'All-Consuming Faith: Language, Material Culture and World-Transformation among Protestant Evangelicals', *Etnofoor* 9:29–47.

    1998, 'Charismatic Christianity and the Dilemmas of Globalization', *Religion* 28:245–56.

    1999, 'God's Children: Physical and Spiritual Growth among Evangelical Christians', in S. Palmer and C. Hardman (eds.), *Children in New Religions*, New Brunswick: Rutgers University Press.

    (forthcoming), 'Materialising the Self: Words and Gifts in the Construction of Evangelical Identity', in F. Cannell and M. Green (eds.), *Words and Things in the Anthropology of Christianity*.

Coleman, S. and Elsner, J. 1995, *Pilgrimage: Past and Present in the World Religions*, Cambridge, Massachusetts: Harvard University Press.

Comaroff, J. 1985, *Body of Power, Spirit of Resistance: The Culture and History of a South African People*, University of Chicago Press.

Coney, J. 1995, ' "Belonging to a Global Religion": The Sociological Dimensions of International Elements in Sahaja Yoga', *Journal of Contemporary Religion* 101:109–20.

Connery, D. 1966, *The Scandinavians*, New York: Simon and Schuster.

Corten, A. 1997, 'The Growth of the Literature on Afro-American, Latin

American and African Pentecostalism', *Journal of Contemporary Religion* 12:311–34.

Cotton, I. 1995, *The Hallelujah Revolution: The Rise of the New Christians*, London: Little, Brown and Company.

Cox, H. 1984, *Religion in the Secular City*, New York: Simon and Schuster.

1995 *Fire from Heaven: The Rise of Pentecostal Spirituality and the Reshaping of Religion in the Twenty-First Century*, Reading, Massachusetts: Addison-Wesley.

Csordas, T. 1994a, *The Sacred Self: A Cultural Phenomenology of Charismatic Healing*, Berkeley: University of California Press.

1994b, 'Introduction: The Body as Representation and Being-in-the World', in T. Csordas (ed.), *Embodiment and Experience: The Existential Ground of Culture and Self*, Cambridge University Press, pp. 1–24.

1995, 'Oxymorons and Short-Circuits in the Re-Enchantment of the World: The Case of the Catholic Charismatic Renewal', *Etnofoor* 8:5–26.

1997, *Language, Charisma, and Creativity: The Ritual Life of a Religious Movement*, Berkeley: University of California Press.

Dahlgren, C. 1982, *Maranata: En Sociologisk Studie av en Sektrörelses Uppkomst och Utveckling*, Vänersborg: Plus Ultra.

Da Silva, A. 1985, *Framgångsteologin: Svärmeri eller Väckelse?*, Uppsala: Teologiska Institutionen.

Daun, Å. 1988, 'Svenskhet som Hinder i Kulturmötet', in Å. Daun and B. Ehn (eds.), *Blandsverige: Kulturskillnader och Kulturmöten*, Stockholm: Carlssons, pp. 322–47.

Daun, Å. and Ehn, B. 1988, 'Inledning', in Å. Daun and B. Ehn (eds.), *Blandsverige: Kulturskillnader och Kulturmöten*, Stockholm: Carlssons, pp. 9–16.

Davie, G. 1994, *Religion in Britain since 1945: Believing without Belonging*, Oxford: Blackwell.

Dewhurst, C., MacDowell, B. and MacDowell, M. 1983, *Religious Folk Art in America: Reflections of Faith*, New York: E. P. Dutton.

Douglas, M. 1970, *Natural Symbols: Explorations in Cosmology*, London: Barrie and Rockliff.

Driessen, H. 1992, 'Celebrations at Daybreak in Southern Spain', in J. Boissevain (ed.), *Revitalizing European Rituals*, London: Routledge, pp. 80–94.

Durkheim E. 1915 *The Elementary Forms of the Religious Life: A Study in Religious Sociology*, trans. J. Swain, London: Allen and Unwin.

Eddy, M. B. 1875, *Science and Health with Key to the Scriptures*, Boston, Massachusetts: Christian Science Publishing Society.

Ehn, B. 1993, 'Nationell inlevelse', in B. Ehn, J. Frykman and O. Löfgren,

Försvenskningen av Sverige. Det Nationellas Förändringar, Stockholm: Natur och Kultur, pp. 203–65.

Ehn, B., Frykman, J. and Löfgren, O. 1993, *Försvenskningen av Sverige. Det Nationellas Förvandlingar*, Stockholm: Natur och Kultur.

Eire, C. 1986, *War against the Idols: The Reformation of Worship from Erasmus to Calvin*, Cambridge University Press.

Eisenstadt, S. 1968, *Max Weber: On Charisma and Institution Building*, University of Chicago Press.

Ejerfeldt, L. 1986, 'Svensk Civilreligion', in *Religiösa Reaktioner på Olof Palmes Död*, Stockholm: Religionssociologiska, pp. 13–18.

Ekman, U. 1988, *Gud, Staten och Individen*, Uppsala: Livets Ord.

1989, *Financial Freedom*, Uppsala: Word of Life.

1992, *Judarna, Framtidens Folk*, Uppsala: Livets Ord.

Eldebo, R. 1985, 'Svenska Missionsförbundet', in A. Hofgren (ed.), *Svenska Trossamfund*, Stockholm: EFS-Förlaget, pp. 58–64.

Elisha, O. 1998, 'Sacred Attentiveness: Charismatic Christians and the Indeterminacy of Spiritual Gifts', unpublished paper, Department of Anthropology, New York University.

Ellis, J. 1982, *Visible Fictions. Cinema: Television: Video*, London: Routledge.

Engel, L. 1989, *Livets Ordare*, Stockholm: Religionssociologiska Institutet.

Ewen, S. 1988, *All Consuming Images: The Politics of Style in Contemporary Culture*, New York: Basic.

Farah, C. 1978, *From the Pinnacle of the Temple*, Plainfield, New Jersey: Logos.

Featherstone, M. 1990, 'Global Culture: An Introduction' in M. Featherstone (ed.), *Global Culture: Nationalism, Globalization and Modernity*, London: Sage, pp. 1–14.

Fenn, R. 1982, *Liturgies and Trials: The Secularization of Religious Language*, Oxford: Blackwell.

Fernandez, J. 1986, *Persuasions and Performances: The Play of Tropes in Culture*, Bloomington: Indiana University Press.

Flake, C. 1984, *Redemptorama: Culture, Politics, and the New Evangelicalism*, Garden City, New York: Anchor Press Doubleday.

Forrest, J. 1988, *Lord, I'm Coming Home: Everyday Aesthetics in Tidewater, North Carolina*, Ithaca: Cornell University Press.

Forstorp, P.-A. 1990, 'Receiving and Responding: Ways of Taking from the Bible', in G. Hansson (ed.), *Bible Reading in Sweden: Studies Related to the Translation of the New Testament 1981*, Stockholm: Almqvist and Wiksell, pp. 149–69.

1992, *Att Leva och Läsa Bibeln: Textpraktiker i Två Kristna Församlingar*, Linköping University Press.

Frankl, R. 1987, *Televangelism: The Marketing of Popular Religion*, Carbondale: Southern Illinois University Press.

Freedberg, D. 1989, *The Power of Images: Studies in the History and Theory of Response*, Chicago University Press.

Freston, P. 1994, 'Popular Protestants in Brazilian Politics: A Novel Turn in Sect–State Relations', *Social Compass* 41:537–70.

1996, 'The Protestant Eruption into Modern Brazilian Politics', *Journal of Contemporary Religion* 11:147–68.

Freund, J. 1969, *The Sociology of Max Weber*, New York: Vintage.

Friedman, J. 1994, *Cultural Identity and Global Process*, London: Sage.

Frykman, J. 1993, 'Nationella Ord och Handlingar', in B. Ehn, J. Frykman and O. Löfgren, *Försvenskningen av Sverige. Det Nationellas Förvandlingar*, Stockholm: Natur och Kultur, pp. 119–201.

Gaunt, D. and Löfgren, O. 1984, *Myter om Svensken* Stockholm: Liber.

Geary, P. 1986, 'Sacred Commodities: The Circulation of Medieval Relics', in A. Appadurai (ed.), *The Social Life of Things: Commodities in Cultural Perspective*, Cambridge University Press, pp. 169–91.

Gell, A. 1988, 'Technology and Magic', *Anthropology Today* 4:6–9.

1992, 'The Technology of Enchantment and the Enchantment of Technology', in J. Coote and A. Shelton (eds.), *Anthropology, Art and Aesthetics*, Oxford: Clarendon, pp. 40–63.

1998, *Art and Agency: An Anthropological Theory*, Oxford: Clarendon.

Giddens, A. 1990, *The Consequences of Modernity*, Cambridge: Polity.

1991, *Modernity and Self-Identity*, Cambridge: Polity.

Gifford, P. 1987, ' "Africa Shall Be Saved": An Appraisal of Reinhard Bonnke's Pan-African Crusade', *Journal of Religion in Africa* 17:63–92.

1988, *The Religious Right in Southern Africa*, Harare: University of Zimbabwe.

1993, *Christianity and Politics in Doe's Liberia*, Cambridge University Press.

1998, *African Christianity: Its Public Role*, London: Hurst.

Goethals, G. 1985, 'Religious Communication and Popular Piety', *Journal of Communication* 35:149–56.

Goody, J. 1977, *The Domestication of the Savage Mind*, Cambridge University Press.

1993, *The Culture of Flowers*, Cambridge University Press.

Graham, W. 1987, *Beyond the Written Word: Oral Aspects of Scripture in the History of Religions*, Cambridge University Press.

Gregory, C. 1982, *Gifts and Commodities*, London: Academic Press.

Gustafsson, G. 1988, 'Religiös Struktur och Vardaglig Religiositet', in U. Himmelstrand and G. Svensson (eds.), *Sverige: Vardag och Struktur*, Stockholm: Norstedts, pp. 461–88.

1991, *Tro Samfund och Samhälle: Sociologiska Perspektiv*, Örebro: Libris.

Gustafsson, O. 1987, 'Örnen har Landat – Utkast till ett Forskningsprojekt', *Svensk Missionstidskrift* 3:45–59.

Hackett, R. 1995, 'The Gospel of Prosperity in West Africa', in R. Roberts (ed.), *Religion and the Transformations of Capitalism*, London: Routledge, pp. 199–214.

1998, 'Charismatic/Pentecostal Appropriation of Media Technologies in Nigeria and Ghana', *Journal of Religion in Africa* 28:258–77.

Hadden, J. 1989, 'Religious Broadcasting and the Mobilization of the New Christian Right', in J. Hadden and A. Shupe (eds.), *Secularization and Fundamentalism Reconsidered Vol. III*, New York: Paragon House, pp. 230–51.

1990, 'Precursors to the Globalization of American Televangelism', *Social Compass* 37:161–7.

Hadenius, S. and Lindgren, A. 1990, *On Sweden*, Stockholm: Swedish Institute.

Hagin, K. 1966, *Right and Wrong Thinking*, Tulsa: Faith Library.

1985, *How to Turn your Faith Loose*, Tulsa: Faith Library.

Hambre, C., Hammar, M., Hiding, L., Lindh, M., Moritz, I., Olsson, S., Rudman, C. and Strand, T. 1983, *Framgångsteologi – En Analys och Prövning*, Stockholm: EFS-Förlaget.

Hannerz, U. 1983, *Över gränser: Studier i Dagens Socialantropologi*, Lund: Liber.

1991, 'Scenarios for Peripheral Cultures', in A. King (ed.), *Culture, Globalization and the World-System*, New York: Macmillan, pp. 107–28.

1996, *Transnational Connections*, London: Routledge.

Harding, S. 1987, 'Convicted by the Holy Spirit: The Rhetoric of Fundamental Baptist Conversion', *American Ethnologist* 14:167–81.

Harré, R. 1989, 'Perfections and Imperfections of Form: Cults of the Body and their Aesthetic Underpinnings', *International Journal of Moral and Social Studies* 4:183–94.

Harris, H. 1998, *Fundamentalism and Evangelicals*, Oxford: Clarendon.

Harris, O. 1989, 'The Earth and the State: The Sources and Meanings of Money in Northern Potosí, Bolivia', in M. Bloch and J. Parry (eds.), *Money and the Morality of Exchange*, Cambridge University Press, pp. 232–68.

Harvey, D. 1989, *The Condition of Postmodernity*, Oxford: Blackwell.

Haste, H. (ed.) 1986, *Breven till Olof Palme: Korrespondens med Barn och Ungdom*, Oskarshamn: Pogo.

Haynes, J. (ed.) 1999, *Religion, Globalization and Political Culture in the Third World*, London: Macmillan.

Heelas, P. 1996, 'Introduction: Detraditionalization and its Rivals', in P. Heelas, S. Lash and P. Morris (eds.), *Detraditionalization*, Oxford: Blackwell, pp. 1–20.

1999, 'Prosperity and the New Age Movement: The Efficacy of Spiritual Economics', in B. Wilson and J. Cresswell (eds.), *New*

Religious Movements: Challenge and Response, London: Routledge, pp. 51–77.

Hellberg, C.-J. 1987, *Gud och Pengar: Om Framgångsteologi i USA och i Sverige*, Stockholm: Verbum.

Hexham, I. and Poewe, K. 1997, *New Religions as Global Cultures: Making the Human Sacred*, Boulder, Colorado: Westview.

Himmelstrand, U. 1988, 'Den Sociologiska Analysen av Sverige', in U. Himmelstrand and G. Svensson (eds.), *Sverige: Vardag och Struktur*, Stockholm: Norstedts, pp. 13–22.

Hollenweger, W. 1972, *The Pentecostals: The Charismatic Movement in the Churches*, Minneapolis: Augsburg.

1997, *Pentecostalism: Origins and Developments Worldwide*, Peabody, Massachusetts: Hendrickson.

Hollinger, D. 1991, 'Enjoying God Forever: An Historical/Sociological Profile of the Health and Wealth Gospel in the USA', in P. Gee and J. Fulton (eds.), *Religion and Power Decline and Growth: Sociological Analyses of Religion in Britain, Poland and the Americas*, London: British Sociological Association, Sociology of Religions Study Group, pp. 53–66.

Hoover, S. 1988, *Mass Media Religion: The Social Sources of the Mass Media Church*, Newbury Park, California: Sage.

1990, 'Ten Myths about Religious Broadcasting', in R. Abelman and S. Hoover (eds.), *Religious Television: Controversies and Conclusions*, Norwood, New Jersey: Ablex Publishing, pp. 23–40.

Horsfield, P. 1984, *Religious Television: The American Experience*, New York: Longman.

Horton, M. (ed.) 1990, *The Agony of Deceit*, Chicago: Moody Press.

Hultén, O. 1984, *Mass Media and State Support in Sweden*, Stockholm: Swedish Institute.

Hunt, D. and McMahon, T. 1985, *The Seduction of Christianity*, Eugene, Oregon: Harvest House.

Hunt, S. 1995, ' "The Toronto Blessing": A Rumour of Angels?', *Journal of Contemporary Religion* 10:257–71.

1998, 'Magical Moments: An Intellectualist Approach to the Neo-Pentecostal Faith Ministries', *Religion* 28:271–80.

Hunt, S., Hamilton, M. and Walter, T. (eds.) 1997, *Charismatic Christianity*, London: Macmillan.

Hunter, J. D. 1987, *Evangelicalism: The Coming Generation*, University of Chicago Press.

Huntford, R. 1971, *The New Totalitarians*, London: Allen Lane.

Jacobson-Widding, A. (ed.) 1991, *Body and Space: Symbolic Models of Unity and Division in African Cosmology and Experience*, Stockholm: Almqvist and Wiksell.

Jaffe, A. 1999, 'Packaged Sentiments: The Social Meanings of Greeting Cards', *Journal of Material Culture*, 4:115–41.

James, W. (ed.) 1995, *The Pursuit of Certainty: Religious and Cultural Formations*, London: Routledge.

Jenkins, R. 1992, *Pierre Bourdieu*, London: Routledge.

Johannesen, S. 1994, 'Third-Generation Pentecostal Language: Continuity and Change in Collective Perceptions', in K. Poewe (ed.), *Charismatic Christianity as a Global Culture*, Columbia: University of South Carolina Press, pp. 176–99.

Kälstad, T. 1986, 'Mordet på Olof Palme: Religionpsykologiska Synpunkter,' in *Religiösa Reaktioner på Olof Palmes Död*, Stockholm: Religionssociologiska Institutet, pp. 1–12.

Kapferer, B. 1995, 'From the Edge of Death: Sorcery and the Motion of Consciousness', in A. Cohen and N. Rapport (eds.), *Questions of Consciousness*, London: Routledge, pp. 134–52.

Keane, W. 1994, 'The Value of Words and the Meaning of Things in Eastern Indonesian Exchange', *Man* 29:605–29.

    1996, 'Money as Matter and Sign', *Etnofoor* 9:71–81.

    1997, *Signs of Recognition: Powers and Hazards of Representation in an Indonesian Society*, Berkeley: University of California Press.

    1998, 'Calvin in the Tropics: Objects and Subjects at the Religious Frontier', in P. Spyer (ed.), *Border Fetishisms: Material Objects in Unstable Spaces*, London: Routledge, pp. 13–34.

Kenyon, E. W. 1942, *The Two Kinds of Knowledge*, Seattle: Kenyon's Gospel Publishing Society.

    1970, *The Hidden Man: An Unveiling of the Subconscious Mind*, Seattle: Kenyon's Gospel Publishing Society.

Kiernan, J. 1988, 'The Other Side of the Coin: The Conversion of Money to Religious Purpose in Zulu Zionist Churches', *Man* 23:453–68.

Kilminster, R. 1997, 'Globalization as an Emergent Concept', in A. Scott (ed.), *The Limits of Globalization: Cases and Arguments*, London: Routledge, pp. 257–83.

Kramer, E. 1998a, 'Faith in the Material: Objects and Religious Subjects in a Brazilian Pentecostal Church', paper presented at the American Anthropological Association, Anthropology of Religion Section Conference, 2–5 April, Kansas City.

    1998b, 'The Ritual Value of Words and Money in Brazilian Neo-Pentecostalism', paper presented at the American Anthropological Association Conference, 2–6 December, Philadelphia.

Küchler, S. 1988, 'Malangan: Objects, Sacrifice and the Production of Memory', *American Ethnologist* 15:625–37.

References 251

Lareau, A. and Shultz, J. 1996, *Journeys through Ethnography: Realistic Accounts of Fieldwork*, Boulder, Colorado: Westview.

Lash, S. and Urry, J. 1987, *The End of Organized Capitalism*, Cambridge: Polity.

1994, *Economies of Signs and Space*, London: Sage.

Lears, T. 1983, 'From Salvation to Self-Realization: Advertising and the Therapeutic Roots of the Consumer Culture, 1880–1930', in R. Fox and T. Lears (eds.), *The Culture of Consumption: Critical Essays in American History, 1880–1980*, New York: Pantheon, pp. 1–38.

Lehmann, D. 1996, *Struggle for the Spirit: Religious Transformation and Popular Culture in Brazil and Latin America*, Cambridge: Polity.

Leidner, R. 1993, *Fast Food, Fast Talk: Service Work and the Routinization of Everyday Life*, Berkeley: University of California Press.

Lindberg, A. 1985, *Väckelse Frikyrklighet Pingströrelse: Väckelse och Frikyrka från 1800-talets Mitt till Nutid*, Ekerö: Pingstkolornas Skriftserie.

Linderman, A. 1996, *The Reception of Religious Television*, Uppsala: Acta Universitatis Upsaliensis.

Lindermeyer, O. 1995, ' "The Beast of the Revelation": American Fundamentalist Christianity and the European Union', *Etnofoor* 7:27–46.

Lindholm, H. and Brosché, F. 1986, *Varför Är Trosförkunnelsen Farlig?*, Uppsala: EFS-Förlaget.

Little, J. 1995, 'Video Vacana: Swahyaya and Sacred Tapes', in L. Babb and S. Wadley (eds.), *Media and the Transformation of Religion in South Asia*, Philadelphia: University of Pennsylvania Press.

Löfgren, O. 1987, 'Deconstructing Swedishness: Culture and Class in Modern Sweden', in A. Jackson (ed.), *Anthropology at Home*, London: Tavistock, pp. 74–93.

1993, 'Nationella Arenor', in B. Ehn, J. Frykman and O. Löfgren, *Försvenskningen av Sverige. Det Nationellas Förvandlingar*, Stockholm: Natur och Kultur, pp. 21–80.

1997, 'Scenes from a Troubled Marriage: Swedish Ethnology and Material Culture Studies', *Journal of Material Culture* 2:95–113.

Londos, E. 1985, 'Frikyrkohemmens Bilder', in A. Gustavsson (ed.), *Religiösa Väckelserörelser i Norden*, Lund: Centrum för Religiosetnologisk Forskning, pp. 217–22.

Luckmann, T. 1967, *The Invisible Religion*, New York: Macmillan.

Lukes, S. 1973, *Émile Durkheim: His Life and Work: A Historical and Critical Study*, Harmondsworth: Penguin.

Lyon, M. and Barbalet, J. 1994, 'Society's Body: Emotion and the "Somatization" of Social Theory', in T. Csordas (ed.), *Embodiment and Experience: The Existential Ground of Culture and Self*, Cambridge University Press.

Mansfield, A. and McGinn, B. 1993, 'Pumping Irony: The Muscular and the Feminine', in S. Scott and D. Morgan (eds.), *Body Matters: Essays on the Sociology of the Body*, London: Falmer, pp. 49–68.

McConnell, D. 1988, *A Different Gospel: A Historical and Biblical Analysis of the Modern Faith Movement*, Peabody, Massachusetts: Hendrickson.

McDannell, C. 1995, *Material Christianity: Religion and Popular Culture in America*, New Haven: Yale University Press.

McGuire, M. 1982, *Pentecostal Catholics: Power, Charisma, and Order in a Religious Movement*, Philadelphia: Temple University Press.

McGuire, M. with Kantor, D. 1988, *Ritual Healing in Suburban America*, New Brunswick: Rutgers University Press.

McLuhan, M. 1964, *Understanding Media*, London: Routledge.

Marcus, G. and Fischer, M. 1986, *Anthropology as Cultural Critique: An Experimental Moment in the Human Sciences*, University of Chicago Press.

Marriott, M. and Inden. R. 1977, 'Towards an Ethnosociology of South Asian Caste Systems', in K. David (ed.), *The New Wind: Changing Identities in South Asia*, The Hague: Mouton.

Marsden, G. 1982, 'Preachers of Paradox: The Religious New Right in Historical Perspective', in M. Douglas and S. Tipton (eds.), *Religion and America: Spirituality in a Secular Age*, Boston: Beacon, pp. 150–68.

1991, *Understanding Fundamentalism and Evangelicalism*, Grand Rapids, Michigan: William B. Eerdmans.

Marshall, R. 1991, 'Power in the Name of Jesus', *Review of African Political Economy* 52:21–37.

Martin, D. 1978, *A General Theory of Secularization*, Oxford: Blackwell.

Martin, D. (ed.) 1990, *Tongues of Fire: The Explosion of Protestantism in Latin America*, Oxford: Blackwell.

Marty, M. and Appleby, R. S. 1992, *The Glory and the Power: The Fundamentalist Challenge to the Modern World*, Boston: Beacon.

Marx, K. and Engels, F. 1964, *The German Ideology*, Moscow: Progress Publishers.

Mauss, M. 1979, 'Body Techniques', in *Sociology and Psychology*, London: Routledge, pp. 95–123.

1990, (1925) *The Gift: The Form and Reason for Exchange in Archaic Societies*, trans. W. D. Halls, London: Routledge.

Melton, J. G. 1999, 'Anti-cultists in the United States: An Historical Perspective', in B. Wilson and J. Cresswell (eds.), *New Religious Movements: Challenge and Response*, London: Routledge, pp. 213–33.

Meyer, B. 1997, 'Christian Mind and Worldly Matters: Religion and Materiality in Nineteenth-Century Gold Coast', *Journal of Material Culture* 2:311–37.

Meyer, D. 1966, *The Positive Thinkers: A Study of the American Quest for Health,*

Wealth and Personal Power from Mary Baker Eddy to Norman Vincent Peale, New York: Anchor.

Miller, D. 1987, *Material Culture and Mass Consumption*, Oxford: Blackwell.

Miller, D. E. 1997, *Reinventing American Protestantism: Christianity in the New Millennium*, Berkeley: University of California Press.

Milner, D. 1990, *Sweden: Social Democracy in Practice*, Oxford University Press.

Moore, R. L. 1994, *Selling God: American Religion in the Marketplace of Culture*, Oxford University Press.

Morley, D. and Robins, K. 1995, *Spaces of Identity: Global Media, Electronic Landscapes and Cultural Boundaries*, London: Routledge.

Mullins, M. 1994, 'The Empire Strikes Back: Korean Pentecostal Mission to Japan', in K. Poewe (ed.), *Charismatic Christianity as a Global Culture*, Columbia: University of South Carolina Press, pp. 87–102.

Neitz, M. 1987, *Charisma and Community: A Study of Religion in American Culture*, New Brunswick: Transaction.

Nilsson, F. 1988, *Parakyrkligt: Om Business och Bön i Sverige*, Stockholm: Verbum.

1990, 'Parakyrkligt i USA och Kristen Höger', in *Kristen Högervåg i Amerikansk Mission?* (Mission Report, Theology Department), Uppsala University, pp. 35–55.

Nilsson, S. 1988, *Ledd av Guds Hand*, Uppsala: Livets Ord.

O'Dell, T. 1993, ' "Chevrolet . . . That's a Real Raggarbil!": The American Car and the Production of Swedish Identities', *Journal of Folklore Research* 30:61–74.

Olsen, T. 1998, 'American Pentecost', *Christian History* 58:10–17.

Olwig, K. and Hastrup, K. (eds.) 1997, *Siting Culture: The Shifting Anthropological Object*, London: Routledge.

Ong, W. 1991, *Orality and Literacy: The Technologizing of the Word*, Routledge: London.

Parkin, D. 1992, 'Ritual as Spatial Direction and Bodily Division', in D. de Coppet (ed.), *Understanding Rituals*, London: Routledge, pp. 11–25.

1995, 'Blank Banners and Islamic Consciousness in Zanzibar', in A. Cohen and N. Rapport (eds.), *Questions of Consciousness*, London: Routledge, pp. 198–216.

Parry, J. 1986, '*The Gift*, the Indian Gift and the "Indian Gift"', *Man* 21:453–73.

Patterson, D. 1982, 'Word, Song, and Motion: Instruments of Celebration among Protestant Radicals in Early Nineteenth-Century America', in V. Turner (ed.), *Celebration: Studies in Festivity and Ritual*, Washington DC: Smithsonian, pp. 220–30.

Peacock, J. 1984, 'Religion and Life History: An Exploration in Cultural Psychology', in E. Bruner (ed.), *Text, Play, and Story: The Construction* and *Reconstruction of Self and Society*, Prospect Heights, Illinois: Waveland Press, pp. 94–116.

Peacock, J. and Tyson, R. 1989, *Pilgrims of Paradox: Calvinism and Experience among the Primitive Baptists of the Blue Ridge*, Washington DC: Smithsonian Institution Press.

Peale, N. V. 1952, *The Power of Positive Thinking*, Englewood Cliffs: Prentice-Hall.

Peck, J. 1993, *The Gods of Televangelism: The Crisis of Meaning and the Appeal of Religious Television*, New Jersey: Hampton Press.

Percy, M. 1996, *Words, Wonders and Power: Understanding Contemporary Christian Fundamentalism and Revivalism*, London: SPCK.

1998, *Power and the Church: Ecclesiology in an Age of Transition*, London: Cassell.

Poewe, K. (ed.) 1994, *Charismatic Christianity as a Global Culture*, Columbia: University of South Carolina Press.

Poloma, M. 1982, *The Charismatic Movement: Is there a New Pentecost?*, Boston: Twayne.

1997, 'The "Toronto Blessing": Charisma, Institutionalization, and Revival', *Journal for the Scientific Study of Religion* 36:257–71.

Randall, V. 1999, 'The Media and Religion in Third World Politics' in J. Haynes (ed.), *Religion, Globalization and Political Culture in the Third World*, London: Macmillan, pp. 45–68.

Reich, R. 1991, *The Work of Nations*, New York: Knopf.

Richardson, M. 1990, 'The Spatial Sense of the Sacred in Spanish America and the American South and its Tie with Performance', in R. Schechner and W. Appel (eds.), *By Means of Performance: Intercultural Studies of Theatre and Ritual*, Cambridge University Press.

Richter, P. 1997, 'The Toronto Blessing: Charismatic Evangelical Global Warming', in Hunt et al. (eds.), *Charismatic Christianity*, London: Macmillan, pp. 97–119.

Robbins, T. 1988, *Cults, Converts and Charisma: The Sociology of New Religious Movements*, London: Sage.

Roberts, O. 1955, *God's Formula for Success and Prosperity*, Tulsa, Oklahoma: Healing Waters.

Robertson, R. 1992, *Globalization: Social Theory and Global Culture*, London: Sage.

Robertson, R. and Chirico, J. 1985, 'Humanity, Globalization and Worldwide Religious Resurgence: A Theoretical Exploration', *Sociological Analysis* 46:219–42.

Robertson, R. and Lechner, F. 1985, 'Modernization, Globalization and the Problem of Culture in World-Systems Theory', *Theory, Culture and Society* 2:103–17.

Roelofs, G. 1994, 'Charismatic Christian Thought: Experience,

Metonymy, and Routinization', in Poewe (ed.), *Charismatic Christianity as a Global Culture*, Columbia: University of South Carolina Press, pp. 217–33.

Rosman, D. 1984, *Evangelicals and Culture*, London: Croom Helm.

Rudolph, S. 1997, 'Introduction: Religion, States, and Transnational Civil Society', in S. Rudolph and J. Piscatori (eds.), *Transnational Religion and Fading States*, Boulder, Colorado: Westview, pp. 1–24.

Rydén, E. 1985, ' "Väckelse Grep Omkring Sig i Min Ungdom": En Studie i Religiösa Väckelser I Småland', in Anders Gustavsson (ed.), *Religiösa Rörelser Förr och Nu: Religionsetnologiska Studier*, Lund: Studentlitteratur, pp. 9–37.

Sahlberg, C.-E., 1985, *Om Herren inte Bygger Huset: Dagen 40 År*, Stockholm: Normans Förlag.

Scase, R. 1977, *Social Democracy in Capitalist Society: Working Class Politics in Britain and Sweden*, London: Croom Helm.

Schaefer, N. 1999, ' "Some Will See Miracles": The Reception of Morris Cerullo World Evangelism in Britain', *Journal of Contemporary Religion* 14:111–26.

Schieffelin, E. 1996, 'On Failure and Performance: Throwing the Medium out of the Seance', in C. Laderman and M. Roseman (eds.), *The Performance of Healing*, London: Routledge, pp. 59–89.

Schultze, Q. 1990, 'Defining the Electronic Church', in R. Abelman and S. Hoover (eds.), *Religious Television: Controversies and Conclusions*, Norwood, New Jersey: Ablex Publishing, pp. 41–51.

1991, *Televangelism and American Culture: The Business of Popular Religion*, Grand Rapids, Michigan: Baker Book House.

1996, 'Evangelicals' Uneasy Alliance with the Media', in D. Stout and J. Buddenbaum (eds.), *Religion and Mass Media: Audiences and Adaptations*, London: Sage, pp. 61–73.

Scobbie, I. 1972, *Sweden*, London: Ernest Benn.

Scott, A. (ed.) 1997, *The Limits of Globalization: Cases and Arguments*, London: Routledge.

Scott T. 1999, 'Religion and International Society', in J. Haynes (ed.), *Religion, Globalization and Political Culture in the Third World*, London: Macmillan, pp. 28–44.

Shaverien, J. 1992, *The Revealing Image: Analytical Art Psychotherapy in Theory and Practice*, London: Routledge.

Shegog, E. 1990, 'Religious and Media Imperialism: A European Perspective', in R. Abelman and S. Hoover (eds.), *Religious Television: Controversies and Conclusions*, Norwood, New Jersey: Ablex Publishing, pp. 329–51.

Shibley, M. 1996, *Resurgent Evangelicalism in the United States: Mapping Cultural Change since 1970*, Columbia: University of South Carolina Press.

Shields, R. (ed.) 1996, *Cultures of Internet: Virtual Spaces, Real Histories, Living Bodies*, London: Sage.

Shilling, C. 1993, *The Body and Social Theory*, London: Sage.

Shupe, A. and Hadden, J. 1989, 'Is there Such a Thing as Global Fundamentalism?' in J. Hadden and A. Shupe (eds.), *Secularization and Fundamentalism Reconsidered Vol. III*, New York: Paragon House, pp. 109–22.

Sjöberg, M. 1988, *Trosförkunnelsen och dess Avhoppare* (RI-rapport 3), Uppsala: Kyrkans Hus.

Sklair, L. 1991, *Sociology of the Global System*, Hemel Hempstead: Harvester Wheatsheaf.

Skog, M. 1993, 'Trosrörelsen i Sverige', *Tro och Tanke 87*, Uppsala: Svenska Kyrkans Forskningsråd, pp. 89–138.

1994, 'Antal Medlemmar i Valda Samfund 1975–1993', *Tro och Tanke Supplement*, Uppsala: Svenska Kyrkans Forskningsråd, pp. 77–94.

Smart, N. 1991, 'Old Religions and New Religions', in W. C. Roof (ed.), *World Order and Religion*, Albany: State University of New York Press, pp. 67–81.

Solomon, N. 1994, 'Judaism', in J. Holm and J. Bowker (eds.), *Picturing God*, London: Pinter, pp. 142–72.

Sontag, S. 1977, *On Photography*, Harmondsworth: Penguin.

Spittler, R. 1994, 'Are Pentecostals and Charismatics Fundamentalists?: A Review of American Uses of these Categories', in K. Poewe (ed.), *Charismatic Christianity as a Global Culture*, Columbia: University of South Carolina Press, pp. 103–16.

Stai, S. 1993, '"Omvendelse og Nettverk" Et Sosiologisk Perspektiv på den Virkningen Omvendelsen har på Nettverstilknytningen for Medlemmene I "Trondheim Kristne Senter"', MA thesis, Trondheim: Religionsvitenskapelig Institutt.

Starrett, G. 1995, 'The Political Economy of Religious Commodities in Cairo', *American Anthropologist* 97:51–68.

Stoll, D. 1990, *Is Latin America Turning Protestant?: The Politics of Evangelical Growth*, Berkeley: University of California Press.

Straarup, J. 1994, 'Förord', in *Tro och Tanke Supplement*, Uppsala: Swedish Church, pp. 5–7.

Strathern, A. 1995, 'Trance and the Theory of Healing: Sociogenic and Psychogenic Components of Consciousness', in A. Cohen and N. Rapport (eds.), *Questions of Consciousness*, London pp. 117–33.

Strathern, M. 1988, *The Gender of the Gift: Problems with Women and Problems with Society in Melanesia*, Berkeley: University of California Press.

Stromberg, P. 1986, *Symbols of Community: The Cultural System of a Swedish Church*, Tucson: University of Arizona Press.

1993, *Language and Self-transformation: A Study of the Christian Conversion Narrative*, Cambridge University Press.

Sundstedt, A. 1972, *Pingstväckelsen och dess Utbredning*, Stockholm: Normans Förlag.

Svensson, G. 1988, 'Utländska Bilder av Sverige: Bespeglingar I det Moderna', in U. Himmelstrand and G. Svensson (eds.), *Sverige: Vardag och Struktur*, Stockholm: Norstedts, pp. 139–61.

Swartling, T. 1988, *Trosrörelsen – En Personlig Erfarenhet* (RI-rapport 2), Uppsala: Kyrkans Hus.

Tambiah, S. 1968, 'The Magical Power of Words', *Man* 3:175–208.

1984, *The Buddhist Saints of the Forest and the Cult of Amulets*, Cambridge University Press.

Taussig, M. 1997, *The Magic of the State*, Routledge: New York and London.

Therborn, G. 1988, 'Hur det Hela Började: När och Varför det Moderna Sverige Blev vad det Blev', in U. Himmelstrand and G. Svensson (eds.), *Sverige: Vardag och Struktur*, Stockholm: Norstedts, pp. 23–53.

Thomas, N. 1991, *Entangled Objects: Exchange, Material Culture amd Colonialism in the Pacific*, Cambridge, Massachusetts: Harvard University Press.

Tilley, C. 1991, *Material Culture and Text: The Art of Ambiguity*, London: Routledge.

Touraine, A. 1981, *The Voice and the Eye: An Analysis of Social Movements*, Cambridge University Press.

Trine, R. 1970, *In Tune with the Infinite*, New York: Bobbs-Merrill Co.

Turner, B. 1984, *The Body and Society*, New York: Basil Blackwood.

1991, *Religion and Social Theory* (2nd edn), London: Sage.

1994, *Orientalism, Postmodernism and Globalism*, London: Routledge.

Turner, H. 1979, *From Temple to Meeting-House: The Phenomenology and Theology of Places of Worship*, The Hague: Mouton.

Turner, V. 1982, 'Introduction', in V. Turner (ed.), *Celebration: Studies in Festivity and Ritual*, Washington DC: Smithsonian, pp. 11–30.

Van der Veer, P. 1989, 'The Power of Detachment: Disciplines of Body and Mind in the Ramanandi Order', *American Ethnologist* 16:458–70.

1996, 'Introduction', in P. van der Veer (ed.), *Conversion to Modernities: The Globalization of Christianity*, London: Routledge, pp. 1–21.

Van Dijk, R. 1999, 'Pentecostalism, Gerontocratic Rule and Democratization in Malawi: The Changing Position of the Young in Political Culture', in J. Haynes (ed.), *Religion, Globalization and Political Culture in the Third World*, London: Macmillan, pp. 164–88.

Walker, A. 1989, *Restoring the Kingdom: The Radical Christianity of the House Church Movement*, London: Hodder and Stoughton.

1997, 'Thoroughly Modern: Sociological Reflections on the Charismatic Movement from the End of the Twentieth Century', in S. Hunt, M. Hamilton and T. Walter (eds.), *Charismatic Christianity: Sociological Perspectives*, London: Macmillan.

Wallerstein, I. 1974, *The Modern World-System*, New York: Academic.

1979, *The Capitalist World-Economy*, Cambridge University Press.

Wallis, R. 1976, *The Road to Total Freedom: A Sociological Analysis of Scientology*, London: Heinemann.

Walls, A. 1991, 'World Christianity, the Missionary Movement and the Ugly American', in W. C. Roof (ed.), *World Order and Religion*, Albany: State University of New York Press, pp. 147–72.

Waters, M. 1995, *Globalization*, London: Routledge.

Wauzzinski, R. 1993, *Between God and Gold: Protestant Evangelicalism and the Industrial Revolution, 1820–1914*, London: Associated University Presses.

Werbner, P. and Basu, H. 1998 (eds.), *Embodying Charisma: Modernity, Locality and the Performance of Emotion in Sufi Cults*, London: Routledge.

Wikström, L. 1988, *RI-Projektet* (RI-rapport 1), Uppsala: Kyrkans Hus.

Williams, C. 1984, 'Speaking in Tongues', in D. Martin and P. Mullen (eds.), *Strange Gifts?: A Guide to Charismatic Renewal*, Oxford: Blackwell, pp. 72–83.

Wills, G. 1990, *Under God: Religion and American Politics*, New York: Simon and Schuster.

Wilson, B. 1973, *Magic and the Millennium*, London: Heinemann.

    1999, 'Introduction', in B. Wilson and J. Cresswell (eds.), *New Religious Movements: Challenge and Response*, London: Routledge, pp. 1–11.

Wilson, D. 1979, *The Welfare State in Sweden: A Study in Comparative Social Administration*, London: Heinemann.

Wilson, J. and Clow, H. 1981, 'Themes of Power and Control in a Pentecostal Assembly', *Journal for the Scientific Study of Religion* 10:241–50.

Wolf, E. 1982, *Europe and the People without History*, Berkeley: University of California Press.

Wuthnow, R. 1990, 'The Social Significance of Religious Television' in R. Abelman and S. Hoover (eds.) *Religious Television: Controversies and Conclusions*, Norwood, New Jersey: Ablex Publishing, pp. 87–98.

Wuthnow, R., Hunter, J. D., Bergesen, A. and Kurzweil, E. 1984, *Cultural Analysis: The Work of Peter L. Berger, Mary Douglas, Michel Foucault and Jürgen Habermas*, London: Routledge.

Index